The Bedside Guardian 2007

The Bedside Guardian 2007

EDITED BY BEN CLISSITT

guardianbooks

First published in 2007 by
Guardian Books, 119 Farringdon Road, London EC1R 3ER
guardianbooks.co.uk

Guardian Books is an imprint of Guardian News and Media Ltd

10 9 8 7 6 5 4 3 2 1

A CIP record for this book is available from the British Library.

ISBN: 978-0-85265-085-1

Design: Two Associates
Text layout: www.seagulls.net

Printed and bound in Great Britain by MPG Books, Bodmin, Cornwall

Contents

SUMMER

Introduction

Each day the *Guardian* publishes the same number of words – more on a Saturday – as you might find in an average-length novel. During the 12 months covered by this book we published 38,650,000 of them in 87,000 pieces. Not to mention the huge amount of bespoke copy, sound and vision carried on our website, guardian.co.uk. Beyond this, every reader has his or her particular way of reading the newspaper. The order in which pages are consumed, the tiny items that are read without fail, the columnists who, for each individual reader, are the quintessence of the *Guardian*.

If you were to collect two dozen *Guardian* readers in a research group and ask them to list the 10 reasons why they read the paper, no two lists would agree. (Some would say you wouldn't be able to get them to agree on anything at all, let alone what they liked about the paper.) That diversity of interest, among both the readers and those who put the paper together, is one of the enduring joys of being part of the *Guardian*. It also makes editing this collection enviable and daunting.

A digest of 100 or so pieces will never truly be able to reflect all the tonalities and textures of a publishing year, but I hope that this collection provides a reasonable narrative of events and a reflection of the richness of thought and expression that makes the *Guardian* a daily delight. Print deadlines, Christmas gift lists and

the like dictate that this annual compendium begins in the previous September and runs until the end of August in the year of
publication. Ordinarily it's an oddity and a mild irritant; this year
it provides the perfect framework for this edition's prevailing
theme: the transference of power from Tony Blair to Gordon Brown.

Just now – as Brown has become embroiled in the true trials of
leadership – the trigger for that change has been obscured. This
collection opens with Patrick Wintour's extraordinary report of
the September day in which it looked as if the chancellor was
mounting a coup against his leader. For a few hours it appeared
that there might be a bloody and very public resolution to the
enduring antipathy that the Granita pact had engendered, as Blair
made accusations of blackmail against his challenger. Give or take
the odd resignation and threat of a fight for the right to lead, what
followed was as smooth a handover as could have been envisaged.

Blair's announcement of his resignation in May and the actual
handover in June saw the *Guardian* at its best. From Steve Bell's
revelation that his mad-eyed caricature of the former PM was
based on that of a predecessor, Margaret Thatcher, through
Jonathan Freedland's generous summation of Blair's 10 years, to
Tim Dowling's exclusive report on Brown's first 100 minutes and
Richard Norton-Taylor's account of how new prime ministers react
when informed of the procedure for launching a nuclear strike.

That was not the only major political change Blair was involved
in, of course. At Stormont in May he was in attendance as Ian
Paisley and Martin McGuinness formally agreed to share power, a
moment brilliantly captured in Michael White's sketch ('A time to
love, a time to hate ...'), which compared the moment to a Richard
Curtis movie.

Those of you familiar with reading contents lists will not need
a résumé here of all that is to follow, but there are a number of
pieces that merit special mention.

David Leigh and Rob Evans have for a number of years been investigating the part BAE played in securing arms deals with Gulf states. Despite the government's decision last December to stop a Serious Fraud Office investigation into the al-Yamamah deal (which the *Guardian* had previously exposed), in June this year Leigh and Evans uncovered allegations that Prince Bandar of Saudi Arabia had been paid £1bn by BAE. The British government had knowledge of these payments.

In terms of investigative reporting, Ian Cobain had an extraordinary year. In 2006 he infiltrated the BNP and became its central London organiser. The result ('Inside the BNP') was a compelling undercover account of the organisation and the private motivations of those who are persuaded to join it. He was also part of the reporting team that revealed details about the alleged al-Qaida associate known as Q ('Free – the man accused of being an Al-Qaida leader') and, with Matthew Taylor, he learned of Boris Berezovsky's plans to overthrow the Putin government ('I am plotting a new Russian revolution').

On the subject of Putin's regime, the last article written by the murdered investigative journalist Anna Politkovskaya ('A condemned woman') is mesmeric. Published posthumously, her account of the inhumanity of the Russian forces in Chechnya and of the scale of harassment she suffered as a result of her determination to expose it is chilling. The ending of the piece acts as a reminder of what ordinary Russians, and the world, have lost: 'The main thing, however, is to get on with my job, to describe the life I see, to receive visitors every day in our editorial office who have nowhere else to bring their troubles, because the Kremlin finds their stories off-message.'

Foreign reporting was again dominated by Iraq. Saddam Hussein's execution on New Year's Day saw a moving and troubling piece by Ewen MacAskill and Michael Howard, while the multiple-award-winning Ghaith Abdul-Ahad continued his run of insightful reporting from places that few journalists manage to reach. His revealing piece ('Welcome to Tehran') about Iran's influence in Basra is truly outstanding.

In a quite different sphere, Ben Goldacre's comprehensive demolition of the credentials and credo of Gillian McKeith is one of the most compelling pieces in this year's collection. Goldacre's Bad Science column has become one of those must-read items for many *Guardian* readers in the four years it has been published for its rigorous good sense. The scale of this piece makes him even more convincing.

It was also a good sporting year – in the press box if not on the pitch. Kevin McCarra captured the grinding poverty of Steve McClaren's England early on ('McClaren's shapeless England fall to pieces'), while Gideon Haigh's beautiful tribute to the retiring Shane Warne and Glenn McGrath is as close as we dare come to mentioning the English cricket team's spectacular Ashes failing. On a brighter note, Richard Williams was pleased to welcome the rookie racing driver Lewis Hamilton, a legitimate reason for fresh British sporting hope ('The first sparks of greatness').

But most of all, the joy in compiling a collection such as this lies in the unexpected jewels one stumbles across. Martin Wainwright's account of the *Guardian* Country Diarists' lunch ('The Country Diary at 100'); Emma Brockes visiting a turkey slaughterhouse just before Christmas ('First, stun your turkey'); Michael Billington's account of seeing Olivier in *The Entertainer* as a 19-year-old on a theatre-going trip to London; Mark Ronson in 'Flowered up' revealing to Lily Allen that he once slept with Michael Jackson (it's OK, Sean Lennon was there too); and Zoe Williams's touching tribute to the M2 ('Life in the fast lane').

Finally, a word on the name change. For the past 13 years this collection has been known as *The Guardian Year*. Despite that, both readers of the book and those inside the paper have carried on referring to it as *The Bedside Guardian*, the name it carried from 1952 to 1993. Although it may seem odd in the digital age to revert to a name from the age of austerity that evokes thoughts of hot milk and biscuits, there is something intimate and relaxing about it, which still reflects a *Guardian* reader's relationship with the paper. David Eldridge has designed a cover that pays tribute to some of the great graphic work accompanying early editions of the volume. It is a unique title and it seems worth revisiting.

BEN CLISSITT

September 2007

Autumn

The day Blair accused his chancellor of blackmail

PATRICK WINTOUR

An all-out power struggle between the chancellor and the prime minister – culminating in allegations of blackmail by Tony Blair and a ferocious shouting match between the two men – appeared last night to have forced Mr Blair to publicly declare as early as today that he will not be prime minister this time next year. That may not be enough for Gordon Brown, who is understood to have demanded that Mr Blair quit by Christmas, with an effective joint premiership until a new leader is anointed by the party.

Mr Blair's statement – possibly to be made when he attends a north London school with the education secretary, Alan Johnson, today – will effectively confirm what cabinet ministers, including David Miliband, have been hinting about his intentions in the past few days. It represents a further shift in position as the prime minister struggles to cling to office and prevent a meltdown in the party. However, Mr Brown found himself under pressure from some MPs to force Mr Blair from office now. The Treasury hinted last night that it could accept a deal in which Mr Blair stood down by the beginning of May, provided the prime minister made a public declaration of this intention within the coming months.

In probably the most astonishing day in the annals of New Labour, the use of the word 'blackmail' to describe Mr Brown's actions over the past few days by Downing Street staff was authorised by Mr Blair, and reflected his view that Mr Brown is orchestrating a coup against him. Downing Street claimed the resignation yesterday of the junior defence minister Tom Watson and six parliamentary aides came with Mr Brown's agreement. The seven men quit the government, demanding that Mr Blair stand down immediately. Later in the evening, another of the letter's signatories, Iain Wright, resigned as a parliamentary private secretary in the Department of Health.

Downing Street's allegations led to counter-accusations from the Brown camp of intimidation of backbench MPs by No 10 aides desperate to cling to office. As a result, the chances of the much-prized 'stable and orderly transition' between the two men looked to have collapsed.

The recriminations came after meetings at Downing Street ended yesterday afternoon with Mr Blair rejecting Mr Brown's terms for allowing him to remain in office, including an acceler-ated timetable for Mr Blair's resignation by Christmas and an effective joint premiership in the interim. Blairites claimed that Mr Brown also demanded a public endorsement of the chancel-lor's leadership candidacy and repudiation of the idea of a fundamental debate about the Labour party's future. Mr Blair's aides demanded that Mr Brown distance himself from what the chief whip, Jacqui Smith, described as 'an attempt to bundle Mr Blair from office'.

At one point Mr Blair was also warned that unless he relented on the date and terms of his resignation there would be more senior resignations from government today. A more emollient account was given by the Treasury, asserting that Mr Blair recog-nised that he would have to move on his position that he would not state whether he would go next year.

The two meetings between Mr Brown and Mr Blair, totalling three and a half hours, occurred after Mr Watson and the parlia-mentary aides resigned. They were part of a group of 15 MPs who wrote privately to the prime minister claiming that he was now an electoral liability. News of the letter leaked to the *Guardian* on Monday. In it the 15 MPs, many of them previously loyal back-benchers, described themselves as modernisers and wrote: 'Sadly, it is clear to us – as it is to almost the entire party and the entire country – that without an urgent change in the leadership of the party it becomes less likely that we will win the next election. That is the brutal truth. It gives us no pleasure to say it. But it has to be said. And understood.'

Ominously for Mr Blair, Jack Straw, the leader of the Commons, went to see him to underline the pressure on him. The transport secretary, Douglas Alexander, refused to pledge support, while David Miliband, the environment secretary, said in an interview that only Mr Brown could save the party and urged his colleagues to avoid civil war. But Patricia Hewitt, the health secretary, accused the letter writers of madness, saying they were forgetting the lessons of Labour's strife in the 1980s, and adding: 'It looks as if they are trying to engineer a coup.' Three of Mr Blair's cabinet allies – Tessa Jowell, the culture secretary, Lord Falconer, the lord chancellor, and John Reid, the home secretary – were all abroad.

At the height of the breakdown in relations yesterday, one Blairite and former cabinet minister close to the discussions said: 'Threatening a serving prime minister in this way borders on the unconstitutional. We are a democracy, not an autocracy living in the era of the Soviet Union circa 1956. There is no way people can be muzzled in the way the chancellor is demanding.'

Jamie Oliver is back

NANCY BANKS-SMITH

Jamie Oliver is such a contemporary hero that the new Robin Hood ('a bit of a geezer') will be based on him. In *Jamie's Return to School Dinners* (Channel 4) he reorganised Lincolnshire (next door to Nottinghamshire), which has lost almost all its primary-school kitchens, by getting local restaurants and pubs to provide school dinners.

He is wholly and peculiarly a product of television. Anything this free of fear on television usually has four legs. Jamie and Mitch (a scrap of a lad who packs his own idiosyncratic school lunches) were being filmed on a windswept Lincolnshire shore – very much a director's idea.

'I'm freezing,' said Jamie. 'Do you want to go and get a hot cup of tea?'

'Yeah, go on then,' said Mitch.

Since he started campaigning for 'proper, good, lovely, home-cooked, healthy food every day of the school year', Jamie has seen three secretaries of state for education in three years. Alan Johnson was the latest. A bowl of fruit was positioned prominently on the table, indicating a keen interest in all things dietary. Jamie tipped out beside it a child's typical packed lunch: crisps, snacks and a fizzy drink of a particularly virulent blue. Johnson was new to the job ('I'm this week's secretary of state') and it showed. I haven't seen anyone so unbriefed since *The Full Monty*. When he said, 'I can't commit to anything after 2008 financially,' Jamie snapped back: 'So does that mean our boys are going to be out of

Iraq in a year and a half?' At this the minister's special adviser bounded from her seat as if gravity had been cancelled.

Alan Johnson must have felt the feebleness of this performance acutely, and moved fast. Three weeks later Jamie was summoned to meet the prime minister, who said: 'To be fair to Alan, after he spoke to you we put our heads together and tried to work it out.' In the garden of No 10, against a backing group of exuberant flowers, he strewed handfuls of roses out of his hat. New money for school kitchens, £240m more for school dinners and even a voluntary ban on advertising junk food to children. 'That sounds a bit wet, Tony,' said Jamie. You've got to love him.

The florescent ghost of Dame Barbara Cartland loomed large in *Reader, I Married Him* (BBC4), a whirl through romantic fiction. Meredith Etherington-Smith – no, honestly – was scathing. 'A lot of romantic fiction is extremely badly written. Think about Barbara Cartland lolling around on a sofa in shocking pink with three pekinese lolling about the place, dictating those things to secretaries. Poor secretaries doing all that Pitman's. Just think about it!' I think about it. In one portrait Dame Barbara is in soulful focus, but the peke on her knee is a blur. It has clearly launched itself straight at the photographer.

Melvyn Bragg wore dinner jacket and black tie to interview Dame Barbara for *The South Bank Show*, clearly feeling it incumbent.

'For 20 years I have done a book a fortnight,' she said in those silvery, pre-war tones.

'Why?' he trumpeted. (Lord Bragg, a prolific novelist, is not without sin in this respect. Dame Edna Everage once begged him: 'Don't write any more, Melvyn dear. Give us a chance to catch up.')

Jilly Cooper is a modern grande dame with added humour. She said: 'Sex is very difficult to write, particularly as you get older. One's experience gets further and further away. Also the terminology changes. Brazilian under my thong. It could be some wonderful Latin man with a whip. And it doesn't mean that at all now, does it? And also, when you're having wonderful sex, you can't have a book to make notes in, can you? Because that would be rude.'

The stars of Mills & Boon seemed less eager to appear. Arthur Applin, author of *The Girl Who Saved His Honour*, is probably no longer with us, but I would have liked to hear from Miranda Lee, who wrote *The Billionaire Boss's Forbidden Mistress*. As Wodehouse said of a romantic novelist: 'A simple apology is all that is required.'

In *Life Begins* (ITV1) Maggie did not have an affair with the director of human resources. Phil did not sleep with the exotic blossom from the flower shop. However, every other person they knew was indulging in sexual excess, which would have made Tiberius blink. Quite like life, really.

One of the many sound ideas pioneered by the Romans was a grammatical form that expected the answer 'no'. Even as you asked the question, you already knew the reply. How useful this would be today. Turn to your *Radio Times*, children. *Spooks* (BBC 1): 'Is the country under siege from sinister forces at the heart of the establishment?' No, it isn't. Don't be silly. *The Boy Who Lived Before* (Channel 5): a five-year-old recalls a previous life on Barra. 'Will a trip to Barra provide positive evidence?' No, it won't. Not only is he five, but he is on Five.

SEPTEMBER 25 2006

Shut up – or else

NATASHA WALTER

Last year the big story of the Labour party conference was not NHS reforms or the leadership struggle, it was the 82-year-old delegate who dared to raise his voice, while Jack Straw was speaking, in order to protest about the war in Iraq. When Walter Wolfgang was bundled out of the hall by bouncers, sympathy for him ran high. And the excessive security around the conference this year has caused much throwing up of hands among old Labourites. Because the one thing that everyone agrees on was that it was not like this in the past. Neil Kinnock, everyone says, would have handled this very differently. Harold Wilson positively liked hecklers. Once upon a time the Labour party tolerated dissent. Oh, how the nice party has become nasty!

This is no more than a delusion, however. Forty years ago, when my father, Nicolas Walter, heckled Wilson at the start of the Labour conference in Brighton, he was not just bundled out for his peaceful protest, but sent to prison for two months. Although I was not born when the heckle happened, I appeared just in time to feature in a family photograph on the front page of the *Sun*.

That forgotten heckle took place in 1966, when the Vietnam war was at its height. Although the British government never went down the dead end that it did with Iraq and sign up to send British troops, it had expressed continued firm support for the American government's actions.

The conference began, as it always did, with a church service attended by many MPs and delegates. Wilson and his foreign secretary, George Brown, were to read lessons, including Micah 4:3: 'Nation shall not lift up a sword against nation, neither shall they learn war any more.' Attendance at the service was by invitation only, but a friendly MP had lent protesters in the Vietnam Action Group his invitation for long enough to enable them to make a few copies. When Brown started reading the first lesson, my father rose and called out, 'Hypocrite! How can you use the word of God to justify your policies?!'

He was dragged out of the church, taken to the police station, remanded in custody for a week and later sentenced to two months in prison. He was not the only protester. The Vietnam Action Group had planned an organised disturbance: members would stand up and start making a statement one by one, so that as one heckler was silenced the next one would keep going. After my father was bundled out and Wilson started reading, they began their organised heckle, which led to each one being jumped on by delegates and police. One of the other protesters, Jim Radford, also ended up with a two-month prison sentence. Their crime? Breaking the little-known Ecclesiastical Courts Jurisdiction Act, which can be used to convict people of 'indecent behaviour' if they create a disturbance in church.

My father is now dead, so I can't ask him whether the Labour party is more or less tolerant of dissent than in the past. But Radford is still alive. Then he was a bearded young man with a wife and three young children, now he is a silver-ponytailed widower of 77, who will be going to this year's conference to take part in the Stop the War demonstration. He insists that he would be in the conference hall heckling again if there was any chance of getting through the security.

'It's very short-sighted of politicians to jump so hard on this kind of protest. They would do much better if they handled it in good humour. There are many ways of dealing with protesters other than beating people up, handcuffing them, throwing them in jail and punitively sentencing them.'

At the time, the Brighton church protesters got as much publicity as Wolfgang, with sympathy coming from unexpected quarters. Even the *Sun* ran a front-page leader: 'Whether you applaud or condemn the actions of these men, is any good done by jailing them?'

Obviously I remember nothing of the event or the direct fallout, but it was something that my parents spoke about with amusement and a certain pride, and I only learned gradually – from the horror on the face of a schoolfriend's mother when I mentioned that my father had once been in prison – that it was an odd thing for a middle-class suburban schoolgirl to chat about.

By 1966 Nicolas was a married man with one baby (my sister), so maybe he should have been more careful about what he did. But the urgency with which people like my parents took the work of protesting meant that it fed through every bit of their lives. When I was a young child I can't remember that my parents had any friends who were not part of that network, and Aldermaston and sit-downs and the duplication of little pamphlets of government secrets were part of the shared history they had with all their friends. It was not some optional extra, it was their lives. That began to change as we grew up, when they began to live a suburban life centred on schools and jobs. But at that time, in 1966, they were still part of this single-minded network.

This kind of protest suited my father. He was a naturally unclubbable man, who relished confrontation and never made a friend if he could make a really good enemy. He loved being part of a movement in which his talent for fury was appreciated. But he took the fallout seriously. The prison sentence completed his alienation from mainstream politics and he wrote what turned out to be quite a popular little book, *About Anarchism*, as soon as he came out of prison.

My father wrote personal letters from prison, but he also wrote a couple of political letters for my mother to circulate. 'It isn't necessarily a bad thing to interrupt a church service,' he wrote, 'and it may be a good thing sometimes. There are plenty of respectable precedents. The conscientious objectors did it in the first world war, the suffragettes did it before them, and the London unemployed did it before them. Long before that, the Quakers did it, and long before that, the Men of Kent interrupted mass in Canterbury Cathedral at the beginning of the Peasants' Revolt. You can't go much further back than that and I'm glad to have taken part in reviving such a good old tradition.'

My mother, Ruth, shared that sense of pride, which for her easily weighed against the inconvenience of having her husband – the father of her children and the only breadwinner of the family – in prison. It could have been tricky for her, as society was a lot more traditional then and neighbours cut her on the street and refused to let their children play with us, while even her own parents cut off contact for some months. But she had a network of friends who shared her views and, overall, she remembers those days with affection – it was a time when a traditional, deferential society seemed to be transforming, and they were the people who were creating that shift.

'Those were good times,' she says now. 'We felt as though it was worth raising our voices for what we believed, so we did. There were a lot of other people who thought like us, that it was worth having a go and trying to change things. There was an optimism about the way things were going. I never thought we'd end up with what we have now, 40 years on. We seem to have regressed in so many ways.'

OCTOBER 12 2006

McClaren's shapeless England fall to pieces: Croatia 2, England 0

KEVIN McCARRA

After all the debate over the shape England ought to adopt, Croatia decreed that it would be a severely dented one. The damage is just as severe for Steve McClaren, whose strategy was supposed to help the team get forward. His players merely moved mechanically and if there is any consolation for the goalkeeper, Paul Robinson, (who missed his kick and let a Gary Neville backpass roll into his net) it is that England, already a goal behind, were unlikely to score in any case.

McClaren, on his fifth match in charge, already has on his record a defeat that will trail him through many fixtures to come. It is sure to be there, mentioned aloud or hovering unspoken over every occasion. He knew the job could be like that, but he has to tremble early. At the minimum, Group E is now converted into a challenge where, before Saturday's draw with Macedonia, it had promised to be a sinecure.

Everything is in doubt, with even the manager's future already overcast. It took Sven-Goran Eriksson four years before humiliation had to be endured in Northern Ireland, his sole defeat in a qualifier. As if the grilling over tactics were not enough, McClaren must face questioning of his worth as a motivator, especially as he had made so much beforehand of character and the requirement for an 'English performance'. The latter term, with its macho overtones, is overblown at the best of times and utterly absurd in the wake of a night such as this.

England, particularly in the first half, enjoyed a good share of possession without having any notion of what could be done with it. This sort of debacle is not complete without a piece of ignominious irony and Neville must bear it. Having missed a chance to score on Saturday, he now has his first goal in England's colours, much as he would love to disown it.

At least it is Robinson who will go down in folklore as the culprit. Having got no boot on the ball he indicated that there had been a bobble, but a shortage of sympathisers is inevitable. Until then he had actually played well enough and pulled off a few saves as he aimed for a seventh consecutive clean sheet with England.

No one was to reach their target in McClaren's side. In a supposedly beefed-up midfield, the trio of Scott Parker, Michael Carrick and Frank Lampard all had an insipidness that seeped out to taint the entire team. Croatia had a far greater sense of the architecture of a performance, establishing a basis for victory in the first half and relishing the topping-off ceremony well before the full-time whistle.

There were very few distractions from their labours. Wayne Rooney – zealous yet no nearer the aplomb that is meant to characterise him – did get behind Robert Kovac when the game was goalless, but his drive sailed high. It was an evening otherwise crammed with woe for England and Rio Ferdinand, already booked, might have been dismissed for a foul on Luka Modric. The centre-half's yellow card had been imposed after his ball control failed him and he felt obliged to bring down Mladen Petric. There was a profusion of evidence that England lacked concentration, confidence, conviction, technique, imagination and everything else essential for the task in Zagreb.

In a sense the formation had been a secondary factor when standards were so low. Not even marking could be guaranteed.

When Niko Kovac crossed deep after an hour neither John Terry nor anyone else marked Eduardo da Silva and the Brazilian-born striker put a looping header over a stranded Robinson for the opener.

It was improbable that Croatia would not make a break-through. England – for whom the substitute Phil Neville injured a hamstring in the pre-match warm-up – will feel ill-starred, but the fates were the least of their trouble. Croatia's nominal wingers Milan Rapaic and Portsmouth's Niko Kranjcar savoured the night efficiently to show that there was definitely no gain in using three centre-backs.

When Rapaic crossed in the 27th minute Robinson had to save a Kranjcar volley. Slaven Bilic's team were far from devastating, but the moments of encouragement never completely dried up. Croatia were more intimidating 10 minutes later. Vedran Corluka sent a well-paced pass down the right and Rapaic, clear of Ashley Cole, went to the byline before delivering a cut-back to Kranjcar. His effort was deflected behind off Ferdinand. Another Kranjcar shot ensued and had to be pushed away by Robinson for a corner.

The goalkeeper – dealing with a Petric header soon after the interval – may have been conned into believing this was his night. He would readily have been pardoned for that and there had been far more pernicious delusions around. McClaren had talked constantly of the need for improvement, but the manager could not have anticipated such vapidity. Afterwards he spoke of the shortage of chances to be expected of a visiting team in a place such as this, but England's aimlessness made it a self-fulfilling prophecy. His next qualifier is in Israel in March, meaning he must suffer five months of reflections, as well as fears, deep down and never to be admitted, that this job will overwhelm him as it has so many others.

OCTOBER 13 2006

A Nobel winner for our times

MARGARET ATWOOD

Orhan Pamuk, the celebrated Turkish novelist, has won the Nobel prize for literature. It would be difficult to conceive of a more perfect winner for our catastrophic times. Just as Turkey stands at the crossroads of the Muslim east/Middle East and the European and North American west, so Pamuk's work inhabits the shifting ground of an increasingly dangerous cultural and religious overlap, where ideologies as well as personalities collide.

It is no exaggeration to say that you have to read Pamuk if you want to begin to understand what's going on in people's hearts, minds and souls, not only in Turkey, but also in Britain, where the current Jack Straw headscarf controversy eerily mirrors the subject matter of Pamuk's recently translated 1996 novel, *Snow* (in which we are reminded that Ataturk's ruthless modernisation campaign included a much-disputed banning of headscarves).

Pamuk has felt the shockwaves from such factional collisions. He has never been one to duck controversy: just a year ago he was facing prosecution on charges of 'un-Turkishness' – he had been so rash as to have mentioned the fate of the Armenians at the beginning of the 20th century, a taboo subject for the authorities. Possibly in response to international outcries, the charges were dropped, but many lesser-known Turkish writers have not been so lucky.

He has already won many literary prizes, including the 2003 Dublin Impac award for his sixth novel, *My Name Is Red*. In Turkey, he is far more than a novelist: people rush to read his novels as if he's a kind of sure-fire prophet or a hugely popular singer or a national psychoanalyst or a one-man newspaper editorial page. There is nothing programmatic about his novels. He simply writes out of the centre of the whirlwind both his characters and his Turkish readers feel swept up in every day.

Where is Turkey going? How will it come to terms with its once glorious, often troubled history and resolve the conflict between old and new? And handle the power struggle between secularists and Islamists? And find self-respect or peace of mind or inner wholeness or a new direction? Pamuk's novels don't provide cut-and-dried solutions, but they follow the tortuous lines of such questionings with anguished and wrenching fidelity. Sometimes his characters are almost literally torn apart by choices they don't know how to make, but are forced to make. His power as a novelist stems in part from his refusal to judge the choices his characters make: their tragedy is that no matter what path they take, they can't be at ease and, worse, some other element in their society is bound to condemn them.

Thus Pamuk's heroes – they are typically heroes, not heroines – wander through the plots of their books as if caught in a particularly anxious and threatening collective dream. It is not unusual for a Pamuk protagonist to end up dead at the hands of persons unknown.

I wrote of his novel *Snow* in the *New York Times Book Review*: 'The twists of fate, the plots that double back on themselves, the trickiness, the mysteries that recede as they're approached, the bleak cities, the night prowling, the sense of identity-loss, the protagonist in exile – these are vintage Pamuk, but they're also part of the modern literary landscape.'

Pamuk's heroes are pestered by Turkey's former pre-eminence: they may stumble upon architectural fragments of the huge, opulent Ottoman empire or see an Armenian church standing empty or be reminded of earlier Russian rulers or glimpse a fly-spotted picture of the once-revered Ataturk, whose attempts to forge a fully westernised, secular Turkey now seem futile. Where has all the power gone? such echoes say. The Christian Byzantine city of Constantinople casts a long shadow and the European west and the Muslim east are seen as mirror-opposite twins ensnared in a net that traps them both.

Pamuk gives us what all novelists give us at their best: the truth. Not the truth of statistics, but the truth of human experience at a particular place, in a particular time. And as with all great literature, you feel at moments not that you are examining him, but that he is examining you.

'No one could understand us from so far away,' says a character in *Snow*.

Reader, it's a challenge.

OCTOBER 14 2006

A condemned woman

ANNA POLITKOVSKAYA

I am a pariah. That is the main result of my journalism throughout the years of the second Chechen war, and of publishing abroad a number of books about life in Russia and the Chechen war. In Moscow I am not invited to press conferences or gatherings that officials of the Kremlin administration might attend, in case the organisers are suspected of harbouring sympathies towards me. Despite this, all the top officials talk to me, at my request, when I am writing articles or conducting investigations – but only in secret, where they can't be observed: in the open air, in squares, in secret houses that we approach by different routes, like spies.

The officials like talking to me. They are happy to give me information. They consult me and tell me what is going on at the top. But only in secret.

You don't get used to this, but you learn to live with it. It is exactly the way I have had to work throughout the second war in Chechnya. First I was hiding from the Russian federal troops, but always able to make contact clandestinely with individuals through trusted intermediaries, so that my informants would not be denounced to the top generals. When Putin's plan of Chechenisation succeeded (setting 'good' Chechens loyal to the Kremlin to killing 'bad' Chechens who opposed it), the same subterfuge extended to talking to 'good' Chechen officials, whom of course I had known for a long time, and many of whom, before they were 'good' officials, had sheltered me in their homes in the most trying months of the war. Now we can meet only in secret because I am a pariah, an enemy. Indeed, an incorrigible enemy not amenable to re-education.

I'm not joking. Some time ago Vladislav Surkov, deputy head of the presidential administration, explained that there were people who were enemies but whom you could talk sense into, and there were incorrigible enemies into whom you couldn't and who simply needed to be 'cleansed' from the political arena.

So they are trying to cleanse it of me and others like me.

On August 5 2006, I was standing in the middle of a crowd of women in the little central square of Kurchaloy, a dusty village in Chechnya. I was wearing a headscarf folded and tied in the manner favoured by many women of my age in Chechnya, not covering the head completely, but not leaving it uncovered either. This was essential if I was not to be identified, in which case nobody could say what might happen.

To one side of the crowd a man's tracksuit trousers were draped over the gas pipeline that runs the length of Kurchaloy. They were caked with blood. His severed head had been taken away by then and I didn't see it.

During the night of 27-28 July, two Chechen fighters had been ambushed on the outskirts of Kurchaloy by units loyal to the pro-Kremlin Ramzan Kadyrov. One, Adam Badaev, was captured and the other, Hoj-Ahmed Dushaev, a native of Kurchaloy, was killed. Towards dawn, not far short of 20 Zhiguli cars, full of armed people, drove into the centre of the village and up to the district police station. They had Dushaev's head with them. Two of the men suspended it in the centre of the village from the pipeline and beneath it they hung the bloodstained trousers I was now seeing. The armed men spent the next two hours photographing the head with their mobile phones.

The head was left there for 24 hours, after which militiamen removed it but left the trousers where they were. Agents of the procurator-general's office began investigating the scene of the fighting and local people heard one of the officers ask a subordinate: 'Have they finished sewing the head back on yet?'

The body of Dushaev, with its head now sewn back in place, was brought to the scene of the ambush and the procurator-general's office began examining the scene of the incident in accordance with normal investigative procedures.

I wrote about this in my newspaper, refraining from comment beyond dotting a few 'i's in respect of what had happened. I reached Chechnya at exactly the same time as the issue of the newspaper with the article. The women in the crowd tried to conceal me, because they were sure the Kadyrov people would shoot me on the spot if they knew I was there. They reminded me that Kadyrov has publicly vowed to murder me. He actually said during a meeting of his government that he had had enough and that Politkovskaya was a condemned woman. I was told about it by members of the government.

What for? For not writing the way Kadyrov wanted? 'Anybody who is not one of us is an enemy.' Surkov said so, and Surkov is Ramzan Kadyrov's main supporter in Putin's entourage.

'Ramzan told me, "She is so stupid she doesn't know the value of money. I offered her money but she didn't take it,"' an old acquaintance, a senior officer in militia special forces, told me that same day. I met him secretly. He is 'one of us', unlike me, and would face difficulties if we were caught conferring. When it was time for me to leave it was already evening and he urged me to stay in this secure location. He was afraid I would be killed.

'You mustn't go out,' he told me. 'Ramzan is very angry with you.'

I decided to leave nevertheless. Someone else was waiting for me in Grozny and we needed to talk through the night, also in secret. He offered to have me taken there in a militia car, but that struck me as even more risky. I would be a target for the fighters.

'Do they at least have guns in the house you are going to?' he continued anxiously. Throughout the war I have been caught in the middle. When some are threatening to kill you, you are protected by their enemies, but tomorrow the threat will come from somebody else.

Why am I going on at such length about this? Only in order to explain that people in Chechnya are afraid for me and I find that very touching. They fear for me more than I fear for myself, and that is how I survive.

Why has Ramzan vowed to kill me? I once interviewed him and printed the interview just as he gave it, complete with all his characteristic moronic stupidity, ignorance and satanic inclinations. Ramzan was sure I would completely rewrite the interview and present him as intelligent and honourable. That is, after all, how the majority of journalists behave now, those who are 'on our side'.

Is that enough to make someone vow to kill you? The answer is as simple as the morality encouraged personally by Putin: 'We are merciless to enemies of the Reich.' 'Who is not with us is against us.' 'Those who are against us must be destroyed.'

'Why have you got such a bee in your bonnet about this severed head?' Vasiliy Panchenkov asks me back in Moscow. He is director of the press office for the interior ministry troops, but a decent man. 'Have you nothing better to worry about?' I am asking him to comment on the events in Kurchaloy for our newspaper. 'Just forget it. Pretend it never happened. I'm asking you for your own good!'

But how can I forget it, when it did happen?

I loathe the Kremlin's line, elaborated by Surkov, dividing people into those who are 'on our side', 'not on our side' or even 'on the other side'. If a journalist is 'on our side', he or she will get awards, respect, perhaps be invited to become a deputy in the Duma. If a journalist is 'not on our side', however, he or she will be deemed a supporter of the European democracies, of European values and automatically become a pariah. That is the fate of all who oppose our 'sovereign democracy', our 'traditional Russian democracy'. (What on earth that is, nobody knows but they swear allegiance to it nevertheless: 'We are for sovereign democracy!')

I am not really a political animal. I have never joined any party and would consider it a mistake for a journalist, in Russia at least, to do so. I have never felt the urge to stand for the Duma, although there were years when I was invited to.

So what is the crime that has earned me this label of not being 'one of us'? I have merely reported what I have witnessed, no more than that. I have written and, less frequently, I have spoken. I am even reluctant to comment, because it reminds me too much of the imposed opinions of my Soviet childhood and youth. It seems to me our readers are capable of interpreting what they read for themselves. That is why my principal genre is reportage;

sometimes, admittedly, with my own interjections. I am not an investigating magistrate, but somebody who describes the life around us for those who cannot see it for themselves, because what is shown on television and written about in the overwhelming majority of newspapers is emasculated and doused with ideology. People know very little about life in other parts of their own country, and sometimes even in their own region.

The Kremlin responds by trying to block my access to information, its ideologists supposing that this is the best way to make my writing ineffectual. It is impossible, however, to stop someone fanatically dedicated to this profession of reporting the world around us. My life can be difficult, more often humiliating. I am not, after all, so young at 47 to keep encountering rejection and having my own pariah status rubbed in my face, but I can live with it.

I will not go into the other joys of the path I have chosen: the poisoning, the arrests, the threats in letters and over the internet, the telephoned death threats, the weekly summonses to the procurator-general's office to sign statements about practically every article I write (the first question being 'How and where did you obtain this information?'). Of course, I don't like the constant derisive articles about me that appear in other newspapers and on websites that have long presented me as the Madwoman of Moscow. I find it disgusting to live this way; I would like a bit more understanding.

The main thing, however, is to get on with my job, to describe the life I see, to receive visitors every day in our editorial office who have nowhere else to bring their troubles, because the Kremlin finds their stories off-message, so that the only place they can be aired is in our newspaper, *Novaya Gazeta*.

This piece was written shortly before Anna Politkovskaya's assassination on October 7 2006, and appears in the English PEN anthology of work by writers of conscience, Another Sky: Voices of Conscience from Around the World *published by Profile Books.*

OCTOBER 20 2006

About a boy

XAN RICE

This is the story of a 13-month-old African boy. Of a father who, after burying his wife and two infant sons, took his only remaining child to an orphanage to give him a better chance of survival. Of a pop superstar desperate to adopt a kid from a continent she had never visited. And of a government so grateful for her promise of more than a million pounds in aid that it bent the rules to help her, turning the adoption into a PR nightmare. This is the story of David Banda – the most famous baby in the world.

It begins in Lipunga, a small, neat village of 300 people in the foothills of far western Malawi, in early September last year. Yohane and Marita Banda are expecting their third child. They are nervous. Their first son, Garnet, died from malaria aged two years and eight months. The second, Babel, also a boy, died from an undetermined illness aged 18 months.

Now Marita, 28, is feeling ill. So Yohane borrows a bicycle, lays her on the trailer hitched behind it, and pedals 13 miles along a dirt road to the nearest clinic. They are sent home with medication, but are back in the clinic that night.

'I took her back there on the bicycle,' recalls Yohane, a pleasant 32-year-old man with a physique that speaks of physical labour.

This time the clinic summons an ambulance and Marita spends a week in hospital. After being discharged, she travels from Lipunga across the nearby border into Zambia, where her parents live. David is born on September 24, delivered by traditional birth attendants. He is healthy, but his mother is not. By the time

Yohane reaches the village, she is clinging on to life. Marita dies on September 30, six days after giving birth.

Yohane is devastated, but his problems are not over. He still owes 10,000 kwacha (£40) to his in-laws as part of the dowry. They want nothing to do with David. So Yohane returns home to Lipunga wondering how – as a single parent who works in his tomato and onion 'garden' all day – he is going to ensure that his week-old son does not suffer the same fate as his siblings.

After a discussion with his mother, Asianti, who also spends all day tending her vegetables, Yohane meets with the village chief, Henderson Geza. Geza, a small 69-year-old man with bright eyes, knows how tough it has become for single parents to look after a child in poor villages like Lipunga: his own grandson was sent to an orphanage for a few months after the child's mother died. Yohane and Geza agree that the best option is to ask the church's permission to send David to the Home of Hope, an orphanage 25 miles away.

'It was a very sad day for us,' says Asianti. 'Our only consolation was the child had a better chance of staying alive.'

Eleven months later, Madonna, the 48-year-old superstar with homes in the UK and US and a fortune of nearly £250m, tells *Time* magazine that she is going to raise $3m to help some of the estimated 900,000 orphans in the southern African country. She says that in the past few years she has 'felt more responsible for the children of the world'.

Madonna, who has never been to Africa before, plans a trip to Malawi with her husband, Guy Ritchie, who has quietly visited the country earlier in the year. Preparations are also under way for the trip's second, secret purpose: the Ritchies are planning to go home with an adopted child. Lourdes, 10, and Rocco, six, will soon have a baby brother.

In Malawi, all adoptions are organised through the ministry

for gender, child welfare and community services. At the Ritchies' request, ministry officials have been asked to visit orphanages and identify a dozen babies for them to choose from. The search has begun.

David is now nearly a year old and in good health. Yohane visits him twice a week, using a borrowed bicycle to make the 50-mile round-trip. Usually he brings food that he has grown in the village. Asianti sometimes comes along, too, pedalling her own bike. Though 56, her work in the fields means she is fitter than most women half her age.

'We were very close to my child,' says Yohane. 'Whenever I left the orphanage, David would cry.'

Madonna and Ritchie arrive in Malawi on a private jet on October 4, check into the Kumbali Lodge near the president's house in the capital and immediately begin visiting orphanages around the country to observe the challenges facing the country. But before the day is out a government official tells the press that the singer is looking to adopt a child and, in a display of well-intentioned naivety, asks the media to respect the couple's privacy.

Madonna's spokeswoman immediately denies the report, but the damage is done. While it seems highly unlikely that the Ritchies want events to unfold as they do – they are reportedly furious at the leak and the government soon clams up on the topic – the official's slip-up ensures that the adoption occurs under the full view of the world's media. And with the British tabloids on the trail, there is little doubt that the identity of the latest addition to the Ritchie family will soon come out before the child leaves the country. A week after the Ritchie's arrival, it does. The child is David Banda.

If the news of the adoption of a tiny black boy by a white pop diva isn't enough, there is an added sensation – Madonna and Guy Ritchie are adopting a boy with a living father. And how are they going to get around Malawi's tough adoption rules, which require that foreigners be resident in the country for 18 months before adopting a child to ensure that welfare officials have time to moni-tor their suitability?

'Only children without any living parents and circumstances that make it unlikely that they can ever return to their extended family are selected for adoption,' says the director of a well-established infant home in Malawi, who asks not to be named. 'This was a very unusual case.'

On September 30, several days before the Ritchies arrived in Malawi, Yohane says that he was visited in Lipunga by Penston Kilembe, the country's director of social welfare, and asked whether he would allow David to be adopted by a well-vetted foreign couple. After sitting down with Asianti and other members of the extended family, Yohane agreed that it would be best to let David go. The thinking was this: if David stayed in Malawi, he would remain close to his father, but would be unlikely ever to break the cycle of poverty. The best he could realistically hope for would be to become a herder, a petty trader or a subsis-tence farmer. By going abroad – even as the child of another family – he could become whatever he wanted. The decision may seem callous to some in the west – a father abandoning his only son. In Malawi, it seems selfless.

'My interest is in the child's best chance for health and educa-tion,' says Yohane, who denies that he was coerced or manipulated into making the decision – a claim reportedly made by his brother last week. 'It was a hard choice to make, but when it seemed likely that David would have a better life with a new family, I could not say no.'

The legal hurdles disappear swiftly. A high court judge passes an interim order allowing the Ritchies to take David home with them, waiving the normal requirement of 18 months' residency for any foreign nationals looking to adopt a Malawian child. Under the order, the court will make a second ruling after 18 months to formally approve the adoption – assuming welfare officials are happy with the child's new environment. Technically, the ruling may be legal – Malawi has signed an international convention allowing intra-country adoptions, even if it conflicts with the constitution – but it was certainly highly unusual in application.

At the court hearing, Yohane meets the Ritchies for the first time, finds them to be 'nice people' and formally consents to David's adoption. The Ritchies agree that David will visit his father in Malawi 'within three or four years', according to Yohane.

If not starstruck, the government clearly feels deeply indebted to Madonna for her pledges to help out the country's orphans and to raise international awareness of their plight.

'Madonna has a big programme in this country,' Andrina Mchiela, the principal secretary in the welfare ministry, says. 'She is a daughter of Malawi. There is no mistrust and her integrity cannot be questioned.'

As for the fact that David has a father who regularly visits him, Mchiela says that by placing his son in an orphanage Yohane has demonstrated his intention to seek a better life for his child.

'It was like when Moses was left in the basket in the hope that someone would rescue him. Madonna has rescued the baby. All we can say is, "Bon voyage, David."'

It's now Wednesday. Thanks to her visit, Madonna's songs are still being played in Malawi's nightclubs. 'Holiday' is a particular favourite. David has spent his first full day in the United Kingdom.

It is nearing midday. Asianti has been tending her fields since 5am. With a giggle, she sums up the happenings of the past two weeks.

'My son is a father who was poor and did not know much. Now he has a child that will be cared for by a rich and famous woman!'

Yohane is spraying his tomato crop nearby. He is wearing a pair of old tweed trousers, a yellow and blue T-shirt that says 'Dada' and blue sandals. He appears tired of all the media attention, but sits down to answer questions without complaint.

'I will miss David,' he says. 'I miss him already. But I know that it's for the best.'

OCTOBER 24 2006

Licensed to kill

KIRA COCHRANE

To die at the wheels of a speeding driver is so common – 3,201 people died on the roads last year – that we rarely hear individual stories. Unless an incident has some special edge of celebrity or gore or misery, then this occurrence is so ordinary – 271,017 people were injured on our roads last year – that it is not really a story at all. And, when individual stories are told, the dead are so frequently described as 'angels' or 'innocents' or 'perfect' human beings that their distinguishing features melt together, replaced instead by a saintly glow.

Let me just clarify then: my older brother, Gleave, who was killed, aged eight, by a speeding driver, was certainly not perfect. But, with his enthusiasm and easy laughter, he was the kind of kid you might actually have liked.

For instance, he did send his teachers into despair with his endless chatter. Every time they tried to catch him out, though – stopping a lesson mid-sentence, warning him to shut up with the usual, tricksy 'Perhaps you'd like to teach the class, Gleave?' – he would repeat back their last few lines, verbatim. But he was caring, too. Our father had died of a heart attack when Gleave was four, I was two and my mother was pregnant with my younger brother, Frazer. To use an outdated notion, Gleave became the man of the house. Shortly before he died, I remember him sitting on my bed and stroking my hair as I cried about something or other. He didn't say much. He just understood.

On December 10 1983, while the rest of us put up the Christmas decorations, Gleave cycled around the corner to his best friend Robert's house. A couple of hours later, at tea time, he was supposed to return, but instead we received a phone call. Standing by the side of the road, waiting to cross, Gleave had been hit by a car and was being taken to hospital. My mother rode in the ambulance with him, while Frazer and I stayed with Robert's family. Robert's teenage sister, Caroline, said that it would almost certainly be OK. He had probably just broken an arm or a leg. In fact, he had broken his neck. At hospital he was DOA. With which, Gleave became just another statistic.

I bring you this miserable little tale partly to humanise these deaths – which so acutely need humanising – but also to explain why I felt so emotional when I first heard about the *Top Gear* presenter Richard Hammond's 288mph crash while filming for the programme last month.

On the one hand I felt incredibly sorry for him and empathised especially with his wife and young children. I know what it's like to hear that someone you love has been hurt – and may either die or be brain damaged – because of a road crash. Thankfully, Hammond now looks set to make a full recovery. In yesterday's *Mirror* he described the accident and its aftermath, his sympathy for his family ('The one thing I feel awful about is that they had to see [me] in that state') and his comic anger that he doesn't have any scars ('Do you realise how annoyed I am that I've got no marks on me? Absolutely nothing at all, nothing for the pub. There are people who fall off their trikes at the age of four who've got better injuries than me.') And money won't be a problem, judging by reports of a £2m, two-year 'golden handcuffs' deal with the BBC.

Primarily, though, when I heard about Hammond's crash I felt absolutely, boilingly livid. We have an obsession with speed in this country, a misguided notion that it is our right to buck the speed limit, to drive as fast as we like on the public highways, because – or so the argument goes – good drivers can handle high speeds, can't they? And at the heart of this attitude has been *Top Gear*, a programme that glamorises speeding, rails against speed cameras and sticks two fingers up at the basic laws of physics and biology – the fact that the faster you drive, the more likely you are to kill or be killed.

Looked at statistically, for instance, Gleave never stood a chance. The driver who killed him was travelling at 43mph in a 30mph area – not that fast or reckless, you might think. Any pedestrian though, let alone a child, knocked down at 40mph has just a 5 per cent chance of survival. (By comparison, a pedestrian hit at 20mph has a 95 per cent chance.) The driver was travelling with his wife and daughter and was going so fast in the dusk that he didn't even recognise Gleave as a human being as he knocked him into the gutter. He only stopped a few hundred yards later because he suspected he had hit a dog.

Hammond, of course, was on a racetrack, so there wasn't any danger of him harming anyone else. But this stunt was just another aspect of *Top Gear*'s central purpose: to deify and fetishise speed. In the recent past, the show has tested brakes by aiming cars at cardboard cut-outs of Richard Brunstrom, the chief constable of North Wales. Why? Because Brunstrom has had the temerity to promote Arrive Alive, a charity that campaigns for more speed cameras. The fact that speed cameras have led to 42 per cent fewer people being killed and injured on the roads where they are erected – saving an estimated 1,000 lives overall – is apparently insignificant. Anything that slows the *Top Gear* presenters down (with caravans apparently the worst offender) is fit for immediate destruction.

After Hammond's crash I waited to see whether the show's best-known presenter, Jeremy Clarkson, would be sorry or silent. In the past, he has said that 'speeding is no big deal', has professed support for groups that break speed cameras and suggested that these might be 'filled ... with insulating foam that sets rock hard'.

In the event, Clarkson emerged from Hammond's crash more bullish than ever. He is set to showcase his love of speed this week at the MPH exhibition in Birmingham, with its promises of 'high-octane car chases' and 'outrageous stunts'. He reported that he first heard of Hammond's accident as he was 'doing a rather pedestrian 175mph in an Aston Martin round the programme's test track in Surrey' and that his only responsibility was to ensure that Hammond 'has a show to come back to'. Those who question *Top Gear*'s approach are just 'people with beards and dirty finger-nails' and 'lesbians' (it says so much that this is a serious insult in Clarkson-world).

And this attitude – with its facile sexism and machismo – is typical of Clarkson and his acolytes. That is one of the things that is so frustrating about *Top Gear*. Its love of speed, its addiction to racing metal – speeding, to put it in context, causes twice as many road accidents as drunk-driving – is nothing more than willy-waving of the worst kind. 'The only thing that sounds better than a Ferrari is telling someone you have one,' Clarkson has boasted pathetically. But this rampant, empty machismo costs life after life. It is estimated that each of us has a 1 in 17 chance of being killed or seriously injured in a road crash.

As fate would have it, Gleave's death wasn't the only incidence of road violence to hit my family in my early years. Three years on from his death – when I was nine, and my younger brother, Frazer, was six – the shadow of a speeding car crossed our paths again. Our house sat at the end of a quiet cul-de-sac at the bottom of a short, steep hill and I was looking after Frazer, who has autism, as we played in the snow outside. We were building a snowman, perfectly content, when a car hurtled down (it can't have taken more than a few seconds for it to slip silently from the top of the hill to the bottom), losing control on the ice and smacking into Frazer. As he lay in a deep bank, blood spreading around him, I screamed for our mother. I was certain he was going to die.

Fortunately, the snow was sufficient cushion to save him. Frazer was only cut and concussed. We heard later, though, that before we had gone out to play the teenager driver had been speeding up and down the hill repeatedly, skidding each time at the end of the cul-de-sac, trying to impress one of the neighbourhood girls.

Any approach to driving that is about preening arrogance – rather than getting from A to B – is always likely to involve more speed and less attention to the road than is necessary. Yet at the moment, when it comes to the speeding laws, Clarkson and his ilk seem to be shouting loudest and winning the argument.

OCTOBER 31 2006

Climate change: what the government must do now

GEORGE MONBIOT

It is a testament to the power of money that Nicholas Stern's report should have swung the argument for drastic action, even before anyone has finished reading it. He appears to have demonstrated what many of us suspected: that it would cost much less to prevent runaway climate change than to seek to live with it. Useful as this finding is, I hope it doesn't mean that the debate will now concentrate on money. The principal costs of climate change will be measured in lives, not pounds. As Stern reminded us yesterday, there would be a moral imperative to seek to prevent mass death even if the economic case did not stack up.

But at least almost everyone now agrees that we must act, if not at the necessary speed. If we're to have a high chance of preventing global temperatures from rising by 2C (3.6F) above pre-industrial levels, we need, in the rich nations, a 90 per cent reduction in greenhouse-gas emissions by 2030. The greater part of the cut has to be made at the beginning of this period.

To see why, picture two graphs with time on the horizontal axis and the rate of emissions plotted vertically. On one graph the line falls like a ski jump: a steep drop followed by a shallow tail. On the other it falls like the trajectory of a bullet. The area under each line represents the total volume of greenhouse gases produced in that period. They fall to the same point by the same date, but far more gases have been produced in the second case, making runaway climate change more likely.

So how do we do it without bringing civilisation crashing down? Here is a plan for drastic but affordable action that the government could take. It goes much further than the proposals discussed by Tony Blair and Gordon Brown yesterday, for the reason that this is what the science demands.

1. Set a target for reducing greenhouse-gas emissions based on the latest science. The government is using outdated figures, aiming for a 60 per cent reduction by 2050. Even the annual 3 per cent cut proposed in the early day motion calling for a new climate change bill does not go far enough. Timescale: immediately.

2. Use that target to set an annual carbon cap, which falls on the ski-jump trajectory. Then use the cap to set a personal carbon ration. Every citizen is given a free annual quota of carbon dioxide. He or she spends it by buying gas and electricity, petrol and train and plane tickets. If they run out, they must buy the rest from someone who has used less than his or her quota. This accounts for about 40 per cent of the carbon dioxide we produce. The remainder is auctioned off to companies. It's a simpler and fairer approach than either green taxation or the EU's emissions trading scheme and it also provides people with a powerful incentive to demand low-carbon technologies. Timescale: a full scheme in place by January 2009.

3. Introduce a new set of building regulations, with three objectives. (A) Imposing strict energy-efficiency requirements on all major refurbishments (costing £3,000 or more). Timescale: in force by June 2007. (B) Obliging landlords to bring their houses up to high energy-efficiency standards before they can rent them out. Timescale: to cover all new rentals from January 2008. (C) Ensuring that all new homes in the United Kingdom are built to the German Passivhaus standard (which requires no heating system). Timescale: in force by 2012.

4. Ban the sale of incandescent lightbulbs, patio heaters, garden floodlights and other wasteful and unnecessary technologies. Introduce a stiff 'feebate' system for all electronic goods sold in the United Kingdom, with the least efficient taxed heavily and the most efficient receiving tax discounts. Every year the standards in each category rise. Timescale: fully implemented by November 2007.

5. Redeploy money now earmarked for new nuclear missiles towards a massive investment in energy generation and distribution. Two schemes in particular require government support to make them commercially viable: very large wind farms,

many miles offshore, connected to the grid with high-voltage direct-current cables and a hydrogen pipeline network to take over from the natural gas grid as the primary means of delivering fuel for home heating. Timescale: both programmes commence at the end of 2007 and are completed by 2018.

6. Promote the development of a new national coach network. City-centre coach stations are shut down and moved to motorway junctions. Urban public transport networks are extended to meet them. The coaches travel on dedicated lanes and never leave the motorways. Journeys by public transport then become as fast as journeys by car, while saving 90 per cent of emissions. It is self-financing, through the sale of the land now used for coach stations. Timescale: commences in 2008 completed by 2020.

7. Oblige all chains of filling stations to supply leasable electric car batteries. This provides electric cars with unlimited mileage: as the battery runs down, you pull into a forecourt; a crane lifts it out and drops in a fresh one. The batteries are charged overnight with surplus electricity from offshore wind farms. Timescale: fully operational by 2011.

8. Abandon the road-building and road-widening programme and spend the money on tackling climate change. The government has earmarked £11.4bn for road expansion. It claims to be allocating just £545m a year to 'spending policies that tackle climate change'. Timescale: immediately.

9. Freeze and then reduce UK airport capacity. While capacity remains high there will be constant upward pressure on any scheme the government introduces to limit flights. We need a freeze on all new airport construction and the introduction of a national quota for landing slots, to be reduced by 90 per cent by 2030. Timescale: immediately.

10. Legislate for the closure of all out-of-town superstores and their replacement with a warehouse and delivery system. Shops use

a staggering amount of energy (six times as much electricity a square metre as factories, for example) and major reductions are hard to achieve: Tesco's 'state of the art' energy-saving store at Diss in Norfolk has managed to cut its energy use by only 20 per cent. Warehouses containing the same quantity of goods use roughly 5 per cent of the energy. Out-of-town shops are also hardwired to the car – delivery vehicles use 70 per cent less fuel. Timescale: fully implemented by 2012.

These timescales might seem extraordinarily ambitious. They are, by contrast to the current glacial pace of change. But when the United States entered the second world war it turned the economy around on a sixpence. Carmakers began producing aircraft and missiles within a year, and amphibious vehicles in 90 days, from a standing start. And that was 65 years ago. If we want this to happen, we can make it happen. It will require more economic intervention than we are used to and some pretty brutal emergency planning policies (with little time or scope for objections). But if you believe that these are worse than mass death then there is something wrong with your value system.

Climate change is not just a moral question: it is the moral question of the 21st century. There is one position even more morally culpable than denial. That is to accept that it's happening and that its results will be catastrophic, but to fail to take the measures needed to prevent it.

NOVEMBER 1 2006

Being Muslim in Britain today: how we spent last Friday

REAR ADMIRAL AMJAD HUSSAIN (48)

Head of the Royal Navy's defence logistics and most senior Muslim in the armed forces, Bristol

I have developed my moral code according to my religion, but I would describe myself as practising rather than pious: although I was born in Rawalpindi, in Pakistan, I used to say my ethnicity was Irish, because I resented the question.

I pray when I have the time, but my day is not driven by it. I think a lot of Muslims are angry that a noisy minority is driving perceptions of us. There are only about 350 Muslims in the Royal Navy – 0.1 per cent of the total – but I like the organisation and it isn't worried about my background.

On Friday I left at 7.30 for a meeting at Whitehall to discuss changes in the structure of the defence industry. My job is to oversee the running of the navy's engineering and logistics: I essentially make sure the ships aren't falling apart. At 10am I attended the naval board meeting with other admirals. It lasted two and a half hours and was held in a room fitted with the latest IT. Nelson used to meet here, so it's a nice mix of the technical and the traditional. Lunch consisted of a sandwich at the Liberal Club with the commander-in-chief of the navy, Admiral Sir James Burnell-Nugent. Then I travelled to Portsmouth to spend the afternoon discussing a contract for tugs and boats, and at 6pm I headed over to HMS Victory for a Trafalgar Night dinner – the anniversary of the battle is October 21. At 11.30pm a car took me home to Hertfordshire.

AHMED HAJI (39)

Computer studies student, east London

I moved to England from east Turkestan in 1998, worked in a Turkish leather shop and learned English. I came for political asylum. I'm happy here: England gives good rights to Muslims. I can pray anywhere, knowledge is available. I would like to become a computer engineer. I met my wife in 2001 – we talked and fell in love.

We have lived in Newham since February. It is lonely here. There are more Turkish people in Stoke Newington, where I lived for four years. I applied for a council flat there, but they didn't have any, so arranged temporary accommodation here.

I pray before dawn, study until my daughter wakes, and drop her off at school. Then I help my wife give breakfast to our other children. Every Friday I go to mosque for an hour, then study in the library. I pick up my daughter at half three, help with her homework. At seven we have dinner, then the children go to bed. I work until 11, then pray another three prayers and go to bed.

TAHIR BHATTI (42)

GMB trade union racial equality officer, Hendon, north London

I was at the GMB's National Race Conference. The majority, including myself, voted to allow women to wear the veil. All motions from today will go to the general vote at congress next year. If the motion passes, it will be added to our rule book and it will be my job to distribute the information to members in their workplaces.

Meeting delegates from other areas, I hear about different issues from the ones I deal with. For example, Poles are having difficulty finding work due to the language barrier. I speak Urdu, Punjabi, Hindi and Gujarati. Recently I received a call from a company where 99.9 per cent of the 2,500 staff are migrant workers. I help them with applying for visas for their spouses or children. I also try to stop employers paying immigrants below the minimum wage.

My drive home was punctuated by conversations on my mobile, finalising plans for our Black History Month celebrations the next day: the refreshments, speeches, dance and documentaries we planned to show on the BNP and racism.

I am a member of the local mosque committee. The Forest Gate raids[1] suprised a whole community. The police acted without enough information. But the community is split between those born here and migrants like myself. The youngsters react more strongly to these events.

SAIRA KHAN (36)

Businesswoman, Chiswick, London

I woke up at six and spent half an hour reading the *Qur'an*. I'm basically re-reading it from scratch in the light of everything that's happening: I want to clarify my own thinking, revisit certain passages and be sure how I personally interpret them. I went to the gym before a business meeting at 9.30. Then I went home, worked and had lunch with my husband, Steven.

We met in 1998. He is white and not Muslim. Although there were some difficulties with the wider family, there were no problems with my direct family – I just sat down and talked with my parents, who are Kashmiri, and it was fine.

In the afternoon I had another business meeting, did more work at home, cooked dinner and spent the evening in with

1 On June 2 2006, shortly before 4am, the Metropolitan police raided a house in Lansdown Road, Forest Gate, east London, as part of an anti-terrorist operation. Mohammed Abdulkahar – who was shot in the shoulder – and his brother Abul Koyair were arrested, but were later released without charge. The Independent Police Complaints Commission described the shooting as an 'accident'. [Ed.]

Steven. At 11pm I went to bed. I don't pray five times a day. I do say a particular prayer when I get into the car or something – it translates roughly as 'God watch over me as I start a new thing' – because it's what you get taught when you are young. I always say the *kelma*, six little prayers before you go to sleep.

NAZISH JILANI (22)

Home Office researcher, Ilford, Essex

My phone alarm woke me at 5.30am and I got up to pray in my bedroom. I try to be as observant as possible. My phone alarm rings five times a day to remind me to pray.

Dressing in my room, I picked a black hijab to wear. I tend to choose dull colours for work, so I don't stand out. At 6.30am I ate my breakfast, then left to get the train to work at my office in High Holborn.

I was at my desk at 8am. I checked my emails and had a chat with the team I work with. At lunchtime I prayed before going to a meeting in the House of Commons, where I sat at the back and took notes. More work at my desk until 5.30pm and then I left to join a friend at a meeting on peace in the Middle East.

I arrived home, where I live with my parents and brother and sister, at 8pm. My little sister is on half-term and wanted to go to a film, so I took her to see *The Departed*. We went to bed at 10.30pm, but before bed I prayed once more.

LUTFI RADWAN (44)

Organic farmer, near Kidlington, Oxfordshire

We all got up at 7.30am. The first prayer of the day is meant to be at sunrise, but if we oversleep we do it as close to sunrise as possible. I let the chickens out, checked their feed and water and looked in on the sheep. Then I helped get the kids get ready for school and had a cup of tea.

I'm half-Egyptian and half-English and my wife is of Pakistani descent. We've got five children between two and 18. During Ramadan we rose at 4am and had breakfast together before fasting all day: Eid has just passed, but we're still appreciating everything a bit more, even if it's just a cup of tea.

By 11am the morning egg collections are over and my wife goes to Oxford to deliver them. For me, religion is about being part of a community and making a difference locally. Trying to live sustainably is as much a part of being Muslim as anything else. An Islamic environmental ethic has much in common with the green movement's idea of responsibility for our individual footprint. I grew up in London and believe that many aspects of urban society – for Muslims and non-Muslims alike – actually increase our sense of separation and alienation.

When the children got back from school they helped collect eggs and looked at our newly hatched chicks before doing their homework. We're a musical family: we often play and sing together. This Friday my son was performing songs he had composed at a club in Oxford, so after I'd locked the chickens up we went to that. When we got back we still had some late-night baking to do for the Saturday farmers' market.

KHADIJA RAVAT (34)

Teacher of Qur'anic Arabic, Leicester

I woke at 7am, prayed, then had breakfast. It wasn't a teaching week because of mid-term, so I showered and went into college for a quick meeting about classes.

I find it useful to wear the niqab when I'm teaching, because I know that people are concentrating on what I'm writing on the board. Even when I'm teaching only women I wear a long gown, because I don't want my clothes to take over.

I came back home and had pasta for lunch, then visited a friend who had been in hospital. I returned and said the afternoon prayer. I went through my emails, then finally got round to last night's washing-up. I drove to where my husband works and picked him up and we made the journey to West Yorkshire, where my mother lives. We spent the weekend there celebrating Eid.

I don't want the veil to be the biggest thing about me, but recently I feel as if it has been. It's just a symbol of what I'm trying to do. There are many other issues I'd rather talk about.

IMRAN HUSSAIN (27)

Shopkeeper and bus driver, Birmingham

I woke up at 4.30am for prayer. I didn't go to the mosque, because it was cold and I didn't have time to get ready, so I prayed at home. I got some sleep afterwards, but had to get up at 8.30 to take my mum to hospital. She's diabetic.

In the afternoon I went to Friday prayers. Mosque is always busy on Friday. I have mixed feelings about that: it makes me proud that so many Muslims drop what they're doing to come and sad that people (myself included) don't make it the rest of the week. Still, it's nice to be able to catch up with people. Non-Muslims use pubs as a meeting point – we use mosques.

In a mosque, everyone is equal. I find mosques relaxing. I leave behind my phone and my car keys and forget about my two jobs. I try to pray on time five times a day and try to read the *Qur'an* every day. I read the translation, because I don't understand Arabic. After prayers I had lunch with my parents and did some errands for my family and business.

UMMAR RASHID (24)

Architect, London

I walked past the mosque on the way to the tube at about 7am and it reminded me of my lack of faith. I'd describe myself as a struggling Muslim, maybe even a fraudulent one. I was at university during 9/11 and remember thinking, 'I'm never going to get through an airport again.' It was around then I first identified myself as a Muslim and grew my beard, but I'm not devout. I don't drink and I fast – sometimes.

I recently went to a mosque in Manchester for Eid prayers and it pissed me off. The imam could have engaged with current issues like the veil or John Reid's 'parent' remarks[2] – instead he chose platitudes and spoke in Urdu.

The day was spent like most others: building models for design projects that the firm is working on. At lunchtime I had miso soup and a sandwich, while other Muslims were going to Friday prayers.

After work I went to a Halloween-themed burlesque cabaret show at Bethnal Green Working Men's Club and watched my friend make a fool of himself. It was a good night. I didn't get home until 4am.

2 In September 2006 John Reid used his first speech to a Muslim audience since becoming home secretary to ask Muslim parents to keep a close eye on their children and to act if they suspected they were being radicalised by extremists. [Ed.]

NOVEMBER 14 2006

Britney and Kevin aren't the first to find chess sexy

STEPHEN MOSS

Phil Maggitti, an editor on the satirical US website *Pug Bus*, is evidently not a chess player. His site was planning to sponsor a competition to find a name for the four-hour sex video – currently the subject of a tabloid and internet bidding war – featuring Britney Spears and her husband, Kevin Federline, but Maggitti says his interest initially waned when he read a description of what they got up to: 'They did nothing all day but have sex – and play the odd game of chess.'

'At first we were put off by the "odd game of chess" reference,' says Maggitti, 'but then we learned that by "odd" the source really did mean "odd".'

Sadly, I have no idea how odd their games were – whether Ms Spears perhaps played an unusual line of the Dutch defence or Mr Federline opted for the modern Benoni. But Maggitti is wrong to assume that chess is inherently unsexy. It makes perfect sense for Spears and Federline to be jumping from sex to chess and back again in their four hours of passion, because the two are natural bedfellows.

Nor do you need a special chess set to sexualise the game. Spears and Federline were reportedly playing with a hand-carved erotic set for which they had paid $15,000, but the standard pieces will do.

'Chess is better than sex,' the former world champion Bobby Fischer is reputed to have said. The German academic and chess player Eckhard Freise agreed: chess is better than sex, he said, because there are more positions. They are intimately connected because both are about control. The notion of 'bondage' is important in chess: tying your opponent in knots so that, ultimately, you can do with him/her (probably him) what you will. Some chess players talk about 'killing' their opponents; others about 'fucking' them.

Sex bubbles just beneath the surface. Occasionally, it is explicit, as when the British grandmaster Danny Gormally thumped an Armenian grandmaster at the Chess Olympiad in Turin in June after a row over a beautiful female player they were both trying to mate at a party. Chess is not a genteel pursuit, it is a violent struggle for survival and domination. Demonstrations of potency and fears of emasculation are central to chess.

Why is the game played predominantly by hormonally challenged teenage boys and pot-bellied men with limited social lives? Why is the queen the most powerful piece? Why does the king hide away until the end of the game, when the battlefield has been cleared and it's safe to emerge? Freud would have a field day with chess.

Winter

Fashion victim

HADLEY FREEMAN

Fashion trends, by their very nature, burn brightly but briefly. Last summer's essential skinny jeans are now trampled underfoot as customers rush to get next season's high-waisted style. When a person embodies a particular trend, her rise might seem, momentarily, unstoppable. But one need only wait just a few months for her brutal demise – and few falls from fashion grace have been as unexpected and as humiliating as that of Rachel Zoe this month. Once you typed her name into the internet and you were greeted with endless adoring websites, extolling her genius and her famous friends; now it's pages of sniggering blogs cackling over the end of 'the Queen of the Underworld'.

But perhaps the biggest surprise is that she lasted so long. For more than two years, Zoe (pronounced to rhyme with 'so') has been one of the most influential people in the fashion world. If you have wondered why every other teenage girl is wearing over-sized sunglasses, or just why you've even heard of Nicole Richie, Zoe is the one to blame.

She is the regular stylist to Richie, Lindsay Lohan and Mischa Barton from *The OC* – probably three of the celebrities most copied by the lucrative teenage market – as well as frequently dressing Keira Knightley, Kate Beckinsale and Cameron Diaz. If we are now in an era when celebrities control the fashion world, Zoe has been its ruling force. Her appeal has spanned the style spectrum, from *Vogue* to *Heat*, and she has probably kick-started more trends for young women in the past two years than Kate Moss. In an interview with Vogue earlier this year she said, 'My mission, when I moved here [to Los Angeles], was to try, somehow, to merge the worlds of fashion and celebrity.' She did this so successfully that merely by wearing her impeccably chosen clothes, her clients became celebrities even if they didn't actually do anything else. Richie was the most obvious case in point.

Zoe's fondness for vintage gowns and long headscarves made Richie and Lohan look like Hollywood icons, even when they were photographed falling out of another nightclub at 5am. Several designers are said to consult her before working on their collections in order to ensure their clothes are worn by her influential clients. She co-designed a dress worn by Knightley with Calvin Klein's Francisco Costa. At Paris fashion week in October, one show was delayed by an hour because Zoe, now a crucial front-row presence, was running late.

Celebrity stylists have existed for as long as there have been celebrities, but none before has been famous on Zoe's scale. Partly because, unlike most stylists, she often attends red-carpet events with her clients, posing with them for the cameras. Moreover, unusually, she is said to dress some of her more image-conscious clients on a daily basis, not just for special events – ensuring they look as attention-grabbingly stylish as possible should they happen to be photographed en route to Starbucks.

But the main reason Zoe became so well-known is that her style is so distinctive. In the *Vogue* interview she summed up her look, in true fashion description-style, with as few verbs and as many repetitions of the word glamour as possible: 'It's very 60s to 70s glamour. It's Mod meets Grecian. A lot of gold and a lot of bronze, shimmer and glamour, but relaxed glamour, very unstructured, bold accessories.' Her mantra is 'shine and gold, shine and gold, always'.

What this pile-up of adjectives and references actually amounts to is vintage, brightly patterned dresses; long, loose tops over extra-skinny trousers; bug-like sunglasses and huge designer handbags.

To those outside the fashion world, it looked like 70s Hollywood housewife with a *Valley of the Dolls* lifestyle – *Tatler* memorably dubbed the look 'dead socialite' in honour of the ladies-who-didn't-lunch of yesteryear, such as Jackie Onassis, Nan Kempner and Talitha Getty, on whom the look was based.

It is how Zoe dresses and how she dressed her clients. Photographs of her emerging from restaurants and nightclubs with Richie, Barton and Lohan look like images from a quadruplets' convention. Richie, in particular, seemed to be morphing into Zoe, even cutting and dyeing her hair to match. The *New York Post* referred to Zoe's clients as the 'Zoebots'.

As befits a very modern phenomenon, she was brought down in a very modern way. Shortly after it was announced that Richie had sacked the woman she once described as 'like a best friend', the following item appeared on Richie's MySpace page last week: 'What 35-year-old raisin-face whispers her order of three pieces of asparagus for dinner at Chateau every night, and hides her deathly disorder by pointing the finger at me, and used her last paycheck I wrote her, to pay for a publicist instead of a nutritionist? HINT: Her nickname is Lettucecup.' Lohan then posted a smiley face and added, 'Hmmmm ... no comment.'

Zoe quickly retaliated, through gritted teeth, by issuing her own statement.

Zoe has long had to counter allegations that she promotes unnatural thinness. There have been rumours that she ships in illegal diet drugs for her 'girls', as she refers to her clients, and that she refuses to sully her bejewelled hands by dabbling with any clothes over a size zero (UK size 4). She has vehemently denied both accusations. Nevertheless, her look is dependent on thinness because it takes a very small body frame not to look like a sofa in a Pucci kaftan. 'It is a very stylish look, but you have to be very thin to wear it, so it has become synonymous with the size zero debate [the argument about whether celebrities and models are becoming too thin],' says Jo Elvin, editor of *Glamour*.

On top of that, everything about the aesthetic is geared to emphasising skinniness: extra-large bags make the arms look frail, oversized men's watches make the wrists look twig-like, oversized sunglasses render the face almost shrunken. The *LA Times* claimed that, 'Fashion insiders have whispered privately that Zoe is single-handedly bringing back anorexia.'

She is tiny, and although all of her clients have dismissed claims that she promotes skinniness, it is notable that since Knightley, for example, has come under her aegis, she has grown visibly thinner, to say nothing of Richie.

Asked why she had broken off with Zoe, Richie, whose weight was said to have dropped to six stone, told an American magazine that she 'wanted to surround herself with positive people and influences'. When she appeared at the American Music awards this month, dressed by her new stylist, Cristina Ehrlich, she looked undeniably, if only relatively, healthier.

It would be ridiculous to blame Zoe for today's obsession with skinniness. But her dominance in the fashion world has notably coincided with the escalation of the trend, and her clients have been the most high-profile, and most extreme, examples of it. Perhaps it needed to become as extreme as possible in order to spark the reaction against it.

'Nicole does dress fabulously, but we do have a responsibility about who we hold up as fashion icons,' says Elvin.

'The tide has turned against this emphasis on skinniness, and I think women are now feeling that it's all a bit sad, really,' adds Jane Bruton, editor of *Grazia*.

It will take more than the demise of a stylist to reverse the belief that thin is in. But the end of the Zoebots may well signify the end of the size zero era.

DECEMBER 13 2006

Life is beautiful

ALAN RUSBRIDGER

Alice Herz-Sommer is, I think, the most optimistic person I have ever met. She sits in her armchair in her single-roomed north London flat beaming at the beauty of life and treasuring the moment. She is 103 and cannot quite believe her luck.

This is not wholly what you expect as you read the summary of her life. It is true that she is an immensely gifted pianist, who has found great sustenance from her art and who, even now, practises for three hours a day. But she has also experienced more unhappiness than any optimist has a right to expect.

With her Jewish background, she endured the miseries of the Prague ghetto, spent two years in the Theresienstadt (Terezin) concentration camp, where nearly 35,000 prisoners perished. Her husband was moved to Auschwitz in 1944: she never saw him again. She lost many in her extended family and most of the friends she had grown up with.

All this she tells with a near-perfect recall of dates, names and places. If she was ever bitter about the hardships she endured or the losses she suffered, it is all wiped clean. Instead, there is an almost evangelical zeal in communicating the necessity of optimism.

She lives on her own in Belsize Park. Until she was 97 she went swimming every day at the pool in nearby Swiss Cottage. Her daily routine still involves playing the piano from 10am to 1pm. Her musical memory is, she says, still excellent. She begins by playing a Bach prelude before working her way through the repertoire –

Schubert, Beethoven and so on – that she has always played. Twice a month she plays with a violinist and occasionally trios with her daughter-in-law, a cellist.

Her story begins in 1903, the year she was born in German-speaking Prague, then still part of the Austro-Hungarian empire. Her mother came from a musical Moravian family and was a childhood friend of Gustav Mahler. Sommer remembers hearing the first performance of Mahler's 2nd Symphony in Prague when she was about eight.

'Still now when I listen to Mahler my mother is next to me,' she says.

As a young girl, she knew Franz Kafka – he was the best friend of her elder sister's husband. She started playing the piano when she was five and was soon taking lessons with a distinguished pupil of Liszt, Conrad Ansorge ('as a pianist, extraordinary; as a teacher, not so good'). Her sister was simultaneously taking lessons from Alexander Zemlinsky, under whom she sang in a performance of Mahler's 8th Symphony. By her mid-teens Alice was giving lessons and touring as a pianist, playing Schumann, Bach, Beethoven, Suk and Smetana.

She met her husband-to-be, also a musician, in 1931 and married him two weeks later. 'He spoke five languages. He was an extremely gifted man, extremely gifted,' she says. Their only son, Raphael, who went on to be a concert cellist, was born in 1937.

Everything in this busy, fulfilled and creative life changed in March 1939, when Hitler occupied Czechoslovakia.

'This was a hard time for Jews,' she says with some understatement. 'Nothing was allowed. The food was very poor. We could only buy things for half an hour in the afternoon. We had to give away all our belongings. We were poor, we had nothing. For me the greatest punishment was having to wear the yellow star, here on the left side. When I went on the street my best non-Jewish friends didn't dare to look at me. I didn't know if I should go and speak with them. It was a very, very, very hard time, this I must say.'

Most Jews were sent to a ghetto, but for a while Sommer, her husband and her son were allowed to stay in their own flat. 'Above us was living a Nazi and beneath us a Nazi.'

Then, in 1943 – a year after Sommer's mother had been sent away with only a rucksack – the three were sent to Theresienstadt.

'The evening before this we were sitting in our flat. I put off the light because I wanted my child to sleep for the last time in his bed. Now came my Czech friends: they came and they took the remaining pictures, carpets, even furniture. They didn't say anything. We were dead for them, I believe. And at the last moment the Nazi came – his name was Hermann – with his wife. They brought biscuits and he said, "Mrs Sommer, I hope you come back with your family. I don't know what to say to you. I enjoyed your playing – such wonderful things, I thank you." The Nazi was the most human of all.

'When you know history – wars and wars and wars … It begins with this: that we are born half good and half bad – everybody, everybody. And there are situations where the bad comes out and situations where the good comes out. This is the reason why people invented religion, I believe.'

The following day the three of them spent an hour and a half on the train to Theresienstadt – bizarrely, a 'show camp' for Red Cross inspections and simultaneously a staging post for tens of thousands of inmates who were shipped off to their deaths in other camps. The Red Cross inspectors noted the cultural activity: the inmates included numerous artists, writers and musicians.

'We had to play music because the Red Cross came and the Germans were trying to show what a good life we had,' says Sommer. 'It was our luck, actually. Even so, hundreds and hundreds were dying around us every day. It was a hard time.'

They lived in barracks for two years. They were given black-water coffee for breakfast, white-water soup for lunch and, in the evening, black-water soup.

'We lost weight. People ask, "How could you make music?" We were so weak. But music was special, like a spell, I would say. I gave more than 150 concerts there. There were excellent musicians there, really excellent. Violinists, cellists, singers, conductors and composers.'

The conductor Rafael Schächter recruited 150 singers and conducted 15 or more performances of the Verdi *Requiem*, some of which Sommer sang in. And she gave her own concerts. 'I played twice, three times a week. The audience were mostly old people – very ill people and unhappy people – but they came to our concerts and this was their food.'

Sommer's son, Raphael, took part in performances of Hans Krasa's children's opera *Brundibar* – given as part of the Nazis' attempts to show how 'normal' life was in Theresienstadt. Out of 15,000 children who were sent to the camp, he was one of only 130 to survive the war.

'In 1944 my husband was among thousands who were sent away. His last words to me were, "You mustn't do anything voluntarily." I didn't understand what was in his mind. This was on Monday. Three days afterwards, again thousands were sent away, mothers and children of the men who had already been sent. In the second transport the women went voluntarily because they wanted to meet their husbands. They never met them. So my husband saved our lives.

'He was sent to Auschwitz first and then sent to work in Dachau and – six weeks before the end of the war – he died from typhus. I brought up my son alone.'

Does she think she had a particular toughness? 'Yah, I tell you something. I had a twin sister – same mother, same father, same upbringing. She was extremely gifted, but a terrible pessimist, but I was the contrary. This is the reason I am so old, even now. I am sure. I am looking for the nice things in life. I know about the bad things, but I look only for the good things. The world is wonderful. It's full of beauty and full of miracles. Our brain, the memory, how does it work? Not to speak of art and music ... It is a miracle.'

On May 9 1945 the Russian army arrived to relieve the camp. 'We knew already that Hitler had lost the war so we expected to be relieved. I remember my brother took his violin and went immediately to Prague. I stayed in the camp for a month or two, because I was told there was an epidemic. When I came back home it was very, very painful, because nobody else came back. The whole family of my husband, several members of my family, all my friends, all the friends of my family, nobody came back. It was a hard time. Then I realised what Hitler had done.

'I never spoke a word about it, because I didn't want my child to grow up with hatred, because hatred brings hatred. I succeeded. My son had very good friends in Germany and they invited him to play and [they] appreciated him. And I never hated either, never, never.'

In 1949 she went to Israel with her sisters and taught music in Tel Aviv. 'I must say, when I moved to Israel there was not a day without political tension, but [to experience] democracy! After Hitler and Stalin, you feel what it means. You can read, speak, trust everyone. It was a beautiful life in Israel, inspiring. Musicians, scientists and writers – they all came and lectured. It was a cultural centre. I was very happy.'

I ask her about her feelings of identity. 'My parents were not Jewish. I am not. My husband was not. We are Jewish without religion. I belong to this group because of my ancestors, of course. I don't need religion. I understand when we are in a terrible situation we are needing hope. Religion, for me, is a symbol of hope. It helps, this hope. I know about religion, but even in the darkest time I never believed.'

At the prompting of her son, she moved to London 20 years ago. Until recently she went to the University of the Third Age three times a week to study history, philosophy and the history of Judaism. She has now stopped, because of problems with her back.

Sommer feels very at home in England. 'It's because English people are so polite and this politeness is not superficial. The English respect each other more than others. They are cheerful and helpful and I admire their humour. English humour is not laughing, it is distance. They observe life and always stay stoic. Admirable people. I love them, I love them.'

In 2001 Sommer had to endure the grief of losing her cellist son, who died suddenly while on tour, aged 65. She found comfort in playing the piano and still loves it. 'I love work. Work is the best invention, the best. Playing the piano is still a discipline. It makes you happy to have something. The worst thing is boredom. Boredom is dangerous.

'My fingers are not as good as they were, but [where it's a problem] I change the fingering. I have a very good memory. I start every day with an hour of Bach. I play all the 48 *Preludes* – not the *Fugues* – which is very difficult, even when you try one page without mistakes. After Bach, I play my other pieces in order not to forget.'

Every Saturday, she plays Scrabble with another musical survivor of the camps, the cellist Anita Wallfisch, who played in the Auschwitz camp orchestra. 'We don't speak about the past,' says Sommer.

All her family and friends are dead. 'I have never met anyone of this age. Never. When I was young, somebody of 60 was regarded as an old man.' Does she ask herself why she survived? 'My temperament. This optimism and this discipline. Punctually, at 10am, I am sitting there at the piano, with everything in order around me. For 30 years I have eaten the same, fish or chicken. Good soup, and this is all. I don't drink, not tea, not coffee, not alcohol. Hot water. I walk a lot with terrible pains, but after 20 minutes it is much better. Sitting or lying is not good.

'In any case, life is beautiful, extremely beautiful. And when you are old you appreciate it more. When you are older you think, you remember, you care and you appreciate. You are thankful for everything. For everything.'

DECEMBER 14 2006

'I've never done anything for less than £15'

ESTHER ADDLEY

It was only the fact that she was abused as a child, Jackie says, that ever enabled her to go through with the sex. She hated the sex, she says, really hated it. 'But I was abused when I was a kid and when you have been abused by a bloke you just learn to turn yourself off. When you come out on the game you turn your feelings off.'

Most of the women working on the streets of Ipswich have been abused, she says, and they all feel the same. 'Everyone has the same past. I can't name one girl who likes the job.' A heroin habit also helps. 'Heroin stops you feeling, it really does. If you want to cry, you just can't cry. The feelings are just not there. I know. And when your feelings are suppressed, that's when you come out to work.'

Jackie was a street sex worker in Ipswich, on and off, for three years until a few months ago.

Most of the time, she says, she would come out every night. A good night would mean she'd take home between £40 and £80, representing two punters wanting full sex and paying full price. On a bad night there would be between 15 and 20 women working and the customers were scarce or, worse, willing to exploit the women's desperation.

'The refugees – I shouldn't say this – but the refugees were the worst. They would offer you £5. Especially at this time of year, when it's freezing and the men know you need the money. But I've never done anything for less than £15. You can get a bag [of heroin] for £15.'

Jackie, 34, doesn't use heroin any more – or at least not very often – and she's no longer working the streets. In March a man with whom she was living and who, she says, kicked her out every time she went to work, finally locked her out.

'I thought, to hell with that, I'm worth more than that.' That moment coincided with getting a methadone prescription from drugs services allowing her to reduce her habit, and gradually she stopped working.

Like most of the women who have worked the streets of Ipswich, Jackie knew all of the five women who are known or believed to have been murdered, except Tania Nicol.[1]

Annette Nicholls's last official sighting was last Tuesday, but Jackie says that on Thursday or Friday – she can't remember which – Ms Nicholls knocked at her flat and shouted through the letter box. Because her partner was asleep she ignored her. 'I feel really

1 Gemma Adams, 25, Tania Nicol, 19, Anneli Alderton, 24, Paula Clennell, 24, and Annette Nicholls, 29, were found dead near villages south of Ipswich during a 10-day period in December. They all worked as prostitutes in the town. On December 21 Steve Wright, a former fork-lift truck driver from Ipswich, Suffolk, was charged with their murders. In May 2007 he pleaded not guilty at Ipswich crown court. [Ed.]

terrible about that. It's preyed on my mind ever since.' Ms Nicholls, as far as Jackie knew, was homeless. So what did she do? 'I think she would go home with the punters.'

Paula Clennell was last seen on Sunday evening, and Jackie says she saw her the day before. In the summer Jackie found a keyring belonging to Ms Clennell, which had pictures of her three daughters on it, all of whom had been taken into care. She returned it after bumping into her a few weeks later.

Anneli Alderton, meanwhile, became a friend in prison a couple of years ago. Jackie last saw her a couple of weeks ago, dressed in white boots and hotpants and clearly heading out to work. As for Gemma Adams: 'She was one of the good ones. Kept herself to herself, didn't really cause the punters trouble.'

She doesn't like to criticise them, Jackie says, but Ms Clennell and Ms Nicholls occasionally resorted to tactics some other women never would. 'They used to rob the punters, and that just gives us a bad name.' Last Tuesday, she says, the day on which she was last officially seen, Ms Nicholls had stolen a customer's phone and sold it for 'gear'.

Jackie discovered heroin quite late, aged 28, after the father of her third child introduced her to the drug. 'I had a three-bedroomed house, a front garden, two boys and a girl, everything I needed in life. As soon as I got into that life everything got taken off me.'

Her parents, discovering she was on heroin, persuaded her to come to Ipswich, where they live, from Sunderland. Soon, however, she was living in a women's hostel, then, on and off, with a partner. At one point she lived in a tent in a cemetery. Now she lives with a new partner, but her two teenage sons are in foster care, her daughter has been adopted.

Recently, a newspaper report of an arrest for shoplifting called her a prostitute, a word she loathes.

'We call ourselves "working girls". When you say "prostitute" it's a dirty word.' Neither of her parents have had any contact since. 'They haven't even texted,' she says.

So what does she hope for the future? 'I hope to not go back to that way.' All the same, she says she feels guilty. 'I don't know why, it's just that the feeling's there. That's what I keep saying to my partner. I could have been out still working and it could have been me.'

DECEMBER 21 2006

Farewell to the blond tease and his trash-talking mate

GIDEON HAIGH

One was bouncy, beamish, a prankster, a prestidigitator; the other was tall, taut, utterly dependable, the natural straight man. Shane Warne and Glenn McGrath: it was hard to imagine one without the other. And now, it would seem, we will not have to.

Steve Waugh was great. Ricky Ponting is. But no two cricketers so separated Australia from the rest of the cricket pack in the last decade or so as Warne and McGrath: the best slow bowler of all and the best seam bowler of his era. It is a freak of nature that they should have coincided and ended up playing more than 100 Tests together. To call them a combination, implying planning and foresight, is not quite right. They were more, as Palmerston described his coalition with Disraeli, an 'accidental and fortuitous concurrence of atoms'.

When they walked off the Oval together at the end of last year's fifth Test, the sardonic smiles masked a brooding determination. Australia had lost the Ashes. That would never do. The physical expense of going on was acute, but the psychological toll of stopping would have been too great.

Their last two years have been full of personal upheaval: McGrath took time off to be with his wife; Warne, rather more publicly, took time off from his wife. But target 2006-07 became their objective and is now to be their swansong.

Warne seems to have been around for ever and not long at all, so vivid is the memory of him in England in 1993 as a 23-year-old blond blur with turn to burn. But the man who bowled the ball of the last century has kept serving up candidates for the ball of this, even if they have not been as rippingly obvious. For all the talk about his flipper and his zooter, his woofer and his tweeter, it was his subtly but scientifically varied leg-break that remained the eternal mystery ball. As Graham Thorpe observed last year in comparing the Australian with his statistical shadow, Muttiah Muralitharan: 'Warne was always varying the degree he spun the ball, while Murali generally just tried to spin the ball as much as he could.'

In his private life, of course, Warne has always been the soul of indiscretion. Even now he marches to a different drum in this Australian XI, listening for his personal bongo while others keep in step with the martial snare. That, though, has involved one of his most amazing feats, persuading Australians to cut him the slack he always thought was his due. He is like the eternally mischievous kid brother: incorrigible to a degree that has become endearing.

The 1993 Ashes series where Warne made his name was watched at the Australian Institute of Sport Cricket Academy by McGrath, also 23, who got by on four hours' sleep a night so he could follow the feats of Allan Border's all-conquering team. Little did McGrath know, but he was watching the opening of the vacancy that he would fill. Craig McDermott was injured; Merv Hughes was injuring himself. McGrath played in the first home Test of the southern summer as a kind of research and development project. His breakthrough tour was 18 months later in the West Indies, when he met the challenge of Curtly Ambrose and Courtney Walsh with his own brand of homespun hostility.

McGrath's bowling career began on a dirt track on a poultry farm with an upturned water-trough for a wicket. It retained that unadorned, unrefined, self-sufficient practicality. 'Keep everything simple' was his golden rule. 'Don't complicate things for the sake of it.' He brought to fast bowling the philosophy of the Model T, mass-producing deliveries just short of a length, just wide of off-stump, just doing enough, just about unimprovably.

Warne and McGrath both epitomised Australian excellence and embodied Australian aggression. Warne was a tease, a flirt, a provocateur, tripping up even the nimble feet of Mark Ramprakash. 'Come on, Ramps, you know you want to,' he taunted the young batsman in a famous spell at Trent Bridge in July 2001. 'That's the way, Ramps, keep coming down the wicket.' So Ramps did – too far, and another English Ashes challenge stumbled and staggered to a halt.

McGrath, meanwhile, was the trash-talker extraordinaire. New Zealand's Adam Parore, in his autobiography, *The Wicked-Keeper*, a few years ago, took the trouble to transcribe a standard McGrath monologue: 'You guys are shit. We can't wait to get rid of you so we don't have to play you. Get the South Africans over here so we can have a real game of cricket. We can't be bothered playing you guys. You're second-raters.' Rubbish, of course, but annoying rubbish, the kind that one recalls and ruminates on, as did Parore.

Above all, these two Australians have been winners, each a talisman for the other. McGrath has been on the winning side in 82 out of his 122 Tests (67.2 per cent), Warne in 90 of his 143 (62.9 per cent). No bowlers with more than 200 Test wickets have played in a greater proportion of victories. It is a safe bet that no bowlers can have contributed so much to victories so often.

The farewells of Warne and McGrath will elicit tributes aplenty. What they mean for Ponting's Australians is less clear. Cricket in this country has nursed a dread of a sudden glut of retirements since the Sydney Test of January 1984, which first Greg Chappell, then Dennis Lillee and finally Rod Marsh chose as the stage for their final curtain call. They left in charge Kim Hughes, who proved unequal to the burden, and Border, who took a while to feel comfortable with it, and the Australia XI for three years marked time, when it was not retreating.

McGrath now has a near body double in Stuart Clark, who has been probably the most consistent component of Australia's attack this summer. But while Warne has an effective understudy in Stuart MacGill, the wrist-spin ranks thin drastically thereafter. Warne made leg-spin look easy – much easier than it was, in fact, as numberless imitators have discovered. No new Warne looms, any more than does a new Bradman.

That is something, however, Australian cricket will have to deal with on its own. McGrath's wife is sick. Warne's is sick of him. Age is only one factor in their decisions. Their personal futures are as important as their pasts. These are not simply retirements about where Warne and McGrath have been; they concern where the pair want to end up.

DECEMBER 21 2006

Inside the BNP

IAN COBAIN

Early one evening in October, outside an entrance to Liverpool Street station in London, a few dozen men and women are standing around in small groups whispering into mobile telephones, shuffling their feet, smiling and nodding discreetly to one another.

It is unseasonably warm and people are spilling on to the pavement from the Hamilton Hall, a pub a few yards away. It's also a Saturday and throngs of noisy football supporters are weaving in and out of the station on their way home from matches around the capital.

The small groups of men and women become larger and gradually merge into one company, but they blend in beautifully with the people around them. Nobody sees their congregation, nobody else notices that they are one. These people are using what they call an RVP – a clandestine rendezvous point. If it sounds like an extraordinarily secretive way to meet your friends on a Saturday evening, that's exactly what it is. But then, these are people who use pseudonyms to conceal their true identities. Their emails are encrypted, with only a chosen few possessing the codes needed to decipher them. They are people who employ carefully coded language to express their views and who will, before speaking plainly, quite literally look over their shoulders.

This is the strange world of what may be the United Kingdom's fastest-growing political party: these people have proclaimed themselves to be the Torch-Bearers of British Culture, the guardians of our national identity.

Welcome to life inside the British National Party.

My first meeting with a BNP activist was in the Amato Café in Soho's Old Compton Street on September 7. His name was Steve Tyler, he was slightly scruffy and he had a goatee beard and dyed hair. He must have been about 60. His companion was a young Brazilian woman. They were obviously close. As she left, and our meeting began, Steve muttered something about his friend wanting help bringing her sister into the country. That was my first surprise. The second came when Steve admitted that he is not British at all: he is Australian. Despite this, Steve clearly regards immigration as the greatest problem facing his adopted home.

'The whole world is pouring down on us,' he said. 'It's a huge problem and it's going to get worse.' Not that he is a racist, you understand – 'I'm on the liberal wing of the party ... most of the people in the party are' – and he doesn't blame the immigrants themselves – 'If I was a 19-year-old Kurd, I'd be trying to get into the country.' It's just that there is such a deluge, he explains. And really, something must be done about it! 'I don't want to be lying on my deathbed thinking that I could have done something about it, but didn't.'

For generations people like Steve have struggled to capture more than a tiny percentage of the votes at local or general elections. That has begun to change following Nick Griffin's attempts to clean up the BNP's image since becoming chairman seven years ago. In last May's local elections, the party won 229,000 votes and now has more than 50 council seats.

To put this in some context, around seven million votes were cast last May, and 364,000 people voted for the Green party. But support for the BNP is clearly growing. In some parts of the country – in areas of West Yorkshire and East Lancashire, in pockets of the Midlands and on the eastern outskirts of London – the extreme right has achieved the political legitimacy that has eluded it for generations. It is also recruiting new members hand over fist. But what sort of people are now joining the party? What is its electoral strategy? Is it dedicated purely to the pursuit of democratic politics? And where is it obtaining its funds? In an attempt to answer these questions – and to take a look behind Griffin's façade of normality – the *Guardian* decided that it would join the BNP.

I signed up under an assumed name last June, using a fake address in central London from which I could pick up BNP correspondence, a new email account and a dedicated mobile phone. I was keen to become active, I said on my application form, but I wanted to remain behind the scenes.

In my first meetings with BNP activists I hinted heavily that I worked in the public sector and could lose my job if my membership became known. Over the months that followed there were times when members would question me closely about my views and my background, and it would be unclear to me whether they were merely curious or suspicious. Before most meetings I would feel some fear of exposure, but when asked about my work, I found I could reply, quite truthfully: 'Trust me, if you knew what I did for a living, you would understand exactly why it is that I can't tell you.'

After talking about my 'work for the government', Steve turned to the question of police surveillance. 'The police will watch leading members, of course, but they can't watch everybody who joins. They're too busy watching Islamic terrorists these days. And it's no secret that most police officers probably support us. Certainly those working in central London know the problems we face … '

'The problems we face.' I heard phrases like this uttered by BNP members many times and, after several months, came to understand their precise, nuanced meanings. 'Nice areas' I quickly understood to signify predominantly white areas. 'Quiet areas' are places where black and minority ethnic people live, but keep a low profile and don't compete too hard for jobs, school places or sexual partners. 'Troublesome areas' are places where black people do just the opposite. 'No-go areas' are places where black and ethnic minority people are in a majority. 'Ethnics' speaks for itself, as does 'our people'. And 'the problems we face'? They are, quite simply, that there are black people living among us whites.

In my seven months as a party member I heard very few racist epithets and no anti-semitic comments. Such language appears almost to be frowned upon in Griffin's post-makeover BNP. Perhaps it is a tribute to the Race Relations Act 1976 and the Public Order Act 1986 – and to the gently shifting mores of British life – that racists rarely feel able to express themselves, even among like-minded people. But some of the fear and the hatred remains: it just emerges in code.

On the evening of Sunday September 24 I was sitting in the Orange Tree pub in Richmond, south-west London, opposite a man who had contacted me by email. He had told me that his name was Nick Russell and that he was the London regional organiser for the BNP. One these statements was true; the other I knew to be a lie.

Nick is indeed a dedicated party activist. His real name, however, is Nick Eriksen. He is 47, a former civil servant, and he once served as a Tory councillor in Southwark, south London. An intense man, with bitten nails and a permanent frown, he appears forever to be on the brink of losing his temper. His complaints that night were endless: the sale of a local real-ale brewery, the iniquity of Britain's divorce laws, interference from Brussels and, of course, immigration.

'Yes, I suppose if I was a half-starved Somali goatherd I would want to come to Britain ... the South Africans will never stage a proper World Cup. How could they? It's a black country. They've got the infrastructure the whites left them, but it's a mess now ...

I hear there are a hundred thousand Bulgarians and Romanians waiting to get in ... I would have thought the number of people we had living in Britain in the 30s or 40s was the optimum population.' And so it goes on.

Nick, I discover in time, is an almost archetypal BNP member. I had joined a party that draws in people who are not only xenophobic, but harassed and malcontented; people who feel themselves to be unfairly put-upon, to be slightly under siege. It is a party of people for whom British society, as it is and as it is developing, has no appeal, and no room. It was also a party that was about to appoint a *Guardian* journalist to one of its key positions.

Nick was looking for a central London organiser. He already had almost a dozen district organisers working under him, in different parts of the capital, but central London had been neglected for years. The party had decided to bring its members living in central London into one branch and then get some of them active: distributing leaflets, writing to newspapers, contesting council byelections.

The party, Nick explained, is particularly keen to gain a foothold in the London assembly. The next elections to the assembly, in 2008, will be held under a proportional representation system, and the BNP will capture a seat if it wins just 5 per cent of the vote. 'Around 7 per cent or 8 per cent will give us two seats, which would be good, as it could be a bit lonely for just one person.'

Nick explained that the lists of local members and former members would be sent to me in encrypted emails. He slid a brown envelope across the table: inside was a CD that held the software that would enable me to decode them. He also asked me to write down the elaborate password I must use with the software: 'the KING was born on 31 FEBRUARY'.

It will also be my job to organise social events four times a year: 'We'll tell you which venues you should use.' And one last matter:

Nick thinks that perhaps I should use a pseudonym, just to be on the safe side. 'Why not? It's not against the law. It's a free country.' I could even use it when meeting other BNP members. Nobody need ever know my real name. Nick suggests I call myself Ian Taylor.

A couple of months later, when Nick eventually tells me his real name, he explains that he adopted his pseudonym because he is an English teacher. (An inordinate number of members claim to be teachers or retired teachers or married to teachers – I'm never sure whether they are telling the truth.)

'It's ludicrous that you could lose your job for being a member of the party,' he says. 'But there's nothing wrong with using another name. We have a long tradition in this country of using different names. George Orwell wasn't really George Orwell. Cliff Richard isn't Cliff Richard.'

Before I leave the Orange Tree, we are joined by Chris Forster, who stood as a BNP candidate in Richmond at the last council elections. A rather raffish-looking Cockney in his 60s, Chris explains that he was a National Front supporter in the 1970s. He talks about a number of murders and child sex attacks that he hears are happening in West Yorkshire, which are being ignored by the media, and which – we are expected to understand – have been committed by Asians.

Nick and Chris agree that the news from such areas is unremittingly depressing. 'And that's not to mention Lambeth.' From time to time they become so despondent about 'the problems we face' that they fall silent and just shake their heads. Nevertheless, they insist that it is a great time to be joining the BNP. The party is completely skint, it seems, but they assure me that more and more people are joining every day. Up to a hundred new members a week. An electoral breakthrough must be just over the horizon. It must be!

Shortly after this meeting, Sadie Graham, the BNP's group development officer, writes from Nottingham to thank me for becoming the central London organiser and to offer advice. This includes the suggestion that I contact my 'regional security officer' before holding any meetings. From York, the party's group support officer, Ian Dawson, telephones to give me details of my dedicated email account – londoncentral@bnp.org.uk – which sits on the BNP server. He then sends me my password for the account: 27sortcode87.

The following week I receive an email with an encrypted attachment. Using the software from Nick I open it to find an Excel spreadsheet listing 192 current and lapsed members living in the three central London boroughs, plus the north London boroughs of Camden and Islington. I am also sent a second list of people who have joined in the previous few months or expressed an interest in joining. Someone has made notes against a handful of applicants' and members' names, observing that they appear to be of 'Italian origin' or 'Greek origin'.

While some of the members of my new flock are from the BNP's traditional constituency – the white working class – there are also some scattered around some of the wealthiest areas of the capital, living in Chelsea townhouses, Belgravia mansions and apartments in Knightsbridge. They include dozens of company directors, computing entrepreneurs, bankers and estate agents, and a handful of teachers. One member is a former Miss England, another is the American chief executive of a City investment corporation, while one is a servant of the Queen, living at Buckingham Palace.

Among my members, I discover, is Simone Clarke, principal dancer with the English National Ballet. During a subsequent conversation, Ms Clarke says that she believes immigration 'has really got out of hand', despite her partner, both on and off-stage, being a Cuban dancer of Chinese extraction. She adds: 'If everyone who thinks like I do joined, it would really make a difference.'

Another is Richard Highton, administrator of the Optical Consumer Complaints Service, which handles complaints about opticians. 'Everyone you speak to is fed up and thinks the same,' he says. 'I would have thought central London is a breeding ground for discontent at what we have at the moment.'

Then there is Peter Bradbury, a leading practitioner of complementary medicine and board member of the General Naturopathic Council, which works in partnership with a charity established by Prince Charles. He explains that he first joined the party many years ago and was a friend of its late founder, John Tyndall.

Gregory Lauder-Frost, former political secretary of the Conservative Monday Club, the rightwing pressure group, emails to say he is unable to be an active member, as he spends most of his time at his home in the country. And Annabel Geddes – the entrepreneur who created the London Dungeon and who was a director of the London Tourist Board in the 1980s after she sold the business – apologises for having lapsed and promises to send a cheque to renew her membership. Annabel volunteers the opinion that Asian immigrants are a 'bloody bore', while black people are 'ghastly'.

'I'm a racist,' she declares proudly. 'We've got to keep little UK basically Anglo-Saxon.' She pauses, and asks whether I agree.

'Well madam,' I reply, 'I am the central London organiser of the British National Party ... '

DECEMBER 23 2006

First, stun your turkey

EMMA BROCKES

At Manor Farm in Bedfordshire, Richard Brown is about to kill the last turkey of the season. It's an 18kg whopper, known in the business as a catering bird. Mr Brown has performed in front of witnesses before. A woman from environmental health once came and was sprayed with turkey blood when a vessel in the bird's mouth exploded in the final stages of strangulation.

'She was wearing a beige raincoat,' he says. 'Ready?'

As the debate on the ethics of food production grows, so too does the conviction that you shouldn't eat anything you can't envisage being killed without retching. This is the meat-eaters' test, an attempt to narrow the gap between production and consumption that gives rise to a squeamishness among shoppers only the supermarkets benefit from. The irony is that sanitised meat in a cellophane wrapper comes, in all likelihood, from an animal that led a more gruesome life than anything you'll find dripping blood in a farm shop. So here we are, prepared to get back to basics.

This is a family farm, 365 hectares of arable and livestock, which Mr Brown himself grew up on. His father first bought turkey eggs in 1934 – in his last year at school – and Mr Brown's son and daughter-in-law work on the place.

'We're not free range or organic,' he says, 'but we're the next best thing. The turkeys are half under cover and half outdoors.'

'Barn-raised?'

He looks amused. 'If you like.'

Most good farm turkeys are killed in the first few weeks of December and allowed to hang – it improves the flavour. Mr Brown has done 1,200 this season, at a rate of roughly 200 a day, 30 an hour. He has slight RSI from all the lifting.

The key to humane killing is lighting and speed in the moments before slaughter, the birds are kept in a dark anteroom and the walls of the slaughterhouse are a soothing dark green. After he has stunned a bird and wrung its neck, he whizzes it through a defeathering machine and hands it to six seasonal labourers, who finish it by hand. The whole process takes 15 minutes.

Anyone can kill a turkey, but you need a slaughterman's licence to stun it. The stunner hangs on the wall like a shower head. Mr Brown disappears into the holding room and comes out carrying a monstrous turkey, its bright white feathers just visible in the gloom. In one swift movement he hangs it from a shackle by its legs, picks up the stunner, zaps it in the head, pulls its neck between his knees and snaps the bird's neck between the skull and the first vertebra. It's as fluid as a tennis serve and as silent – there's not even a crackle from the stun gun or a meep from the turkey.

Afterwards, the bird's wings flap for about 10 seconds. Mr Brown says that's the nerve endings: it is well and truly dead. When they've stopped, the wings fall in an arc on either side of the bird. At the top of its legs it has fluffy bloomers you could stuff a duvet with. The head goes pulpy from the blood draining into it and the skin turns green and purple. There's blood on the wing tips.

'Come round here,' says Mr Brown, but the photographer and I are scared of brushing too close, in case the bird twitches to life like Glenn Close in *Fatal Attraction*. Mr Brown rolls his eyes. 'Immature feathers still bleed,' he says, snapping off a feather.

We look away. 'Gross.'

I have a theory that one's sympathy for an animal is relative to the size of its eyes, insects notwithstanding. A turkey has tiny, beady eyes, so, apart from the thing with the feather, this has all been quite painless for us. Mr Brown thinks it's a question of exposure. His young grandchildren help out on the farm. Sometimes they name the pigs and then, from their spots, recognise them hanging in the fridge.

'They'll say, "Oh look, it's Freida."' It doesn't worry them unduly. 'They see the whole cycle. They're not afraid. They understand that's what we're here for.' He shrugs. 'We're producers of food.'

DECEMBER 23 2006

Optimism incarnate

MARTIN KETTLE

Dance is hope, optimism incarnate, an affirmation of our humanity. It needs to be valued all year, not just at Christmas.

Dancing is the Cinderella of the performing arts, but at Christmas it gets to go to the ball. For the theatres and the broadcasters, Christmas is the biggest dance festival of the year. Professional dancers never work harder than they do at this time of year, with all those *Nutcrackers* and *Swan Lakes* taking over the opera houses and the big halls. Last Christmas the BBC offered wall-to-wall Darcey Bussell – not that I'm complaining about that. This year the schedules are as dance-filled as ever: *Giselle*, *The Red Shoes*, a documentary about the Royal Ballet and, towering over them all, tonight's finale of *Strictly Come Dancing*.

Actually, the strange thing is not that dancing gets so much mass-media exposure at Christmas. The strange thing is that it gets so little exposure for the rest of the year. For 11 months out of every 12 dance gets on with it, a low-key fact of cultural life, an unobtrusive, occasional activity for millions. And the rest of us barely notice.

As it happens, dance in this country is on a terrific high right now. At the top end of the market, Monica Mason has restored the Royal Ballet's ambition and morale: its recent triple bill – with new ballets by Wayne McGregor and Christopher Wheeldon – was breathtaking; rightly one of the hottest tickets of 2006. In London, all year round Sadler's Wells offers an amazing variety of dancing riches from classical to hip-hop. Yet somehow the fashionable spotlight is always focused elsewhere.

Why is this? It is not as if the arts in general are a ghetto. The other arts are always in the news. A new West End musical, a famous actor in a major new role, a tenor with a tantrum at the opera – all these are big, newsworthy stories. The media takes them seriously and rightly so. But how often does dance get that sort of heavyweight treatment?

With a few exceptions, the movers and shakers of the cultural world share this blind spot. Intellectuals like to obsess about the visual arts, the theatre, opera and music. Dance, in such company, counts for relatively little. Incredibly, there are almost no serious books about dance. Dance has no Simon Schama, no Bryan Magee, no Harold Bloom. Maybe intellectuals don't dance. I suspect the simpler truth is that the men who dominate the western cultural establishment look down on a performance art in which women compete on equal terms and that is particularly attractive to women.

The reason we get lots of dance around now is easy to explain. It's because, whatever the cultural establishment says, dance is incredibly popular. A lot more popular, if truth be told, than most of the other subsidised performing arts. *Swan Lake* and the *Nutcracker* fill the seasonal seats without fail. And Covent Garden's *Giselle* on Boxing Day will pull in a TV audience twice as large as for any opera.

But it's not just classical ballet that's popular. It's dancing in general. Dancing is popular in the truest and deepest sense of the term. It is of the people. No other performance art can match it. Look at the stunning success of *Strictly Come Dancing* and all the imitators it has spawned. Yes, it's partly the kitsch and the camp and the sequins ... and even old Brucie himself. In the end, though, the show's success is down to a magic ingredient. It has a direct line to our deep human need to dance. It presses the button that says: I could do that, and I'd love to.

The truth is that dance and drawing are the two great universal art forms. Dance is universal in a way that not even singing can rival. That's surely because dance is so explicitly and recognisably an affirmation of what it is to be human. Every pattern and gesture says: we are more than dumb, doomed beasts. It says: we are individuals ('look at me') and communities ('look at us'). And it says, very importantly, that the world can be a better place. Dance is hope. Gene Kelly's *Singin' in the Rain* is optimism incarnate. A Dance of Death is the ultimate contradiction.

All the musical arts express this idea of perfectability. Dance, though, does it in the most directly physical and aspirational way. And it does it in almost every cultural tradition on the planet. This is a potent thought. For if there is one form of human activity that stretches across genders, across age-groups, across social classes and across cultural borders, it is dance.

This universality makes dance intensely democratic – far more so than the other performing arts. We all dance, or at least we all try. In a multicultural world this makes dance uniquely treasurable. Dance is a defiance of mind-forged manacles of every kind.

It is one of the reasons why *Billy Elliott* is such a powerful experience. It says there is no barrier to what a working-class boy can become.

If dance is so fundamental, so universal and so enjoyable, then why don't we value it more highly? The more you think about it, the greater the potential of dance, not just to symbolise a better world but to help make the real one better. I'm unconditionally in favour of subsidising the arts for what they are. But think about dance from the public-policy perspective too. It makes people physically healthier. It encourages them to express themselves and to control their bodies. It provides a communal activity that gets people out of their houses and off the streets. It provides an umbrella under which different cultural traditions can all prosper.

Investing in dance ought to be a no-brainer. But we don't do anything like enough of it. Provision is pathetically small and is skewed towards the cities, the middle classes and the very young. All the kids who play Billy Elliott in the theatre are from private schools; a real working-class Billy would have a job getting an audition to play himself.

Maybe things will change as a result of Tony Hall's forthcoming review of dance for the education and culture departments. It will require a leap of the imagination as big as any dancer's leap if it is to happen – not least in the current spending climate. But the dancer can make the magnificent leap. So why can't we?

JANUARY 1 2007

How Saddam died on the gallows

EWEN MACASKILL
AND MICHAEL HOWARD

Camera footage of the final minutes of Saddam Hussein released yesterday shows him being taunted by Shia hangmen and witnesses, a scene that risks increasing sectarian tension in Iraq. As he stood at the gallows he was tormented by the hooded executioners or witnesses shouting at him to 'Go to hell!' and chanting the name 'Moqtada', the radical Shia Muslim cleric and leader of the Mahdi army militia Moqtada al-Sadr.

The grainy images, which appeared to have been taken on a mobile phone, disclose exchanges between Saddam and his tormentors, the moment when his body drops through the trapdoor, and his body swinging, eyes partly open and neck bent out of shape. In what Sunni Muslims will perceive as a further insult, the executioners released the trapdoor while the former dictator was in the middle of his prayers.

Sunni Muslims, who were dominant under Saddam but are now the victims of sectarian death squads, will see the shambolic nature of the execution as further evidence of the bias of the Shia-led government. They have repeatedly claimed that the Iraqi government, helped by the US and British, conducted a show trial, based on revenge rather than justice. Saddam's team of defence lawyers claimed that the hanging had been simply 'victors' justice'.

The unruly scenes will also dismay the US and British governments, who are also privately alarmed at the sectarian bias of the government, led by the prime minister, Nouri al-Maliki. The United States and Britain believe at least some members of the Iraqi government are complicit in sectarian killings, particularly by members of the police force.

The Iraqi government last night denied the execution had been sectarian or designed for revenge. Hiwa Osman, an adviser to the Iraqi president, Jalal Talabani, told the BBC: 'This whole execution is about justice.'

As Saddam was buried in his home village, Ouja, outside Tikrit, yesterday morning, the leaked footage appeared on the internet and on Arabic television stations. While Saddam was professing Muhammad as God's prophet, he was interrupted by shouts. One of the people observing the execution chants 'Moqtada! Moqtada! Moqtada!' Saddam dismissively repeats the name 'Moqtada'. The noose around his neck, he appears to smile and shoots back: 'Do you consider this bravery?'

Another voice shouts at him to 'Go to hell!'

Saddam, seemingly accusing his enemies of destroying the country he once led, replies: 'The hell that is Iraq?'

A Shia shouts 'Long live Mohammed Baqir al-Sadr!', a member of Moqtada's family thought to have been assassinated by Saddam's security services.

Another onlooker pleads for dignity: 'Please don't. The man is facing execution. Please don't. I beg you, no!'

As Saddam continues with his prayers, saying 'I profess that there is no God but God and that Muhammad ... ' – the executioners release the trapdoor.

There is a shout: 'The tyrant has fallen!'

Although many Sunni Muslims also suffered under him and were glad to see him go, the manner in which the execution was carried out will have created some sympathy for Saddam. The fact that the execution took place at the start of the main Muslim religious holiday will further inflame Sunni opinion.

The tit-for-tat killings between the majority Shias – who suffered badly under Saddam – and the previously dominant Sunnis has created a de facto civil war that could break up the country. Sunni insurgents, particularly a branch of al-Qaida, have sought to fan the civil war by carrying out a series of devastating car bomb attacks on Shia population centres, especially Sadr City in Baghdad and towns such as Hilla and Najaf.

The response among Sunnis to the hanging and the video was to swear revenge. A man from Mosul, a mixed city in the north, told Reuters: 'The Persians have killed him. I can't believe it. By God, we will take revenge.' He was referring to Iraq's new leaders' ties to Shia Iran, and the Shia in general.

Accusations that the government had mishandled the execution were not confined to Sunni regions. In the Kurdish region, there was also criticism.

'This execution should have been for all of Saddam's victims and instead they have hijacked it and turned it into a sectarian event,' said Anwar Abdullah, a student at the technical institute of Sulaymaniyah.

Rebwar Suliman, 21, whose uncle and grandfather were killed by Saddam's secret police in Kurdistan in the 1980s, said: 'It does a dishonour to the Kurds.'

Saddam was buried in the dead of night, prompting an outpouring of grief and anger from fellow members of his tribe and other Sunni Arabs. His body was flown by US military helicopter to Tikrit and then taken to the village where he was born. Hundreds of mourners visited his tomb inside a marble-floored hall built by Saddam. Others attended the Great Saddam Mosque in Tikrit.

The funeral came as it was reported that the US death toll in Iraq since the invasion had reached 3,000. The US military disclosed yesterday that an American soldier had been killed by a roadside bomb in Baghdad on Saturday, the 2,999th death since

MARCH 6 2007

A Eurostar train enters the historic Barlow Shed for the first time, as preparations are made for the switch of the Eurostar service to the newly restored St Pancras International. MICHAEL WALTER/TROIKA

JUNE 21 2007

A prospective buyer tries one of over 40 grand pianos displayed in Conway Hall in London ready for an auction sale. THOMAS EISL

MAY **14 2007**

Gallery-goers explore inside the dense vapour of Antony Gormley's
Blind Light installation at the Hayward Gallery. DAVID LEVENE

JULY 13 2007
First night of the BBC Proms at the Royal Albert Hall in London.
GRAEME ROBERTSON

APRIL 26 2007
Stephen Hawking experiences the weightlessness of space first-hand
on a zero-gravity trip over the Atlantic. ZERO GRAVITY CORP/AP

the invasion in 2003. But yesterday the website www.icasualties.org also listed the death of Specialist Dustin Donica, 22, on December 28 as previously unreported, bringing the total to 3,000.

George Bush is expected to face renewed domestic political pressure following the latest milestone. Although the 3,000 figure is symbolically important for Americans, Iraqis suffer that rate of casualties on a monthly basis.

JANUARY 6 2007

Married to the Mob

IAN COBAIN, DAVID WARD AND TOM KINGTON

To judge by her Friends Reunited profile, Ann Hathaway could not be living a life more ordinary: married with a couple of kids, she informed her old chums from Moorclose secondary modern in Rochdale, and recently back in town after a few years in Italy. 'Miss the weather,' she wrote. 'Ha ha – *ciao.*'

However, to read Ms Hathaway's file at the prosecutor's office in the southern Sicilian town of Gela would be to encounter an entirely different woman. For almost 20 years, according to the Italian authorities, she has been happily married to the Mob. By last night, moreover, a warrant had been issued for her arrest, accusing her of 'mafia association' after investigators said they had uncovered evidence that she helped her husband run an underworld empire while he was behind bars.

It was all a terrible shock to her neighbours in the Middleton area of Rochdale, Greater Manchester, where Ms Hathaway, 44, has been renting a modest terrace house, from where she was declining to comment last night. 'I know she speaks foreign,' said one neighbour, 'but as far as I know she's a very nice girl.'

Ms Hathaway's Friends Reunited posting recounts how she 'went dancing in Italy and lived in Milan for a couple of years' after taking her O-levels at Moorclose. 'I then went to live in Sicily with my husband. Seven years later we moved to Rome and I stayed there for 16 years.' She returned to Rochdale for Christmas, a little more than a year ago, and 'decided to stay with my two daughters and give good old England a go!'

What Ms Hathaway did not mention is that her husband, Antonio Rinzivillo, and her brother-in-law, Crocifisso, were among the leading members of a mafia clan that bore their family name, until their arrest almost five years ago. The clan specialises in drug-dealing, extortion and arms-trafficking. Antonio has been convicted of murder and is incarcerated in Tolmezzo prison, north of Venice. His brother Crocifisso is in jail in Rome.

The clan's godfather, Giuseppe 'Piddu' Madonia, has been in prison since 1992 and is considered to be one of the most loyal lieutenants of Bernardo Provenzano, the ultimate head of the Cosa Nostra, who was finally captured last April after more than 40 years on the run.

About 80 members of the gang were rounded up in a wave of arrests across Italy last month during Operation Choice Cuts – so named because the Rinzivillo clan is said to have a stranglehold on the local meat trade. Although most of the arrests were in Sicily, the family's tentacles are said to have spread as far north as Lombardy. Many of those arrested are accused of laundering the proceeds of drug-trafficking through public sector construction contracts, which were acquired through bribery. Drugs and firearms were seized, along with property and businesses valued by police at €20m (£13.5m).

A warrant was issued for the arrest of Ms Hathaway, whom Italian authorities allege was no mere gangster's moll, but rather an influential figure within the clan. Prosecutors say allegations against her range from acting as a messenger to receiving and investing cash. 'She was tough, not your usual housewife,' one prosecutor told the *Guardian*. A second Italian source – who claims to have listened to bugged telephone conversations – said that Ms Hathaway could be heard speaking fluent Italian with both a Sicilian and northern England accent; she did not make any clear threats, he said.

With her husband behind bars Ms Hathaway continued to live in the Rome suburb of Prima Porta until her return to England at the end of 2005. Speaking at her home in England yesterday, Ms Hathaway would say only: 'I'm not saying anything. I'm not going to confirm or deny anything. Do you want to speak to my solicitor?'

JANUARY 22 2007

Life in the fast lane: the M2

ZOE WILLIAMS

Let me talk you through the beauty of it: as you join it from the south it has five mighty lanes. There is never any traffic. The only bad thing that can happen to you is that you run out of petrol on the one farthest from the hard shoulder. That happened to me once and when the AA man arrived he assumed my sister (27) and my brother (23) were my children. This is one of the top five bad days of my life. It is testament to the motorway's healing powers that it has remained my favourite highway.

Start from London, to experience the full force: you cross the incredibly windy bridge over the Medway. There is a train bridge adjacent. Race the train! The countryside of Rochester unwraps itself before you like the credit sequence of a pastoral sitcom about vets. Slow down if you will, to wait for a big gust of wind, then put your foot down as you veer wildly from one lane to another. It's like a video game, particularly if you are a bad driver and have a very old automatic car whose handling isn't great at the best of times.

Services-wise, there ain't much meat on her, but what there is is choice, as Spencer Tracey used to say of Katharine Hepburn, in his not-at-all-demeaning account of their life-long love affair. Medway is a Moto. Its loos are very clean, on account of the rigorous, no-nonsense natures of the people of Thanet. To my knowledge it has never run out of the key sections of pick-and-mix, unlike some services I could mention, which run out of white mice almost immediately, but don't actually bother replacing any until they're down to their last chocolate brazil. It was among the first motorway service stations to start proselytising about fruit portions, over the distracting olfactory hum of frying bacon. It's interesting that, while Burger Kings are the same the country over, there is variation within the genre 'Upper Crust', and I think this one is among the classiest. It's something to do with not always thinking that everyone wants the brie and bacon, and sometimes mixing it up a bit with a coronation chicken. I have never been scammed by a broken quiz machine, nor found anything in a soup that wasn't part of the description, nor been cheeked by the Saturday staff. I really can't fault any part of the M2 experience.

JANUARY 23 2007

The wreckers return

STEVEN MORRIS

Jane and Mary huffed and puffed as they rolled the oak wine cask across the shingle towards the Sea Shanty car park. 'Honestly, we just came for a walk and a chat,' said Mary, a retired teacher, 'but then we saw all this stuff here and the police told us we could help ourselves. So we did.'

They were not the only ones. Branscombe beach, usually deserted at this time of year, was heaving yesterday with hundreds of – depending on your point of view – looters, salvagers or beach-combers. While a desperate rescue operation was under way to try to prevent ecological disaster a mile off the Devon coast, a scramble of a different kind was taking place, one unlikely to have cheered the insurers of the 62,000-tonne cargo ship that was stricken in last week's storm.

Among the goodies that had fallen off the back of MSC Napoli were motorbikes – 15 disappeared yesterday – steering wheels, carpets, beauty creams, shoes, golf clubs, oil paintings and camcorders. The salvagers carried, dragged and hauled what they could from the beach. And when they couldn't, they made sledges from wooden pallets. One gang brought their own tractor.

'It's great isn't it? A cross between a bomb site and a car boot sale,' said Mike Lorberg as he hauled away big bags of pet food for his three cats and two dogs.

Scavengers did not lose any time yesterday, with items soon appearing on eBay. Ten steering wheel airbags advertised as coming from the Napoli were up for auction before the end of the day. There were also reports from families who had lost personal possessions being transported by the Napoli, and family photographs and furnishings were among the items strewn on the beach.

The free-for-all began in the early hours yesterday when word got out that a crate of BMW motorbikes, worth £12,000 each, was among the hundred or so containers that had been washed ashore.

Tom 21, a Royal Marine, said: 'We got here at midnight and haven't slept. I couldn't believe my eyes. There's so much stuff – it's like an Aladdin's cave!'

By dawn, visitors were being directed to what they wanted, with the police apparently powerless to stop them.

'I was walking down the cliff path and I met a bloke who just said to me, "If you want trainers they're on the left, and videos are on the right,"' said one visitor.

Hector Bird, 33, from Branscombe, admitted he was now one of those with a new bike on his front drive. He said: 'A whole lot of us came down from the village at 2am. Me and my mates got two off, but we lost one of them to another gang. It was quite nasty at times and for some it came down to who was the biggest bloke. If we hadn't rescued them, they would have ended up in the sea and useless. I feel we are not stealing them, we are helping the authorities clear them up.'

However, Anita Bokdal, a Swedish woman sending goods to Cape Town, said she had been horrified to see photographs of her possessions being collected by beachcombers. 'I can't believe they would do this, those were our personal belongings.'

The official line from the police and from the receiver of wreck, the official in charge of such matters, was that nothing should be moved from the beach.

The very ambitious were contriving ways to recover tractors and cars half buried in the shingle, but most were happy simply to sift the debris and choose the odd item. One man carried a soggy rug over his shoulder, while his wife clutched a couple of oil paintings and a golf club. A mother had to hold her child in her arms because she had crammed her pram with toys and nappies, while an old man was pushing a BMX bike through the surf.

Most of the cosmetics appeared to have been washed up in the shade of the towering Pinnacle Rock. Jess, 19, had chosen some Lancôme anti-ageing cream for her father. 'He'll be pleased with this – it's really expensive, you know.' The shoes were a little more problematic. It was easy enough to find one nice bright pink Croc sandal – much harder to find its partner among the thousands strewn over the high-tide mark.

JANUARY 25 2007

The Country Diary at 100

MARTIN WAINWRIGHT

They are trained observers, skilled at slipping between grebe-frequented reeds or waiting silently for hours by a badger sett, but a few days ago the *Guardian*'s corps of Country Diarists went in search of different prey.

'So you're Graham Long,' said Mark Cocker, adjusting his bird-watching lenses to people-spotting mode. 'And do you think that's Virginia Spiers or Veronica Heath over there?' They do the same job but, by the nature of their far-flung outposts, the diarists seldom, if ever, meet.

The setting that brought them together was far from the fells of Cumbria, which Tony Greenbank patrols, or the Dark Peak, where any lanky lone rambler you spot will probably be Roger Redfern. This nature outing was in the windowless boardroom of the *Guardian*, deep in an office block in Farringdon Road surrounded by the urban sprawl of London.

But like their predecessors in 1974, when the only other Country Diarists' lunch ever held took place at King's Cross (convenient for rapid escape), the corps who scout for us out in the embattled natural world arrived with pockets and minds stuffed with trophies. In the 1970s – when the Welsh diarist Bill Condry attached a luggage label to himself in case he got lost in the metropolis – they brought meadowsweet from a Camden building site and some black aphids. This time, Paul Evans reported a figwort unseasonally in flower at Euston, and Ray Collier had a film canister of Arctic cowrie shells he had collected on Rhum beach.

'I thought I'd do a bit of a detour to look at some weeds,' said Evans, while Collier explained one of those unexpected connections nature throws up, in this case between the unhurried life of the shoreline in the Scottish Hebrides and the frantic round of central London.

'The cowrie's biological name is *trivia*,' he told the diarists' editor, Celia Locks, who organised the get-together to celebrate 100 years of the small but much-read column. 'They were used as counters in games.'

You never know when countryside lore is going to stand you in good stead and, by the same token, the roll-call of Country Diarists is full of surprises. There have been plenty of woodsmen like Collier, who brought his firearms certificate from Inverness in case London's terrorism precautions required photo ID (he does not usually leave his patch, so does not have a passport). But the writers have also included a leading and very intellectual suffragette, Helena Swanwick; Virginia Woolf's Greek teacher, Janet Case, and the poet Rupert Brooke's mistress, Ka Cox, who died after a furious row with the satanist Aleister Crowley, whose black masses were upsetting badgers on her Cornish estate.

Today's 14-strong team takes up only a fragment of the paper, but prompts endless comments and readers' queries – as well as matchboxes and special-delivery ice-packed parcels if diarists are rash enough to ask if anyone has seen a particular bird, rodent or flea. The greatest controversy in its history concerned the (still unsolved) question of whether woodlice instinctively curl up when disturbed. The late Enid Wilson from Keswick, who raised it, was beset with accounts, photographs and preserved specimens. But that has been outdone by Phil Gates's worm.

A lecturer at the University of Durham, Gates wrote a gruesome account of how immigrant New Zealand flatworms predate on our earthworm (a creature itself immortalised by Gilbert White, who puzzled in his *Natural History of Selborne* about why 'worms are so much addicted to venery', AKA sex). Gates described how the New Zealanders wrap themselves round the native earthworm and secrete an enzyme that melts their prey into an easily edible mush.

'I found some in Durham and asked if anyone else had seen these alarming creatures,' he said, as lunch progressed cheerfully from chicken to forest fruits. 'The matchboxes arrived for several months. I got leeches, centipedes and lots of different worms. It was a pleasant reminder that we are writing for people who take a real interest.'

Gates is one diarist who stands out in the team photograph: he has a black eyepatch as a result of an accident when he was 13. He had an artificial eye, but it used to pop out if he sneezed during lectures. When it finally fell into a stream in Hamsterley Forest – where he was investigating micro-life among small, round, whiteish pebbles – he didn't bother to hunt for it, but adopted the patch instead.

The very first diarist, Thomas Coward, was appointed in 1904 after one of the then *Manchester Guardian*'s high command heard tell of his practice in chapel of taking an end seat near the door, so he could slip out if he heard the song of an unusual bird. One of the topics of discussion yesterday was how modern Country Diarists get the job.

Veronica Heath, who has written from Northumberland for more than 30 years, admitted a version of divine right. Her father, Harry Tegner, author of 40 nature books, including *Beasts of the North Country: From Whales to Shrews*, did the column before her for another 30 years. She recalled: 'He was failing a bit in the 1970s and he wrote to the editor saying: "My daughter's a writer – could she send you some diaries instead?" The editor, Alastair Hetherington, said, "Yes, tell her to put one in the post," and I've just gone on doing that ever since.'

She is now the only Country Diarist who types her piece up, from a longhand original, and puts it in her pillar box near Morpeth. Even the late Harry Griffin – who developed exactly sized typing paper during his record 53-year stint and was incandescent when his column was then cut – finally accepted the computer. But Heath and the rest of the team are fully up to date on the technological battles and environmental skirmishes that give their patch little rest.

Another *Guardian* writer, Geoffrey Moorhouse, described the diarists as long ago as the 1960s as patrols who reported from one of the world's most important front lines, between nature on the retreat and the advance of humankind. The paper's current editor, Alan Rusbridger, made the same point when he welcomed the lunchers and told them that their place in the paper was copper-bottom safe.

'What have you seen recently that makes the point about climate change?' he asked, referring to the current stream of readers' letters about far-too-early blossom, birds and bees. Collier was first up with a sighting of a creamy butterburr in bloom on the banks of Loch Ness by a mallard's nest with a clutch of six eggs. What was worse, the unseasonal flowering appeared to have taken place backwards: oversized versions of the leaves that normally follow the flowers had come out first.

'It was upsetting,' said Collier grimly. 'It was wrong.'

Then it was time to go home, led by Colin Luckhurst, the only member of the gathering who was also at the 1974 lunch, looking then like an eager young schoolmaster among silver-haired sages. Eyes were peeled, notebooks made ready and Derek Niemann resolved not to talk to anyone on the train home to Bedford.

'I spent the whole journey here chatting to another passenger,' he said, 'and when we passed an interesting-looking lake I had to keep one eye on her and only the other one on the ducks. If it's light enough and they're still there, I'm going to identify them on the way back.'

FEBRUARY 6 2007

So unlucky in love

LIBBY BROOKS

Kylie Minogue is not, I acknowledge, Everywoman. Everywoman does not regularly sport exotically draped jumpsuits or find her outfits being displayed at the V&A. But since her diagnosis with breast cancer in 2005, Minogue has inadvertently come to encapsulate the dilemmas of modern middle-class womanhood. Her split from the French actor Olivier Martinez, announced at the weekend, simply compounds that status.

The 38-year-old singer is reportedly distraught at the idea that she may not now have children of her own, and considering the 'daunting' possibility of adoption or surrogacy without a long-term partner. Although she had slices of her ovaries frozen for re-implantation before undergoing chemotherapy, time is most definitely not on her side. So it's hard not to feel some sympathy for a woman who, for all her globally branded successes, has regularly reaffirmed that most ordinary and – in this age of single-person households, fractured families and dating websites – most complicated of desires: to meet someone to love for ever and raise a family with.

Having spent a succession of school discos in the 1980s attempting the Locomotion, I must confess to a particular fondness for this woman who began her trajectory in a time when celebrity had not yet begun to eat its own tail. For those of us who grew up with Minogue, there's a certain safety in knowing that beneath the glitter and the gloss there's Charlene from *Neighbours*, in a bad bubble-perm and a frothy wedding dress, stepping out of Erinsborough church with Jason Donovan on her arm to the strains of Angry Anderson's 'Suddenly'. But, at the risk of hanging an entire generation's angst from her slender ankles, the story of Kylie does speak to thousands of women who find themselves wrestling with the fact that the decade in which they are ready to put their foot on the gas in their professional lives is also the one in which they should be taking partnership and procreation in hand.

Throughout her 30s, Minogue's musical reinventions and international acclaim have been accompanied by a catalogue of romantic disappointments. It's always appealing to the can't-have-it-all Jeremiahs to point to the professionally stellar but emotionally empty lady in the corner. Feminism has often been described as a movement against nature. Camille Paglia once wrote: 'The more woman aims for personal identity and autonomy

... the fiercer will be her struggle with nature – that is, with the intractable physical laws of her own body.' There's still a sense that women get away with their public successes only for so long, before being punished by loneliness or infertility.

British adults are having fewer children than ever. This trend – and the cacophonous fertility anxiety that accompanies it – is a largely middle-class phenomenon. With success in the workplace – and the material benefits that brings – now considered the measure of bourgeois fulfilment, it's perhaps unsurprising that some are unwilling to contemplate lowering their professional and consumerist horizons in order to raise children. The hard work of parenting sits ill with our modern absolutes of autonomy and individualism. Where once we debated how to make our children happy, now we ask whether they will make us happy.

Of course there are structural reasons why middle-class women are pursuing their careers into their 30s, enjoying economic independence and professional fulfilment, while controlling their fertility. Many are understandably unwilling to sacrifice their hard-won status in the public sphere, because they are all-too aware of the lowly status of mothering and that having children will penalise them far more than it will their male colleagues.

Meanwhile, despite all evidence to the contrary, an expanding range of birth technologies that promise to ease later conception implies that any woman can choose to be a mother at any time, provided she tries hard enough and spends enough money. But choice here is a vexatious concept. Some things cannot be scheduled – a shocking revelation in our buy-it-now, fix-it-quick, take-it-all society. Falling in love, getting pregnant and good health are three of them. As Kylie Minogue would tell you.

FEBRUARY 6 2007

Children of war

MICHAEL HOWARD

The car stopped at the makeshift checkpoint that cut across the muddy backstreet in western Baghdad. A sentry appeared.

'Are you Sunni or Shia?' he barked, waving his Kalashnikov at the driver. 'Are you with Zarqawi or the Mahdi army?'

'The Mahdi army,' the driver said.

'Wrong answer,' shouted the sentry, almost gleefully. 'Get him!'

The high metal gate of a nearby house was flung open and four gun-toting males rushed out. They dragged the driver from his vehicle and held a knife to his neck. Quickly and efficiently, the blade was run from ear to ear.

'Now you're dead,' said a triumphant voice, and their captive crumpled to the ground. Then a moment of stillness before the sound of a woman's voice.

'Come inside boys! Your dinner is ready!'

The gunmen groaned. The hapless driver picked himself up and trundled his yellow plastic car into the front yard. The toy guns and knives were tossed by the back door. Their murderous game of make-believe would have to resume in the morning.

Abdul-Muhammad and his five younger brothers – aged between six and 12 – should have been at school. But their mother, Sayeeda, like thousands of parents in Iraq's perilous capital city, now keeps her boys at home. Three weeks ago, armed men intercepted their teacher's car at the school gates, then hauled him out and slit his throat. Just like in their game.

'That day they came home and they were changed because of

the things they'd seen,' said Sayeeda as she ladled rice into the boys' bowls. 'The youngest two have been wetting their beds and having nightmares, while Abdul-Muhammad has started bullying and ordering everyone to play his fighting games. I know things are not normal with them. My fear is one day they will get hold of real guns. But in these times, where is the help?'

The boys live with their widowed mother and uncle in a modest family house in al-Amil, a once-peaceful, religiously mixed suburb in western Baghdad that is yielding to the gunmen, street by street. Similar tales of growing up in the war zone are heard across the country. Parents, teachers and doctors contacted by the *Guardian* over the past three months cite a litany of distress signals sent out by young people in their care – from nightmares and bedwetting to withdrawal, muteness, panic attacks and violence towards other children, sometimes even to their own parents.

Amid the statistical haze that enshrouds civilian casualties, no one is sure how many children have been killed or maimed in Iraq. But psychologists and aid organisations warn that while the physical scars of the conflict are all too visible – in hospitals and mortuaries and on television screens – the mental and emotional turmoil experienced by Iraq's young is going largely unmonitored and untreated.

In a rare study published last week, the Association of Iraqi Psychologists (API) said the violence had affected millions of children, raising serious concerns for future generations. It urged the international community to help establish child psychology units and mental-health programmes.

'Children in Iraq are seriously suffering psychologically with all the insecurity, especially with the fear of kidnapping and explosions,' the API's Marwan Abdullah told IRIN, the UN-funded news agency. 'In some cases, they're found to be suffering extreme stress.'

'Every day another innocent child is orphaned or sees terrible things children should never see,' said Sherif Karachatani, a psychology professor at the University of Sulaymaniya. 'Who is taking care of the potentially enormous damage being done to a generation of children?' There are well-founded fears, he said, that the 'relentless bloodshed and the lack of professional help will see Iraq's children growing up either deeply scarred or so habituated to violence that they keep the pattern going as they enter adulthood'.

Because of the dire security, organisations such as the United Nations Children's Fund (Unicef) have only a skeleton presence in Iraq. Save the Children is closing its operations next month after 15 years in the country. The Iraqi Red Crescent Society has been forced to suspend a programme for children suffering from war trauma owing to lack of funding.

The country's overstretched hospitals cannot cope with psychological trauma and many of the best doctors have either fled the country or been killed. The problems are compounded by the stigma that psychological and psychiatric care carries.

'They don't bring their children in for treatment, fearing they will be labelled as mad,' said Dr Karachatani.

The field is left to small local and foreign NGOs and to hardpressed Iraqi psychologists, who are not immune to bloodshed. In December, Harith Hassan, one of Iraq's most prominent child psychologists, was shot dead as he drove to work. A regular commentator in the Iraqi media known for his ruthlessly honest comments about the Iraqi mindset, Hassan had worked with victims of trauma. And he had been déterminé to wean Iraqi youth from their obsession with the gun.

'It's all some of them think about and know,' he had told the *Guardian*. 'The dangers are they will internalise the violence and then reproduce it later.'

As with Abdul-Muhammad and his brothers, stories and images

of beheadings and sectarian atrocities were working their way into play, he said, 'bringing nightmares to life'. But that need not be harmful.

'Getting it out in their play is probably quite healthy,' said Anne Jefferies, humanitarian advocacy adviser with Save the Children. The key thing was to provide a safe environment in which children could play, supervised by adults.

Yet in Baghdad's al-Amil neighbourhood that is not easy. Haunted by the spectre of violence, parents have stopped taking their children to local play areas. The neighbourhood's two amusement arcades are shuttered and there are few safe places to play sports. School attendance is down by as much as 60 per cent.

'Children are often incredibly resilient,' said Lynne Jones, a child psychiatrist with the International Medical Corps, who studied children under war in Bosnia. 'In a number of studies, trauma in children in war zones has tailed off quite rapidly once the violence dies down.' Their continued wellbeing depends on the kind of environment in which they live after that and the values of their families or parents, she said.

Shortly before his murder, Hassan told the *Guardian* of his fears for Iraq's current young generation.

'Do not make the mistake of blaming the occupation and the recent war for all of this,' he said. 'For more than three decades, young Iraqis have been forced to learn how to kill. We must now learn instead about dialogue and compromise. Otherwise, we will continue to produce psychopathic personalities for whom violence is simply a means of negotiating daily life.'

FEBRUARY 12 2007

What's wrong with Gillian McKeith?

BEN GOLDACRE

Call her the Awful Poo Lady, call her Dr Gillian McKeith PhD: she is an empire, a multi-millionaire, a phenomenon, a prime-time TV celebrity, a bestselling author. She has her own range of foods and mysterious powders. She has pills to give you an erection. And her face is in every health-food store in the country. Scottish Conservative politicians want her to advise the government. The Soil Association gave her a prize for educating the public. And yet to anyone who knows the slightest bit about science, this woman is a bad joke.

One of those angry nerds took her down this week. A regular from my website (www.badscience.net) – I can barely contain my pride – took McKeith to the Advertising Standards Authority (ASA), complaining about her using the title 'doctor' on the basis of a qualification gained by correspondence course from a non-accredited American college. He won.

She may have side-stepped the publication of a damning ASA draft adjudication at the last minute by accepting – 'voluntarily' – not to call herself 'doctor' in her advertising any more. But would you know it, a copy of that draft adjudication has fallen into our laps and it concludes that 'the claim "Dr" was likely to mislead'. The advert allegedly breached two clauses of the Committee of Advertising Practice code: 'substantiation' and 'truthfulness'.

Is it petty to take pleasure in this? No. McKeith is a menace to the public understanding of science. She seems to misunderstand not nuances, but the most basic aspects of biology – things that a 14-year-old could put her straight on.

She talks endlessly about chlorophyll, for example: how it is 'high in oxygen' and will 'oxygenate your blood' – but chlorophyll will only make oxygen in the presence of light. It's dark in your intestines and even if you stuck a searchlight up your bum to prove a point, you probably wouldn't absorb much oxygen in there, because you don't have gills in your gut. In fact, neither do fish. In fact, forgive me, but I don't think you really want oxygen up there, because methane fart gas mixed with oxygen is a potentially explosive combination.

Future generations will look back on this phenomenon with astonishment. Channel 4, let's not forget, branded her very strongly, from the start, as a 'clinical nutritionist'. She was Dr Gillian McKeith PhD, appearing on television every week, interpreting blood tests and examining patients who had earlier had irrigation equipment stuck right up into their rectums. She was 'Dr McKeith', 'the diet doctor', giving diagnoses, talking knowledgeably about treatment, with complex scientific terminology and all the authority her white coat and laboratory setting could muster.

So back to the science. She says DNA is an anti-ageing constituent: if you 'do not have enough RNA/DNA', in fact, you 'may ultimately age prematurely'. Stress can deplete your DNA, but algae will increase it: and she reckons it is only present in growing cells. Is my semen growing? Is a virus growing? Is chicken liver pate growing? All of these contain plenty of DNA. She says that 'each sprouting seed is packed with the nutritional energy needed to create a full-grown, healthy plant'. Does a banana plant have the same amount of calories as a banana seed? The ridiculousness is endless.

In fact, I don't care what kind of squabbles McKeith wants to engage in over the technicalities of whether a non-accredited correspondence-course PhD from the United States entitles you, by the strictest letter of the law, to call yourself 'doctor': to me, nobody can be said to have a meaningful qualification in any biology-related subject if they make the same kind of basic mistakes made by McKeith.

And the scholarliness of her work is a thing to behold: she produces lengthy documents that have an air of 'referenciness', with nice little superscript numbers, which talk about trials and studies and research and papers ... but when you follow the numbers and check the references, it's shocking how often they aren't what she claimed them to be in the main body of the text. Or they refer to funny little magazines and books, such as *Delicious*, *Creative Living*, *Healthy Eating* and my favourite, *Spiritual Nutrition and the Rainbow Diet*, rather than proper academic journals. She even does this in the book *Miracle Super-food*, which, we are told, is the published form of her PhD.

'In laboratory experiments with anaemic animals, red-blood cell counts have returned to normal within four or five days when chlorophyll was given,' she says. Her reference for this experimental data is a magazine called *Health Store News*. 'In the heart,' she explains, 'chlorophyll aids in the transmission of nerve impulses that control contraction.' A statement that is referenced to the second issue of a magazine called *Earthletter*.

To me this is cargo-cult science, as the great Professor Richard Feynman described Melanesian religious activities 30 years ago: 'During the war they saw aeroplanes with lots of good materials and they want the same thing to happen now. So they've arranged to make things like runways, to put fires along the sides of the runways, to make a wooden hut for a man to sit in, with two wooden pieces on his head as headphones and bars of bamboo sticking out like antennas – he's the controller – and they wait for the aeroplanes to land. They're doing everything right. The form is perfect. It looks exactly the way it looked before. But it doesn't work. No aeroplanes land.'

McKeith's pseudo-academic work is like the rituals of the cargo cult: the form is superficially right, the superscript numbers are there, the technical words are scattered about, she talks about research and trials and findings, but the substance is lacking. I actually don't find this bit very funny. It makes me quite depressed to think about her, sitting up, perhaps alone, studiously and earnestly typing this stuff out.

One window into her world is the extraordinary way she responds to criticism: with legal threats and blatantly, outrageously misleading statements, emitted with such regularity that it's reasonable to assume she will do the same thing with this current kerfuffle over her use of the title 'doctor'. So that you know how to approach the rebuttals to come, let's look at McKeith's rebuttals of the recent past.

Three months ago she was censured by the Medicines and Healthcare Products Regulatory Agency (MHRA) for illegally selling a rather tragic range of herbal sex pills called Fast Formula Horny Goat Weed Complex, advertised as shown by a 'controlled study' to promote sexual satisfaction and sold with explicit medicinal claims. She was ordered to remove the products from sale immediately. She complied (the alternative would have been prosecution), but in response McKeith's website announced that the sex pills had been withdrawn because of 'the new EU licensing laws regarding herbal products'. She engaged in Europhobic banter with the *Scottish Herald* newspaper: 'EU bureaucrats are clearly concerned that people in the UK are having too much good sex,' she explained.

Rubbish. I contacted the MHRA and they said: 'This has nothing to do with new EU regulations. The information on the McKeith website is incorrect.' Was it a mistake? 'Ms McKeith's organisation had already been made aware of the requirements of medicines legislation in previous years; there was no reason at all for all the products not to be compliant with the law.' They go on. 'The Wild Pink Yam and Horny Goat Weed products marketed by McKeith Research Ltd were never legal for sale in the UK.'

Now, once would be unfortunate, but this is an enduring pattern. When McKeith was first caught out on the ridiculous and erroneous claims of her CV (she claimed, for example, to have a PhD from the reputable American College of Nutrition) her representatives suggested that this was a mistake made by a Spanish work-experience kid who posted the wrong CV. Except the very same claim about the American College of Nutrition was also in one of her books from several years previously. That's a long work-experience stint.

She even sneaked one into this very newspaper, during a profile on her: 'Doubt has also been cast on the value of McKeith's certified membership of the American Association of Nutritional Consultants [AANC], especially since *Guardian* journalist Ben Goldacre managed to buy the same membership online for his dead cat for $60. McKeith's spokeswoman says of this membership: "Gillian has 'professional membership', which is membership designed for practising nutritional and dietary professionals and is distinct from 'associate membership', which is open to all individuals. To gain professional membership Gillian provided proof of her degree and three professional references."'

Well. My dead cat Hettie is also a 'certified professional member' of the AANC. I have the certificate hanging in my loo. Perhaps it didn't even occur to the journalist that McKeith could be wrong. More likely, of course, in the tradition of nervous journalists, I suspect she was hurried, on deadline, and felt she had to get McKeith's 'right of reply' in, even if it cast doubts on – I'll admit my beef here – my own hard-won investigative revelations about my dead cat. I mean, I don't sign my dead cat up to bogus professional organisations for the good of my health, you know.

But those who criticise McKeith have reason to worry. McKeith goes after people, and nastily. She has a libel case against the *Sun* over comments they made in 2004 that has still not seen much movement. But the *Sun* is a large, wealthy institution and it can protect itself with a large and well-remunerated legal team. Others can't. A charming but – forgive me – obscure blogger called PhDiva made some relatively innocent comments about nutritionists, mentioning McKeith, and received a letter threatening costly legal action from Atkins Solicitors, 'the reputation and brand-management specialists'. Google received a threatening legal letter simply for linking to – forgive me – a fairly obscure webpage on McKeith. She has also made legal threats to a fantastically funny website called Eclectech for hosting a silly animation of McKeith singing a silly song, at around the time she was on *Fame Academy*.

Most of these legal tussles revolve around the issue of her qualifications, though these things shouldn't be difficult or complicated. If anyone wanted to check my degrees, memberships or affiliations, then they could call up the institutions and get instant confirmation: job done. If you said I wasn't a doctor, I wouldn't sue you. I'd roar with laughter.

If you contact the Australasian College of Health Sciences (Portland, US) where McKeith has a 'pending diploma in herbal medicine', they say they can't tell you anything about their students. When you contact Clayton College of Natural Health to ask where you can read her PhD, they say you can't. What kind of organisations are these? If I said I had a PhD from Cambridge, US or UK (I have neither), it would only take you a day to find it.

However, McKeith's most heinous abuse of legal chill is exemplified by a nasty little story from 2000, when she threatened a retired professor of nutritional medicine for questioning her ideas.

Shortly after the publication of McKeith's book *Living Food for Health*, before she was famous, John Garrow wrote an article about some of the rather bizarre scientific claims she was making. He was struck by the strength with which she presented her credentials as a scientist ('I continue every day to research, test and write furiously so that you may benefit ... ' etc). In fact, he has since said that he assumed – like many others – that she was a proper doctor. Sorry: a medical doctor. Sorry: a qualified conventional medical doctor who attended an accredited medical school.

Anyway, in this book, McKeith promised to explain how you can 'boost your energy, heal your organs and cells, detoxify your body, strengthen your kidneys, improve your digestion, strengthen your immune system, reduce cholesterol and high blood pressure, break down fat, cellulose and starch, activate the enzyme energies of your body, strengthen your spleen and liver function, increase mental and physical endurance, regulate your blood sugar and lessen hunger cravings and lose weight'.

These are not modest goals, but her thesis was that it was all possible with a diet rich in enzymes from 'live' raw food – fruit, vegetables, seeds, nuts and especially live sprouts, which 'are the food sources of digestive enzymes'. McKeith even offered 'combination living food powder for clinical purposes', in case people didn't want to change their diet, and she used this for 'clinical trials' with patients at her clinic.

Garrow was sceptical of her claims. Apart from anything else, as emeritus professor of human nutrition at the University of London, he knew that human animals have their own digestive enzymes and a plant enzyme you eat is likely to be digested like any other protein. As any professor of nutrition – and indeed many GCSE biology students – could happily tell you.

Garrow read the book closely, as have I. These 'clinical trials' seemed to be a few anecdotes in her book about how incredibly well McKeith's patients felt after seeing her. No controls, no placebo, no attempt to quantify or measure improvements. So Garrow made a modest proposal – and I am quoting it in its entirety, partly because it is a rather elegantly written exposition of the scientific method by an extremely eminent academic authority on the science of nutrition, but mainly because I want you to see how politely he stated his case.

'I also am a clinical nutritionist,' began Professor Garrow, 'and I believe that many of the statements in this book are wrong. My hypothesis is that any benefits which Dr McKeith has observed in her patients who take her living food powder have nothing to do with their enzyme content. If I am correct, then patients given powder which has been heated above 118F for 20 minutes will do just as well as patients given the active powder. This amount of heat would destroy all enzymes, but make little change to other nutrients apart from vitamin C, so both groups of patients should receive a small supplement of vitamin C (say 60mg/day). However, if Dr McKeith is correct, it should be easy to deduce from the boosting of energy, etc, which patients received the active powder and which the inactivated one.

'Here, then, is a testable hypothesis by which nutritional science might be advanced. I hope that Dr McKeith's instincts, as a fellow-scientist, will impel her to accept this challenge. As a further inducement I suggest we each post, say, £1,000 with an independent stakeholder. If we carry out the test, and I am proved wrong, she will, of course, collect my stake, and I will publish a fulsome apology in this newsletter. If the results show that she is wrong I will donate her stake to HealthWatch [a medical campaigning group] and suggest that she should tell the 1,500 patients on her waiting list that further research has shown that the claimed benefits of her diet have not been observed under controlled conditions. We scientists have a noble tradition of formally withdrawing our publications if subsequent research shows the results are not reproducible – don't we?'

This was published in an obscure medical newsletter. Sadly, McKeith – who, to the best of my knowledge, has never published in a proper 'Pubmed-listed' peer-reviewed academic journal – did not take up this offer to collaborate on a piece of research with a professor of nutrition. Instead, Garrow received a call from McKeith's lawyer husband, Howard Magaziner, accusing him of defamation and promising legal action.

Garrow, an immensely affable and relaxed old academic, shrugged this off with style. He told me. 'I said, "Sue me." I'm still waiting.' His offer of £1,000 still stands. I'll make it £2,000. But, to me, it's tempting to dismiss the question of whether or not McKeith should call herself 'doctor' as a red herring, a distraction, an unnecessary *ad hominem* squabble. Because despite her litigious-ness, her illegal medicinal products, her ropey qualifications, her abusiveness, despite her making the wounded and obese cry on television, despite her apparently misunderstanding some of the most basic aspects of GCSE biology, while doling out 'scientific' advice in a white coat, despite her farcical 'academic' work, despite the unpleasantness of the food she endorses, there are still many who will claim: 'You can say what you like about McKeith, but she has improved the nation's diet.'

Let me be very clear. Anyone who tells you to eat your greens is all right by me. If that was the end of it, I'd be McKeith's biggest fan, because I'm all in favour of 'evidence-based interventions to improve the nation's health', as they used to say to us in medical school. But let's look at the evidence.

Diet has been studied very extensively and there are some things that we know with a fair degree of certainty: there is convincing evidence that diets rich in fresh fruit and vegetables, with natural sources of dietary fibre, avoiding obesity, moderate alcohol and physical exercise are protective against things such as cancer and heart disease. But nutritionists don't stop there, because they can't: they have to manufacture complication to justify the existence of their profession.

And what an extraordinary new profession it is. They've appeared out of nowhere, with a strong new-age bent, but dressing themselves up in the cloak of scientific authority. Because there is, of course, a genuine body of research about nutrition and health to which these new 'nutritionists' are spectacularly unreliable witnesses. You don't get sober professors from the Medical Research Council's Human Nutrition Research Unit on telly talking about the evidence on food and health; you get the media nutritionists. It's like the difference between astronomy and astrology.

These new nutritionists have a major commercial problem with evidence. There's nothing very professional or proprietary about 'eat your greens', so they have had to push things further: but unfortunately for the nutritionists, the technical, confusing, over-complicated, tinkering interventions that they promote are very frequently not supported by convincing evidence.

And that's not for lack of looking. This is not about the medical hegemony neglecting to address the holistic needs of the people. In many cases, the research has been done and we know that the more specific claims of nutritionists are actively wrong.

I've got too much sense to subject you to reams of scientific detail – I've learned from McKeith that you need theatrical abuse to hold the public's attention – but we can easily do one representative example. The antioxidant story is one of the most ubiquitous health claims of the nutritionists. Antioxidants mop up free radicals, so in theory – looking at metabolism flow charts in biochemistry text-books – having more of them might be beneficial to health. High blood levels of antioxidants were associated in the 1980s with longer life. Fruit and vegetables have lots of antioxidants, and fruit and veg really are good for you. So it all made sense.

But when you do compare people taking antioxidant supplement tablets with people on placebo, there's no benefit; if anything, the antioxidant pills are harmful. Fruit and veg are still good for you, but, as you can see, it looks as if it's complicated and it might not just be about the extra antioxidants. It's a surprising finding, but that's science all over: the results are often counterintuitive. And that's exactly why you do scientific research: to check your assumptions. Otherwise it wouldn't be called 'science', it would be called 'assuming' or 'guessing' or 'making-it-up-as-you-go-along'.

But don't get distracted. Basic, sensible dietary advice that we all know still stands. It's the unjustified, self-serving and unnecessary overcomplication of this basic sensible dietary advice that is, to my mind, one of the greatest crimes of the nutritionist movement. I don't think it's excessive to talk about consumers paralysed with confusion in supermarkets.

Although it's just as likely that they will be paralysed with fear, because McKeith's stock-in-trade is abuse, on a scale that would have any doctor struck off: making people cry for the television cameras – I assume deliberately – and using fear and bullying to get them to change their lifestyles. As a posture it is seductive, it has a sense of generating movement, but if you drag yourself away from the theatricality of souped-up recipe and lifestyle shows on telly, the evidence shows that scare campaigns tend not to get people changing their behaviour in the long term.

So what can you do? There's the rub. In reality, again, away from the cameras, the most significant 'lifestyle' cause of death and disease is social class.

Here's a perfect example. I rent a flat in London's Kentish Town on my modest junior doctor's salary (don't believe what you read in the papers about doctors' wages, either). This is a very poor working-class area and the male life expectancy is about 70 years. Two miles away in Hampstead, meanwhile, where the millionaire Dr Gillian McKeith PhD owns a very large property, surrounded by other wealthy middle-class people, male life expectancy is almost 80 years. I know this because I have the Annual Public Health Report for Camden open on the table right now.

This phenomenal disparity in life expectancy – the difference between a lengthy and rich retirement, and a very truncated one indeed – is not because the people in Hampstead are careful to eat a handful of brazil nuts every day, to make sure they're not deficient in selenium, as per nutritionists' advice. And that's the most sinister feature of the whole nutritionist project, graphically exemplified by McKeith: it's a manifesto of rightwing individualism – you are what you eat, and people die young because they deserve it. They choose death, through ignorance and laziness, but you choose life, fresh fish, olive oil and that's why you're healthy. You're going to see 78. You deserve it. Not like them.

How can I be sure that this phenomenal difference in life expectancy between rich and poor isn't due to the difference in diet? Because I've read the dietary intervention studies: when you intervene and make a huge effort to change people's diets and get them eating more fruit and veg, you find the benefits, where they are positive at all, are actually very modest. Nothing like 10 years.

But genuine public health interventions to address the real social and lifestyle causes of disease are far less lucrative and far less of a spectacle than anything a food crank or a TV producer would ever dream of dipping into.

What prime-time TV series looks at food deserts created by giant supermarket chains – the very companies with which stellar media nutritionists so often have lucrative commercial contracts? What show deals with social inequality driving health inequality?

Where's the human interest in prohibiting the promotion of bad foods; facilitating access to nutrient-rich foods with taxation; or maintaining a clear labelling system? Where is the spectacle in 'enabling environments' that naturally promote exercise, or urban planning that prioritises cyclists, pedestrians and public transport over the car? Or reducing the ever-increasing inequality between senior executive and shop-floor pay?

This is serious stuff. We don't need any more stupid ideas about health in the world. We have a president of South Africa who has denied that HIV exists; we have mumps and measles on the rise; we have quackery in the ascendant like never before; and whatever Tony Blair might have to say about homoeopathy being a fight not worth fighting for scientists, we cannot indulge portions of pseudoscientific ludicrousness as if they don't have wider ramifications for society, and for the public misunderstanding of science.

I am writing this article, sneakily, late, at the back of the room, in the Royal College of Physicians, at a conference discussing how to free up access to medical academic knowledge for the public. At the front, as I type, Sir Muir Gray, director of the NHS National Electronic Library for Health, is speaking: 'Ignorance is like cholera,' he says. 'It cannot be controlled by the individual alone: it requires the organised efforts of society.'

He's right: in the 19th and 20th centuries we made huge advances through the provision of clean, clear water; and in the 21st century, clean, clear information will produce those same advances.

Gillian McKeith has nothing to contribute and Channel 4, which bent over backwards to dress her up in the cloak of scientific authority, should be ashamed of itself.

Adieu to the fair man who gave me football

SIMON HATTENSTONE

Dad died on Sunday. He was 91 and had had what we call a good innings – 91 might be a terrible score to get out on in cricket, but life and sport sometimes go their separate ways.

Dad wasn't a natural sportsman. He preferred to sit in his armchair with a fag or 50 and watch the telly or read a good thriller. (This was before he became cultured and discovered Classic FM.) Occasionally, he developed an interest in sport, but even then it would be the kind you could play or watch with a fag in your mouth. When I was in my teens he took me down to Hurricane Higgins' snooker palace by the Rialto. It was dark and dingy, stank of smoke and beer. He was never a drinker, but he felt at home.

He loved his snooker. Not playing – his biggest break was, like mine, around the eight mark – but watching. He was glued to the telly, hour after hour, day after day, watching the Worlds unfurl on the box. He always had a favourite – the ones who played it as they lived it. First the Hurricane, then the Whirlwind and lastly, of course, the Rocket. A few years ago I interviewed Ronnie O'Sullivan for the first time and came home with one of Ronnie's cues, signed by him for Dad. I can still see Dad's smile. 'And he gave me this? For me?' he said with disbelief. Mum wrote a letter to Ronnie on Dad's behalf to thank him.

Last year he lost his sight and had to give up on the snooker. So I had to report directly to him the Rocket's doings and wrongdoings. A few weeks ago I saw Ronnie at the Masters at Wembley and told him Dad was very ill.

'Tell him, I'm gonna win this one for him,' he said. Ah, that's lovely, I thought, but he's not won a big snooker tournament for close on two years. Anyway, he did.

When Jewish people die the family sit *shiva*, sometimes for a day, sometimes for a working week. The mourners sit on tiny chairs, bottoms next to the ground, and visitors wish them 'long life' and reminisce. It's a surreal scene – something you might expect to find in a Fellini film. Visitor after visitor comes up to me and the first thing they all say about Dad is that he was honest and fair; he never tried to shaft anybody and never expected to be shafted. It makes me proud of him and reminds me of our football days together.

Our football days were limited. It wasn't that he didn't like the game, he just wasn't interested. When I was nine I caught encephalitis and was bed-ridden for the best part of three years. It was when I was ill that Dad and I became much closer. He'd always been working too hard to take much notice beforehand. He used to lie on the spare bed in my room, listen to *Dark Side of the Moon* with me, our eyes shut, and he'd say: 'This is the best bleddy music I've ever heard. Marvellous.'

I started playing football, largely in my bedroom. There was a period when I seemed to break a window a week, sometimes two. Mum and Dad were so relieved I was alive they didn't even give me the bollockings I deserved. When I was better, Dad got us a couple of season tickets at Maine Road. It was a huge sacrifice, because he worked on Saturdays. He started to enjoy the ritual – Big Helen ringing her bell, the couple behind us with their blankets and whisky, the half-time chatter – but he invariably missed the goals, too busy lighting up.

When I think of his sense of fairness it takes me back to a particular day – one of the greatest in my life. It was the last time City won a cup, in 1976, and Dad took me down to the final at Wembley. He decided to make a real day of it, splash out, so we went on the Pullman, ate lunch on the train – fantastic. Best of all, we won, beating Newcastle 2–1, and Denis Tueart's overhead kick is still one of the greatest goals Wembley has seen. Dad missed both goals – he was lighting up, of course.

At the end of the game we walked back down Wembley Way. I was 13 years old and drunk on success, Dad was pleased, but still his sober self. The flip side of his decency was his naivety. It was the mid-1970s, but somehow football violence and sectarianism and the notion of provocation had passed him by. As we were walking, we passed a couple of Newcastle fans. I put my head to the ground. Dad looked at them, smiled and said: 'Well, boys, do you think it was a fair result?'

I waited for them to smack him and prepared to run. But they didn't. They just smiled back, and said 'Aye!'

Of course, they wouldn't have hit Dad. They could tell he was a football innocent – a fair man asking a fair question.

FEBRUARY 17 2007

'It will be sorted'

MATTHEW TAYLOR AND ALEXANDRA TOPPING

Among the bunches of flowers and cards piled up outside the small flat where Billy Cox, 15, was shot and killed, a friend had scrawled a telling message yesterday: 'To Remer: Nuff Luv. All da mandem will miss u heaven's new fallen soldier.' The words, a few centimetres high and written in black pen, gave an insight into the final months of the teenager who, this week, became the latest victim of south London's escalating gun wars.

Billy – who was shot at point blank range at his home in Clapham on Wednesday – was allegedly involved with one of the gangs in his area, the Clap Town Kids. Yesterday a website dedicated to Billy – whose street name was Remer – showed a video of the teenager rapping with friends. Underneath, posts praised the 'fallen soldier'. 'I hope da mandem hu dne it read all des messeges so dai knw dat remer ... was loved by all,' read one.

On the Fenwick estate where Billy died teenagers said 'mandem' was slang for gang and warned Billy's death would have repercussions. 'This isn't going to go by,' said one. 'It will be sorted. Them that did this will know that.'

Yesterday the extent of Billy's involvement in south London's gang wars in which three teenagers have been shot and killed in 11 days remained unclear. Many friends insisted that he was an innocent victim. Others said he had offended a member of another gang or that he owed money for drugs. What was not in doubt was the growing number of teenage gang members who routinely carry and use guns on south London's estates. Some reports suggested that members of the Clap Town Kids had clubbed together to buy a gun to share.

'Getting hold of a gun round here is as easy as going into a McDonald's and getting a McChicken sandwich,' a 16-year-old on the estate told the *Guardian* yesterday. 'If I had the money I could make a phone call and get a gun now ... It wouldn't cost [as much as £150], you could ask anyone to borrow a gun ... they would let you.'

The Clap Town Kids, centred around the Fenwick estate, are part of a web that criss-crosses south London, including the PDC [Poverty Driven Children] in Brixton, Ghetto in Lewisham, and the

Blood Set in Streatham. One former member of the Clap Town Kids said yesterday that gangs were as important as families to many teenagers. 'They [gang members] are like brothers – they protect each other through thick and thin.'

Some residents said Billy had been killed after a text-message argument and yesterday a former member of the PDC told the *Guardian* how a seemingly small slight could trigger a devastating response.

'It could easily have been that he had done something little, and that sparked this,' said Ryan, 19, from Brixton. 'These gangs operate on respect. If someone feels that they have been dissed, they have to act – or it's them that looks bad and they are seen as weak.'

Although Billy was serving a 12-month supervision order for burglary and was on a curfew, many residents said that he had only started getting into trouble in the last year or so. But Ryan said that was not unusual.

'When you get to 14 and 15 and you are living in these places, you have to make a decision about which way you are going to go – it's what I had to do,' he said. 'It's OK sitting here asking why do we get involved, but if you are there and you don't, then you are nothing. You get robbed and beaten up. You get no respect if you are not in a gang – whether it's on the bus or in the street. Even at school and from the police and from the newspapers you get more attention if you are part of it.'

Yesterday Mercedes, 19, who grew up around the Ghetto gang in New Cross, Lewisham, said it was easy for teenagers to be drawn towards gangs.

'I tried everything I could think of to get in [to the Ghetto gang],' she said. 'I would attack people in the street if I thought the "olders" [senior gang members] were watching or rob people or try and go with the guys. When you are up close, it's the gang that matters. You are not interested in jobs or school or anything, you just need to get their respect.' She said that once the gang members reached 14 or 15, they were usually selling drugs and using the guns themselves. 'That is the most dangerous time, cos it's when people have to prove themselves,' she said. 'At that time you earn your reputation and if someone does something to disrespect you, then you have to act or not – it's that pathetic, but when you are in it, it's real.'

She said most of the gangs were made up of teenagers, but older men, who had often been in prison, were still pulling the strings. A 16-year-old, who left the Clapham gang after his friend was killed, agreed, saying older gang leaders were role models.

'They are the nicest people and the most dangerous,' he told the *Guardian*. 'They control everything. They can tell you to sell this or kill that person.'

Yesterday residents on the Fenwick estate were trying to understand exactly why Billy had been taken from them. On the walls and stairwells friends had added 'RIP' to his graffiti tag. But as the media vans began to pack up and move on, a 16-year-old who had just laid flowers outside Billy's flat was already looking forward.

'It's a hard world,' he said. 'You don't stand still in Clapham.'

FEBRUARY 19 2007

Maggie Thatcher pinched my shoes

PAULA COCOZZA

Sometimes fashion moves in mysterious circles and you can find yourself rubbing up against people you would sooner not. How, for instance, would Grace Kelly have felt had she lived to see that her taste in shoes (moccasin-style flats) is shared with Sarah Ferguson? Similarly, Thandie Newton, in her appreciation of the Giles label, has found an unlikely alliance with Su Pollard. In my case, I am walking in ever-closer step with Margaret Thatcher.

It started last spring when she was photographed exiting my favourite shoe shop. Disconcerting, but not entirely damning – if only she had stopped there. But on Remembrance Sunday she appeared on television wearing my very shoes, the ones I wear almost every day, which I have polished with a love and regularity unbestowed on any other shoe. I turned a blind eye that time. But last week she was out and about again – this time in a patent version. Not only does she have my shoes, but she has more than one pair. Why can't she stay out of my shops?

The shoe in question, by Salvatore Ferragamo, is a round-toed court with a grosgrain bow and gilt trim. It has a stout 3cm heel which, I like to think, gives it a twist that sets it apart from your common or garden ballet pump. Appropriately enough for Thatcher, Ferragamo is a shoe house with staying power. In the 1950s, Salvatore himself shod the feet of Audrey Hepburn (her ballet flat with a cross strap is still sold as the 'Audrey' today). The Vara, the shoe Thatcher and I share, has been produced since 1978 – a year before she became prime minister, and a year after I started school.

This might not matter, but as shoes are like signatures it feels as if she has written her name all over my feet. It's not as if there aren't differences between the two of us. I like wearing my shoes with jeans, while Thatcher wears hers with smart tights. When it comes to skirts, I wear mine only with those that end well above the knee (to counteract the sensibleness of the heel), while she wears hers with hems skimming the shin. Perhaps the unifying attraction is that it comes, as few shoes do, in three widths, so it's comfortable, too, although mine is rapidly acquiring discomfort-ing associations. Chiefly, a pinch of a thought that maybe she hasn't got my shoes – maybe I've got hers.

FEBRUARY 20 2007

The politics of wellbeing

MADELEINE BUNTING

A new anxiety is taking hold. The social consensus about what we value and why seems to have fragmented, leaving in its wake an unpleasant cocktail of celebrity, cool, acquisitiveness and depres-sion. The Unicef report that Britain is the worst place to grow up in the industrialised world was a bad enough jolt. The fact that it was published during a series of brutal murders of young men further underlines the pervasive sense that something has gone awry in this country in the quality of relationships – within families, between peers, in neighbourhoods.

It sounds inchoate because it is. How can one characterise social change made up of billions of human relationships? But there is an increasing perception that we have become a nasty country – aggressive, quick to judge or humiliate and profoundly competi-tive. In the constant comparison with others we either crow smugly at our own good fortune or sink into depression at our inadequacy. This gloomy diagnosis seems to be backed-up by research. The British Attitudes Survey shows how we are becoming more preoccupied with our individual concerns and less with those of the community. According to Compass, the political pressure group, we are in the grip of a social recession.

Tomorrow a well-timed debate at the House of Commons, 'The Politics of Wellbeing', featuring two of its leading advocates, will explore the political ramifications of this social recession. A younger generation of politicians is keen to speak to this malaise in the public mood, although they are careful to talk in vague terms about values rather than specific policy proposals. The aim is to project a politics that is more emotionally attuned than the Gradgrind managerialism and target-toting of Labour. But aside from offering opportunities for political positioning, there is a serious question to answer: are politicians to blame for this social recession and can they put it right?

Sure, one can point out that the biggest single cause of unhappiness is inequality, but plenty of countries with greater inequality did better than Britain in the Unicef report. So maybe there's something more at stake – some vacuum of values and, if so, doesn't that go beyond a politician's remit? If we're obsessed with celebrity, self-centred and rude, will a politician's hectoring make any difference?

Oliver James is in no doubt that the politicians are to blame for the social recession. In his new book, *Affluenza*, he particularly targets 'Blatcher' as having missed a historic opportunity to shift the country in the direction of Scandinavian social democracy, instead of the 'selfish capitalism' found in English-speaking countries from the United States to Australia, where depression rates are twice those of mainland Europe.

James lays the blame on a political economy of privatisation, low regulation, low taxation and valuing the success of a business only by its share price, but he never explains why these characteristics are connected – for example, how does privatisation contribute to the pre-occupation with celebrities or hyperconsumerism? Nevertheless, James has a point: turbo-capitalism strips out many of the social contexts which give people meaning and orientate them. International surveys show how desperately insecure the British are – second only to South Korea, according to the Organisation for Economic Cooperation and Development.

The most influential advocate of happiness being a proper subject for government in recent years has been the economist Richard Layard with his book *Happiness*. He attributed the stagnant rates of wellbeing in industrialised countries to trends such as family breakdown, declining trust, rising crime and television eroding social connectedness. He argued for the Benthamite principle of the 'greatest happiness of the greatest number' as the proper aim of government. If that was the accepted goal of society (rather than increasing GDP) it would ensure the priority of tackling inequality and improving mental health services. But politicians are rightly wary of how Bentham translates into politics. Marriage and ethnically homogenous communities lead to higher rates of happiness, while television has a detrimental effect – should government then bring in draconian measures such as banning divorce or TV? Even more crudely, apply Bentham's principle and you could end up advocating Prozac in tap water – it would certainly provide the greatest happiness of the greatest number.

Despite these reservations, James and Layard give politicians plenty to think about. Layard, in particular, has lobbied hard to get politicians to take mental-health services seriously. He's done that by offering the carrot of reductions in the millions of people with depression who are currently on incapacity benefit – that got the Treasury listening. There are real economic costs to our social recession.

James and Layard are challenging the entrenched tradition of materialism in Labour party thinking that believes that all this airy-fairy stuff about wellbeing is a distraction from the real issue of economic growth. It also challenges the more recent managerialist grip of performance indicators and number-crunching that has left Labour sounding robotically soulless.

Brown's team, steeped in the language of the work ethic, will have to find a way to talk about this theme of wellbeing. Perhaps they should take a trip to Denmark – the country that comes closest to having a politics of wellbeing that I've seen. It affects every form of public service from day care through the educational system to looked-after children and the elderly. Denmark invests an enormous amount in training people to nurture human relationships. It has a powerful ideal of human wellbeing and how to develop it. When the Danish built their welfare state, they professionalised and properly remunerated the skills women used in raising families. What Brown won't like is that such a politics of wellbeing is not cheap or easily measurable.

Of course it's not a panacea and Denmark is not a utopia, but this appreciation of the importance of relationships is evident throughout the social infrastructure of the country. In comparison, the British seem mechanistic, obsessed with procedure and distrustful of each other. The costs of that in terms of social recession are beginning to become clear.

FEBRUARY 22 2007

Wags, Bratz and the sexualised adolescent

CATHERINE BENNETT

Concluding two years of research, a task force appointed by the American Psychological Association (APA) has just presented its findings on the sexualisation of girls. Although the task force focuses on US culture, its first and most eye-catching example of sexualisation is available here, too: 'Toy manufacturers,' it regrets, 'produce dolls wearing black leather miniskirts, feather boas and thigh-high boots and market them to eight- to 12-year-old girls'.

The allusion, of course, is to Bratz dolls, whose feather boas are already suspected, by many sexy-toy experts, of having corrupted the minds of innumerable young girls. If their clothes are too provocative, *Time* magazine has also criticised their 'jaded, bored, if not actually stoned' facial expressions. At the *Daily Telegraph*, which presides, somewhat fitfully, over a campaign to protect children from the modern world, a writer promptly shared her disgust for 'these hideous creatures' with their 'heavy-lidded, post-coital gaze' and proposed that parents should begin their revolt against inappropriate toys with a boycott: 'Say no to Bratz.'

My feelings entirely, although my own reservations have more to do with the Bratz dolls' disturbing, detachable feet – a facility that soon results in the toys having to pursue their gruelling timetable of getting dressed, accessorising, grooming, disco-dancing and shopping on no more than a pair of plastic stumps. It is for this reason, I think, that our household's brace of Bratz survived only a week or so before being banished, *sans* feet, to Doll Guantánamo: a cupboard under the stairs, where the Bratz remain to this day, sexualising the vacuum cleaner. Most of their feet have never been found.

Having read the APA study, I wonder how much damage the little sluts might have inflicted had they remained at liberty. Would they have been more likely to lower the aspirations of their young female owner than, say, her subsequent exposure to real-life versions on reality TV? Or her continual non-exposure to prominent women in politics? Were they, with their poutier faces, more likely to help internalise false consciousness than their bustier, Aryan rivals from Mattel? Barbie, after all, was once held by feminist campaigners to be a lethally effective weapon of the patriarchy. Now she is considered ironic.

It is impossible to say. Despite placing the Bratz dolls at the top of an introductory list of sexualisation factors, the American task force struggles to explain why they should present a particular risk to the wellbeing, identities and life chances of very young girls.

'It is worrisome,' the authors will only say, 'when dolls designed specifically for four- to eight-year-olds are associated with an objectified adult sexuality. The objectified sexuality presented by these dolls, as opposed to the healthy sexuality that develops as a normal part of adolescence, is limiting for adolescent girls, and even more so for the very young girls who represent the market for these dolls.'

Worrisome, then, but still not a threat you would want to prioritise until you had seen a longitudinal study, correlating early Bratz ownership with careers in lapdancing. Nor is that the only point in this patchily convincing critique where the task force is obliged to fall back on uneasy feelings, speculation and wishful extrapolation.

'Although much of this research has focused on adult or college-aged women rather than girls or teenagers,' say the authors (after lamenting the sale of children's scent, such as Barbie's Free Spirit), 'portrayals of adult women provide girls with models that they can use to fashion their own behaviour, self-concepts and identities.'

Neither this worrisome vagueness about the origins and effects of girls' sexualisation, nor the fairly unpersuasive idea that banning Bratz and their boas would constitute a worthwhile advance in child protection, has deterred the media from outing the dolls as prime causes of childish unhappiness. Forget explicit content in advertising on pre-watershed BBC television programmes, in ruttish song lyrics by child-focused bands: on Tuesday night, the Bratz manufacturer was forced to defend his dolls against no particularly focused charge on Radio 4's evening news.

Meanwhile, the tale of Coleen McLoughlin has been unfolding. Highlights from her life story – appearing simultaneously in the *Sun* and the *Mirror* – have explored the transformation from schoolgirl nonentity to international celebrity that pretty Coleen has achieved by the simple expedient of going out with the footballer and former patron of prostitutes Wayne Rooney. Everywhere, from broadsheet to tabloid, the media celebrates her accomplishments: getting dressed, losing a few pounds, forgetting about Wayne's 'auld slapper'. How long before her first *South Bank Show*? Or before the makers of BBC2's *The Verdict* put in a request for her to play the judge in their next cutting-edge series? At the very least, acclaim for this modern-day Cinderella will (in the words of that US task force) provide younger girls with a model 'that they can use to fashion their own behaviours, self-concepts and identities'.

When you consider the respect accorded to Coleen and her many C-list colleagues for their achievements in shopping and grooming, the Bratz team start to look a bit up themselves. Coleen and Wayne keep busy watching *Emmerdale*, *Coronation Street*, *EastEnders*, then *Corrie* again. Look on the Bratz website and you will find the dolls have favourite classes (Jade picks chemistry), movies and even 'fave books': 'mysteries' for Cloe, and, for Sasha, 'biographies of successful people'. And what kind of sleazy, disempowering message is that?

FEBRUARY 28 2007

A sense of peril

NILS PRATLEY

Doug Noland, a bearish market strategist in the United States, captured the current predicament for stock-market investors very well last December when he said that 'the current global profits boom is unmatched in its scope, intensity and peril'. In other words, rarely has life been so wonderful for so long – cheap money and low inflation have worked in glorious combination – yet rarely has it seemed so possible that the show could come to a sudden and very painful halt.

Yesterday's little market wobble looks like one of those moments when the second thought was uppermost. Certainly, none of the other explanations looked adequate. The Chinese stock market, the supposed source, is a sideshow in global terms. A plunge of 9 per cent in Shanghai, when it follows a 130 per cent gain last year, is neither here nor there. As for Alan Greenspan's thoughts on the chances of a US recession this year – well, he has said these things before now. And don't blame tensions in Iran: the price of oil and gold would have moved if that was the real worry.

Frankly, if you are in the mood to worry you can find any number of 'top-of-the-market' signals. Private equity seems to be determined to smash its own records for biggest-ever deals virtually every month. Old hands in the property market have been warning for months that asset prices have got out of hand. In the currency markets the entire hedge-fund industry, plus every Japanese saver, seems to be betting that the yen will remain weak.

All are interesting developments, yet the most important

medium-term guide to the direction of markets is probably still the willingness of American consumers to keep spending. At the moment, there is severe pain in the 'subprime' market, as HSBC knows too well. It does not appear to have spread yet, but the banks themselves are clearly terrified that it will. Lending standards are being tightened aggressively. Their actions are nowhere near panic levels, but a credit-crunch is exactly what the bears have been predicting for the final chapter of the bull market. It does not feel like we're there yet, but the sense of peril is not subsiding.

Spring

Obituary: Ian Wooldridge

FRANK KEATING

Ian Wooldridge, who has died aged 75, was an undisputed heavy-weight champion of British sportswriting. For his readers, with his perception, passion and wit, he bridged the chasm between those who are fervently knowledgeable about sports and those who are decidedly not. By his peers over almost four decades, he was considered just about the transcendent British operator. His clubbable urbanity and generosity lent lustre to his peripatetic trade, sometimes considered trivial, if not rather grubby.

But with Ian, sportswriting was never 'below the salt'. He was a top-table eminence, everybody knew it, and most certainly the *Daily Mail*'s proprietors knew it. He played an imperishably crucial part in that newspaper's prominence through the final third of the last century. One of the luminous handful around whom the modern *Mail*'s founding father Sir David English (who died in 1998) built his team, Ian had a singular but always flexible style: he could daub on the primaries with broad strokes or work with a water-colourist's touch – either way, back at base, his copy would invariably be dressed up for the reader in full splash treatment. And he was so agreeable a chap that only one or two of his insecure writing colleagues ever dared publicly to resent his patrician's preferment.

Ian's first and abiding passion was cricket and by 1962, at the comparatively early age of 30, he was the *Mail*'s cricket correspondent. By 1972 – in acknowledgment that the paper's top-of-the-bill had grown weary of watching Geoffrey Boycott bat – he was appointed chief columnist and sportswriter, a title he was to hold to all intents, certainly in repute, until his death.

Mind you, to the end he would boast (as he ordered another dry martini – against doctor's orders) that he was living proof of the old suspicion that those who can do, those who can't quite, coach, and those who are utterly hopeless travel the world on a first-class ticket criticising the others. Dapper, trim, welcoming, lionised ... any job, anywhere was enhanced by Ian's presence. 'Woollers is in already' – from Las Vegas to Melbourne the words greeted your arrival and you knew, no probs, the great man had logged the phone-boxes that worked, booked the best restaurant, told the barman about shaking (not stirring) and that the crucial contacts were already beating a path to his door.

He covered many more than just the routine diary jobs – as well as nine Olympics, cricket tours, golf majors, umpteen championship 'fights of the century' and a myriad of world cups of various shapes and sizes. He relished his big-splash solo stints (mostly in the company of the *Mail*'s star snapper, Monty Fresco). The Cresta Run might have been hairy-scary, but Ian's prose made it a melody; ditto his near-annual run with the bulls at Pamplona.

He took in his stride the 1,200-mile husky-race in Alaska or a white-knuckle ride with the Red Arrows, a round of golf with the Australian prime minister (which he won) or three rounds in the ring (diplomatically lost) against the former heavyweight boxer Idi Amin. The opening ceremony at the 1978 Commonwealth Games in Edmonton, Alberta, was as direly drear as the next one, so I led my piece back to the *Guardian* with Ian's sudden appearance, carrying the flag as manager of the three-man Cayman Islands team.

He always sought the bespoke and telling angle. After one Olympics, when a tiny-tot sensation from the Soviet Union in the gymnastics event enchanted all the British ratings, Ian went to visit the *mignon* mite's state factory-farm in Russia: 'It was a gymnasium where nobody laughed. I longed to see schoolboys sky-larking and fat girls with pigtails doing something hopelessly badly. I longed to see someone dropping in after school for an hour's enjoyment.'

Ian was a child of the New Forest. After Brockenhurst grammar school and national service with the navy, in 1948 he was given a trial as a cub reporter in the Dickensian offices of the *New Milton Advertiser*. To the end, he would quote that first day's work – in the morning, the funeral of local bigwig and coal-merchant Charlie Browning; in the afternoon, Les Tomkins taking 9 for 21 in the local derby against Brockenhurst. (A quarter of a century on, when the Australian fast bowlers Lillee and Thomson were blasting out England, Ian invented for the *Mail* a spoof journal of a coarse Oz bowler – whom he called, with a nice nostalgia, Terror Tomkins).

Young Ian himself was a good enough batsman to have ambitions to play the first-class game – at 17 he batted at number four for Hampshire Schoolboys against the county's 2nd XI. Tom Dean – the county's purveyor of leg-breaks and googlies – was bowling. Ian missed the first three deliveries and was clean bowled by the fourth. All of 33 years later, he met Dean in Port Elizabeth. 'You totally altered my life,' he said. 'If I'd been able to pick your googly, I'd now be a 50-year-old ex-pro running a crumbling pub and, I daresay, contemplating suicide.'

In 1953 he joined the *Bournemouth Times* and made the move to Fleet Street three years later with the *News Chronicle*. He joined the *Daily Mail*'s then sister paper, the *Sunday Dispatch*, in 1960 and the *Mail* in 1961.

Ian was an admirer of American sports columnists and, for a final late-night brandy, he would happily recite the jewels of such as Ring Lardner and Ernest Hemingway, Paul Gallico, James Boswell, Red Smith and all. The United States produced the sports columnists, he reckoned; the Fleet Street forte was sports report-ing. In his time, Ian himself was an accomplished virtuoso at that art. He chronicled, for instance, Ted Dexter's 70 and Tom Graveney's 96, both at Lord's; Ken Barrington's 143 at Port-of-Spain; Basil D'Oliveira's Oval 158; Franz Klammer at the Innsbruck Olympics (arguably his most brilliant-ever piece); Mary Peters at Munich; Muhammad Ali in the Jungle; Arthur Ashe's Wimbledon; Sebastian Coe and Steve Ovett in Moscow ... and on and on to Jonny Wilkinson's drop-goal in Sydney.

Ian, the *Mail*man through and through, was, nevertheless, in the corner of the *Guardian*'s John Arlott (who died in 1991) when the latter spoke at the Cambridge Union in 1969 against playing with apartheid South Africa. He regularly debunked the *Mail*'s 'let's play with apartheid' editorial policy and refused to join in his paper's cynical stunt with the South African runner Zola Budd.

Forty winters ago, during England's Test match at Port Elizabeth – Ian's first tour – some black South Africans who had attempted to watch the cricket were beaten up by police. Ian's telephone line went down, so the *Mail* copytakers in London contacted him through the phone in the committee-room. He had written his piece; now he had to read it at the top of his voice in the presence of about 30 members of the republic's ruling Broederband. He could have altered his intro. Instead, he took a deep breath and dictated: 'The wretchedly evil face of apartheid was displayed here today when ... ' Yes, he would say years later, 'I was fairly proud of myself at that moment.'

In 1997 he had a serious heart operation, but survived it with a bonny optimism – and drinks all round for the discovery that, as his surgeon had apparently told him, 'my lungs and liver are in surprisingly tip-top condition'. He won umpteen sportswrit-ers' awards, wrote and presented a number of films for both BBC and ITV, and wrote five books, notably a fond biography of the pentathlete Mary Peters (1974) and a short and funny memoir, *Travelling Reserve* (1982).

In 1957, he married Veronica Churcher, with whom he had three sons, Kevin, Simon and Max; after that was dissolved in 1979, he enjoyed an immensely happy marriage with Sarah Chappell. She and the children survive him.

Ian Edmund Wooldridge, journalist, born 14 January 1932; died March 4 2007.

MARCH 6 2007

Squalid Britain

JEREMY PAXMAN

Make the most of it. Before the leaves begin to shoot on the trees and the grass thickens on the roadside verges, take a look around you. This is the perfect time of year to appreciate what a squalid place Britain has become. The gutters heave with the spring awakening of Starbucks cartons. The pavements glitter with discarded gum and the sun twinkles on a million soft-drink cans. What is that streaming from the top of the tree? It's a 12ft length of grubby plastic.

It is not just the sordid view from the windows of trains or from cars and buses on the motorways. There can scarcely be a country road in Britain that is not splattered with the evidence of what an ugly, thoughtless people we are becoming. Years ago I remember going to Greece and being depressed by the slick of plastic bags, discarded bottles and soiled nappies at the edge of every road. Nowadays, Britain seems to look at least as sordid. What's gone wrong?

The first port of call is that eminently worthy but dull organisation the Keep Britain Tidy campaign. The logo, the slogan – was there even some irritating jingle, back in the days of black-and-white television? – recall a different country. Keep Britain Tidy has now been rebranded 'EnCams' (short for environmental campaigns? – the name change doesn't exactly seem to have catapulted it into the headlines) and runs from offices in Wigan.

Astonishingly, they seem to think things are getting better rather than worse, according to their most recent survey in November 2006. The top line of their news release claimed that 'litter levels in England have fallen to a five-year low'. This it attributes to 'new laws brought in by government', introducing possible £80 fines. The organisation is largely funded by the government.

How can they claim the country is so clean, when the evidence of our eyes suggests quite the reverse? To be sure, they do think that some problems seem as bad as ever: lots of fag ends, for example, a 2 per cent increase in dogshit (how do they measure these things?).

The organisation is enthusiastic about clean-up campaigns of the kind organised in cities such as Manchester and Nottingham, backed by fines for offenders. These included an £800 penalty for a woman in Manchester for persistently not cleaning up after her dog had pooed in public places. (More effective, it seems to me, would be community service orders requiring such people to spend a few weekends scooping up dog mess, preferably with their bare hands, but that is by the by.) At the end of successful local campaigns you have a cleaner area.

Of course, this is a good thing: one consequence of rubbish on the streets is that they make you ashamed, depressed and angry about where you live. But it seems to me that we long ago moved from an environment in which litter was a local problem. We are no longer a green and pleasant land spotted with filthy places. We are a filthy island in which there is now an occasional oasis of cleanliness.

Just look at the roadsides. Setting out to cycle a one-mile stretch of quiet country road to attempt my own amateurish survey of rubbish, I gave up once I had counted more than 100 items and, it seemed, hardly gone 500 yards. Of course, some of it – hubcaps and so on – looked as if it had fallen there by accident. But most – sandwich wrappers, McDonald's bags, crisp packets and endless plastic bottles – had been deliberately jettisoned. The problem is that the detritus that accompanies our increasingly mobile lives lasts a great deal longer than the time it takes for its contents to pass through us. If it is not cleared up and dumped in one of the increasingly scarce holes in the ground, it stays in the undergrowth for years, a semi-permanent reminder of what a tatty little place we have become.

The reason people throw their trash out of the window of their car is, obviously, that they do not want it inside. They do not want it there because that is space for which they feel personally responsible. 'Outside' belongs to someone else. Or, more likely, to no one. So the litter issue is about more than the uglification of Britain. It tells us something about the sort of nation we have become. People, like animals, do not generally foul their own nests. But they feel free to throw rubbish around for much the same reason morons feel entitled to vandalise bus shelters, smash park benches or use telephone boxes as urinals: they do not feel the public realm is theirs.

On the left, the common coin is to see this sort of antisocial behaviour as the natural consequence of the 'no such thing as society' individualism that underpinned Thatcherism. I guard my things. Indeed, I demand respect from others for them, because they signify my achievement (even if, as often as not, the credit bills on which they were bought will long outlive their shiny consumerist showiness). But it is too easy to blame it all on Margaret Thatcher. Whatever Blairism may be, it has done nothing to dim the obsession with the signifiers of success. The ludicrous 'respect' culture – that sees knife-fights start because someone fails to accord due deference to another person's trainers – is just the most extreme expression of a cast of mind that now seems universal.

The flipside is not merely increasingly frenetic attempts to persuade us to spend money on things we don't need to buy. It also encourages a belief that that which is not obviously personal property has no value. I might respect your trainers – but I couldn't give a toss about the park or the bus shelter that belongs to all of us.

It is stupid, of course, because we all then have to clear it up. And as no government – national or local – wants to take away the money citizens would prefer to spend on shiny new goods, they economise on clearing up rubbish. The difficulty that then arises is that once you get to a point where there is garbage everywhere you look, there is no longer any incentive for others not to add to the mess. The contrast is with visiting a continental city that has the civic pride to keep the streets clean: when foreign visitors see cleanliness is the norm, they feel inhibited about dropping rubbish.

The paper and dogshit will rot away. The real problem, it seems to me, is plastic. The stuff is everywhere – in parks, public spaces, outside office blocks, blowing about on country fields and festooned in the branches of trees.

First off, there are the estimated 10bn plastic bags given to shoppers. Some of them will take anything from 100 to 1,000 years to rot away. It is not as if nothing can be done about it. Five years ago, the Irish government brought in a tax on non-recyclable plastic bags (15 cents for each one) and within three months cut their use by 90 per cent. When he was a minister at the British Department of

Environment, Michael Meacher attempted to introduce a similar arrangement in Britain. The plastics industry objected, of course. But they need not have bothered. Meacher found the idea stifled before it could draw breath: taxes were the Treasury's prerogative, and they weren't going to let a bunch of sandal-wearers take the initiative. Remember this the next time that Gordon Brown poses as an environmentalist. Here is a man whose memorial should be built of discarded supermarket bags.

The people who supply and manufacture plastic bags claim that 'plastic carrier bags are not a significant component of litter' on the grounds that they are outnumbered by discarded cigarette butts. This is an argument on a par with the old excuse that 'the cat ate my homework'. But I suspect we will whistle ourselves breathless waiting for the government to make the packaging industry pay to clear up the rubbish their customers throw around. There aren't any votes in it.

In the meantime, we shall have to try to force government – local and national – to knuckle down to their responsibilities. Local authorities have a statutory duty to ensure streets, parks, playgrounds and pedestrian areas are clean. The sides of roads and motorways are the responsibility of councils and the Highways Agency. They are demonstrably failing to keep pace with the tide of rubbish. In theory, any of us could go to a magistrates' court to get an order forcing them to take their duties seriously. But who has the time? A spokeswoman for the Highways Agency, for example, could not recall a single instance of an individual seeking an enforcement notice against it through the magistrates courts.

What is obviously needed is some combined initiative, individual and collective, voluntary and coercive, before it is too late. Unless we are to revel in a belief that somehow the British are a uniquely sordid people, we should seize the moment. This is the perfect time of year for a national spring-clean, which could involve councils, schools, voluntary groups and community organisations, as well as the statutory authorities. It would be one of those few tasks in life at the end of which you would see a result.

The alternative is to continue sliding downhill into a country that increasingly resembles some vast municipal landfill site. We may be – in every sense – at a tipping point. But we know that people respond to what they see around them. If they see clean and tidy, they act clean and tidy. If they see squalor, they act squalid. Right now, Britain looks pretty vile in many places. Wait five years and see how it looks.

MARCH 6 2007

Olivier had the instincts of a pub comic

MICHAEL BILLINGTON

It was the Christmas hols, 1957. As a 17-year-old provincial theatre junkie, I dashed to London for a mad, packed Saturday: a 2.30 matinee of Gielgud in *The Tempest*; a 5.30 visit to Jean Anouilh's *Dinner With the Family*; an 8.30 trip to the Palace to see Olivier in *The Entertainer*. Of the three, it's the last that stays with me.

In the front-cloth scenes, Olivier's Archie Rice was extraordinary. He was jaunty, spry in white kid-gloves and natty bow-tie, and often incredibly camp.

'You think I'm like that, don't you?' he cried, flapping a limp wrist. 'You think I am! Well, I'm not. But [pointing to the conductor], *he* is.'

I suspect Olivier loved all that. After years of being encased in the role of a great classical actor, here was a chance for him to chat to the audience, do a nifty buck-and-wing dance and sing John Osborne's mock-jingoistic numbers. My memory is that the Saturday second-night house was a popular audience out for a good time and Olivier, who had the instincts of a pub comic, gave it to them in spades. But Olivier's real greatness came out in the family scenes. Under the outward bravura, he displayed a soul-wrenching despair that reminded me of the Macbeth he had played at Stratford two years previously.

There was a moment at the end of the second act when, hearing of his son's death at Suez, Olivier slowly slid down the side of the proscenium arch while singing the blues. For the first time, I realised it was possible to convey tragic emotion in modern dress. It was indisputably thrilling and, listening to it again on a recently issued *Classics for Pleasure* live recording, I found the hairs standing up on the back of my neck just as they did that December day in 1957.

MARCH 15 2007

A right royal frump

JESS CARTNER-MORLEY

About five years ago there was much tabloid excitement at rumours of a budding email romance between Prince William – who was in those days a rather handsome young man with a lovely head of blond hair – and Britney Spears, who was in those days a phenomenally successful young popstrel with equally lovely blond locks.

What a difference a few years have made. Britney is bald; William not far behind. And instead of being accompanied by a miniskirted pin-up, the heir to the throne has by his side a girl in longer-length tweed. It's a funny old world.

The photographs of William and Kate at Cheltenham serve to back up two of my most unshakeable sartorial prejudices: first, that calf-length skirts should be banned by law; and second, that posh people should never wear sunglasses, because they always get them horribly wrong.

They are also an undoubted setback in the royal family's long-running campaign to update their public image. William is 24; Kate is 25. Normal people their age do not wear tweed hacking jackets or buttoned-up longer-length skirt suits on fun days out. Fact.

William has never been exactly fashion-forward, but he now seems positively fashion-backward. You can't wear a shirt and tie and jumper and jacket: the jumper kills dead all the muscularity of the suit and tie, while the suit and tie kill the casualness of the jumper, so you end up looking stuffy and emasculated.

Who should take the blame for Kate's look? By all accounts she has long had tendencies – despite the much-publicised flirtation with Topshop – towards lamb-dressed-as-mutton. Last year she wore a tailored tweed coat by the Fulham designer Katherine Hooker to Cheltenham – livened up on that occasion by a controversial mink hat – so fingers are likely to point in that direction.

More intriguing is the evident influence of Camilla. Kate's matronly dog-walking tweeds and unreconstructed-Sloane shirt collar are more in keeping with the wardrobe of Charles's current wife than that of the glamourpuss William's mother had become by the time of her death. Perhaps the publicity-shy Kate has found a smart way of avoiding becoming the new Diana – by becoming the new Camilla instead.

MARCH 21 2007 – COMMENT IS FREE

After the party

LINDA GRANT

The news that the Communist Party of United States of America is finally opening its archives to the public should at last focus attention away from the McCarthy witchhunts of the early 1950s and the high-profile hounding of the Hollywood Ten, towards the tens of thousands of ordinary Americans who joined the party, lived its dream and eventually became disillusioned.

In the 1930s and 1940s American leftists, unlike their counterparts in Britain, had no mainstream party to join and no hope – despite the perennial candidacy of the Socialist party leaders Eugene Debs and Norman Thomas – of forming a government. The American Communist party was one of the vitalising forces in American life. In her landmark study, *The Romance of American Communism* (shamefully out of print) Vivian Gornick interviewed dozens of former members. She vividly described her own upbringing, among the Jewish garment workers of New York, how ideas lifted these members of the proletariat out of the grind of their everyday lives, how the party made intellectuals of them. To be a communist, one of them remarked, made you bigger than you were, and those who left described the soul-destroying loneliness of life on the outside.

But even without the blind indifference to Stalinism, the persistent self-delusion of those who refused to believe that the Soviet Union was not the workers' paradise of its own propaganda, the party became the mirror image of its own persecutors. As well as those who left, there were those who were flung out, expelled in a series of internal show trials, charged with a deviation from 'the line'. The leadership ossified into a hierarchy of apparatchiks. Those accused of betrayal felt themselves betrayed. They were tossed back into America, having given 20 years or more to the party, severed connections with their families, gone underground at the leadership's behest, and then, as a new directive arrived from Moscow, were discarded. The waste of their lives was what enraged them and often they were not even told what they had done.

The party was also riddled with informers. Who could tell who was a friend and who was an FBI agent? All normal life was mediated through one's membership. Marriage outside the party was discouraged, and yet, wives discovered their husbands were covert government agents.

Back in the early 1990s – researching a novel, *The Cast Iron Shore*, about a young girl who travels to America in the mid-1940s and joins the Communist party – I felt great compassion for those who had given their lives to a struggle that ended in abject failure. American communists never built a revolutionary party and the Soviet experiment was dissolved by the indifference of its own people.

The fascination, for me, in the archives is not to be found in the minutes of the national conferences or the deliberations of the central committee, but those of the local branch meetings, wherein we will find another, secret America. The nature of idealism, the longings that will not leave us alone in peace to pursue our private lives, is part of the history of the human race. Why it fails, over and over again, to achieve the boldest and most humane of its ambitions is perpetually baffling. The Communist party archives will, I hope, provide us with the material to map that unknown territory.

MARCH 24 2007

To cut a long story short

Ernest Hemingway once said his best work was a story he wrote in just six words: 'For sale: baby shoes, never worn.' We challenged some contemporary authors to be equally economical.

'Samaritans.'
'I'm listening.'
'Hello?'
'Hel ...'
'Samaritans ...'
Michel Faber

'It can't be. I'm a virgin.'
Kate Atkinson

Set sail, great storm, all lost.
John Banville

Dream punctured. Build pyre. Curses ... Adolf.
Beryl Bainbridge

See that shadow? (It's not yours.)
Jim Crace

Defenestrated baby, methamphetamine, prison, rehab, relapse.
Jeffrey Eugenides

Juicy offer. Must decline. Still paralysed.
Richard Ford

Bob's last message: Bermuda Triangle, Baloney.
Elmore Leonard

Dad called: DNA back: he isn't.
Helen Fielding

Humorous book: critic died laughing. Sued.
Alexander McCall Smith

'Kiss me.'
'?'
'Kiss me ... '
'?!!'
'Oh, sorry.'
Jon McGregor

Mother's-milk. Ribena. Tetley's. Chibuku-Shake-Shake. Complan.
Morphine.
Marina Lewycka

'Apple?'
'No.'
'Taste!'
'ADAM?'
Oh God.
David Lodge

Evil isn't necessarily unkind. Gran next.
DBC Pierre

MAY 21 1982

Men of 42 Commando Royal Marines storming ashore from a
landing craft at Port San Carlos, East Falkland, on the first day
of the British land campaign to recapture the Falkland Islands
from Argentina (see page 240). JOHN SHIRLEY

MAY 30 2007

American soldiers attached to the Stryker units with injured
Iraqis just after an explosion outside two houses used as bomb
factories in Karradah. SEAN SMITH

MAY 19 2007

Tony Blair returns from the Green Zone back to Baghdad airport, Iraq, in a Puma helicopter with armed escort. DAN CHUNG

JUNE 24 2007

New Labour leader Gordon Brown shakes hands with Tony Blair on stage at a special Labour leadership conference in Manchester. MARTIN ARGLES

JUNE 28 2007

Gordon Brown heads his first cabinet meeting in 10 Downing Street.
MARTIN ARGLES

Megan's baby: John's surname, Jim's eyes.
Simon Armitage

Purse found. 'No notes,' she said.
Andrew O'Hagan

Served the pie, watched him die.
Maggie O'Farrell

Thought love must fade: but no.
George Saunders

He didn't. She did. Big mistake.
AL Kennedy

They awaited sunrise. It never came.
AS Byatt

In the end, everything simply began.
Ali Smith

Stop me before I kill again.
Hari Kunzru

Free to good home. Extraneous coffin.
Barbara Trapido

I repented and turned to Christ.
Ian Sansom

The pillow smelled like my brother.
Patrick Neate

'Hello?'
'Cupcake.'
'Douglas?! I'm ... married.'
[click]
Miranda July

It was a dark, stormy ... aaaaargggh!
John Lanchester

Armageddon imminent. Make list. Tick most.
Ian Rankin

Catherine had treasonable sex. Heads rolled.
Helen Simpson

'The Earth? We ate it yesterday.'
Yann Martel

A&E IOU
Toby Litt

Funeral followed honeymoon. He was 90.
Graham Swift

Womb. Bloom. Groom. Gloom. Rheum. Tomb.
Blake Morrison

Pain, unutterable pain, stertorous exhalation. Death.
Will Self

'Mind what gap?' ... ...
Hilary Mantel

MARCH 26 2007

With love from her to me

LILIE FERRARI

In 1963 I was 14 and, like almost every girl in Britain, I fell in love with a Beatle. 'My' Beatle was George Harrison. From the first photograph I saw of the Fab Four, I was drawn to his dark eyes, serious face and enigmatic demeanour. He rarely smiled, even when he was being funny, and this made him all the more mysterious and enticing. Compared to the uncouth boys I had to deal with at school every day, George was a delicate, idealised vision of what I thought boys ought to be like. If he had pimples, I never saw them. If he swore, I never heard it. I never saw his hair greasy, his armpits damp, his shoes scuffed. In short, he was perfect.

We had just moved to Norwich and I had missed a Beatles concert by a few weeks, but a girl in my class had somehow obtained all the Beatles' home addresses (I daren't think how, looking back) and was selling them at playtime for half a crown each. A bargain, I thought, handing over my two-and-six eagerly. Immediately upon the exchange, 174 Mackets Lane, Liverpool, became the repository of all my fantasies.

That day I hurried home to compose my first letter to George. I had discovered the joy of words and wasn't about to be intimidated into single syllables by writing to a Beatle. I don't remember exactly what I wrote, but in spite of my best intentions I suspect it was a gauche jumble of repressed adoration, along the lines of 'You're the best Beatle' and 'I much prefer "From Me to You" to "Come On" by the Stones.' I don't remember waiting for the postman every morning. By then the Beatles had started their journey into the stratosphere (it was the year the term 'Beatlemania' was coined) and I guess I assumed I was too small a cog in the great Beatle wheel to merit any kind of response.

But one day a letter with a Liverpool postmark did come, addressed to me in careful looped handwriting. I opened it with trembling fingers and, instead of a letter from George, found one from his mum, Louise. After a few niceties and general bulletins about 'the boys'' progress, a question leaped off the page: 'Are you,' she asked, 'by any chance related to a writer called Ivy Ferrari, who writes doctor-and-nurse romances?'

I bellowed a great scream that brought the family running: my mother was Ivy Ferrari, a romantic novelist churning out Mills & Boon paperbacks with titles like *Nurse at Ryminster*, *Doctor at Ryminster*, *Almoner at Ryminster*. I couldn't believe it – I might be a fan of her son, but Mrs Harrison was evidently a fan of my mother. I felt as if I had been raised from one among millions to a special place in Mrs Harrison's head.

Of course I wrote back to tell her that I was indeed Ivy Ferrari's daughter. I was happy to have made the connection – but so, it seemed, was she. I couldn't quite grasp it. Beatles were glamorous. My mum was a harassed woman with inky fingers, unruly hair and scruffy skirts who sweated over a typewriter all day. How could they compare? In the past I might have been indifferent to the overwrought love lives of the fictional staff of Ryminster Hospital, but now they seemed to take on a glamour of their own.

George never wrote to me and my mother never wrote to Mrs Harrison, but the two of us began a correspondence that lasted for several years – years that took her from the Mackets Lane council house to a smart bungalow in Appleton, George from gangling teenage guitarist to married man, and me from schoolgirl to young woman.

I sent Mrs Harrison signed copies of my mother's novels. She sent me signed pictures of the Beatles. I asked her intense questions ('Which one is your favourite, besides George?' Answer: 'John, because he does the tango with me in the kitchen and makes me laugh'). She interrogated me about the mysteries of my mother's creations, such as whether my mum knew any real doctors like Dr David Callender. ('He was fairly tall and tough-looking, with tawny-brown hair and a lean, intent face. His eyes were dark and compelling, so full of fire and life they drew me like a magnet ... ') On my 15th birthday, Mrs Harrison sent me a small piece of blue fabric – part of a suit George had worn at the Star Club in Hamburg. Once, I got a crumpled newspaper cutting containing a photo of the Beatles with their scribbled signatures on it, and a big lipstick kiss, which, she said, had been planted there by John Lennon.

She sent me notes that George wrote her on used envelopes: 'Dear Mum, get me up at 3, love George.' She wrote on the backs of old Christmas cards and odd bits of paper – I never knew why. She told me funny stories about her upbringing in Liverpool, a world of men in caps on bikes and old ladies with jugs of gin. I told her about my life in Norfolk, about my sisters, my pony, the dog, my mother. I told her things I didn't tell anyone else – my fear of failure, my terrible, hidden shyness, my longing to have real adventures, lead a different kind of life to the quiet, rural existence I endured. She was my invisible friend, the silent recipient of everything I had to say.

She always answered my questions, and offered up teasing glimpses of life as the mother of a superstar – 'I'm sitting by the pool with Pattie. Had a lovely time at the film premiere' – remarks tantalisingly combined with more mundane observations about knitting and cakes. Of course, I never mentioned 'real' boys who had caught my eye – that would have been somehow unfaithful to George. That was the only omission I can remember – apart from never articulating how I felt about her son, because I wanted her to think of me as a 'normal' girl and not the wide-eyed obsessive I really was.

After several years the gaps between our exchanges grew longer, as real life began to get in the way of teenage fantasies. I can't remember which of us wrote the last letter, but by the time I was 18 and working in London, the correspondence had petered out.

Soon after we had slipped from each other's lives, I found myself standing a few feet away from George himself, in the Apple boutique on London's Baker Street. He looked tired and unapproachable. The George that I had conjured up in the kitchen of Mackets Lane, propping notes for his mum on the mantelpiece, seemed a kinder, gentler prospect than the gaunt-looking superstar standing before me who might just tell me to get lost. He was close enough to speak to, but I've never been sorry that I backed away in silence.

Mrs Harrison died in 1970 when I was 21. I remember reading about it in the papers. I grieved for her on my own and remembered her small acts of kindness to a girl in Norfolk she had never met. Her son, of course, made an enormous mark on my life without ever knowing it. I even married someone who embodied all the things I thought George represented: quiet strength, spirituality, the same dry humour, the dark good looks. My husband, Colin, had been, among other things, a roadie and the owner of punk record shops. Fortunately, he also had a sense of humour and a high level of tolerance. He learned to live with the omnipresence of George and would sign cards to me 'Love from George and The Other One'.

As the years passed, my life came into focus and George receded. He married, had a son – as did I. I went back to live in a Norfolk cottage, while George retired to a Gothic mansion in Henley. In 1994 I went to Liverpool for the first time with Colin, as a football supporter rather than a Beatles pilgrim: Norwich City were playing at Anfield. I took time out to stand in front of 174 Mackets Lane and tried to imagine Mrs Harrison sitting at the window in the front room, answering my letters. I wanted to weep, but I didn't. When Norwich scored the winning goal that afternoon and we leapt to our feet, I cheered instead for that kindly Liverpudlian who took the time and trouble to light up my teenage years.

I've gradually lost the priceless relics of those years. They would have made me rich if I hadn't been so careless with my belongings; then again, I would never have sold them. So my side of that eccentric correspondence has all but disappeared, along with my youth.

In September 2001 Colin died of Hodgkin's disease. A month later, George was dead, too. It felt as if two distinct parts of my life had ended all at once: my dreamlike girlhood and my real, adult life with a beloved partner and friend. But every day in my study at home I look at something that binds these two parts together. It's a photograph of George taken in 1962 in Hamburg by Astrid Kirchherr (girlfriend of 'fifth' Beatle Stuart Sutcliffe). Colin secretly sought it out, bought it, hand-made a frame for it, and gave it to me on my 40th birthday. It is one of my most treasured possessions.

MARCH 27 2007

Hot flushes and delusions

GERRY ADAMS

At some point in every election campaign every candidate forms a view that they are going to win. This syndrome – known as *candidatitis* – is capable of moving even the most rational aspirant into a state of extreme self-belief. It strikes without warning, is no respecter of gender and can infect the lowly municipal hopeful as well as lofty presidential wannabes.

Screaming Lord Sutch – or his Irish equivalents who stand just for the craic – could be prone to fall victim to candidatitis as much as the most committed and earnest political activist. I believe this is due to two things. First of all, most people standing for election see little point in telling voters that they are not going to win. That just wouldn't make sense. Of course not. So they say they are going to win.

Listen to Michael Howard, the former British Tory leader. He had no chance of beating Tony Blair. Did he admit that? Not on your nelly. Howard sounded as confident as George Bush addressing a rally in his native Texas in the run-up to the last US presidential election.

That's when candidatitis starts. As 'we are going to win' is repeated time and time again it starts to have a hypnotic effect on the person intoning the mantra. By this time it's too late. Which brings me to the second point. The electorate, and others, encourage candidatitis. Unintentionally. Not even the candidate's best friend will say, 'Hold on, you haven't a chance.' The media might, but no candidate believes the media. And most candidates are never interviewed by the media anyway.

So a victim of candidatitis will take succour from any friendly word from any punter. Even a 'good luck' takes on new meaning and 'I won't forget ye' is akin to a full-blooded endorsement. Are we to pity sufferers of this ailment? Probably not. They are mostly consenting adults, though in most elections many parties occasionally run conscripts. In the main these are staunch party people who are persuaded to run by more sinister elements who play on their loyalty and commitment.

In some cases these reluctant candidates run on the

understanding that they are not going to get elected. Their intervention, they are told, is to stop the vote going elsewhere or to maintain the party's representative share of the vote. In some cases this works. But in other cases, despite everything, our reluctant hero or heroine actually gets elected. A friend of mine was condemned to years on Belfast city council when his election campaign went horribly wrong. He topped the poll.

That's another problem in elections based on proportional representation (PR). Topping the poll is a must for some candidates. But such ambition in a PR election creates a headache for party managers. If the aim is to get a panel of party representatives elected, they all have to come in fairly evenly. This requires meticulous negotiations to carve up constituencies. Implementing such arrangements makes the implementation of the Good Friday agreement look easy – and it's taken us nine years to get our first meeting with Ian Paisley. It requires an inordinate amount of discipline on the candidates' behalf. Most have this. Some don't.

Some get really sneaky. Particularly as the day of reckoning comes closer. Hot flushes and an allergy to losing can lead to some sufferers poaching a colleague's votes. This is a very painful condition leading to serious outbreaks of nastiness and reprisals and recriminations if detected before polling day. It usually cannot be treated and can have long-term effects.

So, dear friends, all of this is by way of lifting the veil on these usually unreported problems which infect our election contests. Politicians are a much maligned species. In some cases not without cause. But love us or hate us, you usually get the politicians you deserve.

This might not always extend to governments, given the abandonment by most governments of the election promises that persuaded voters to elect them in the first instance. The lust for power causes this condition, which is probably the most serious ailment affecting our political system and those who live there. It is sometimes terminal. But this comes after elections and is worthy of a separate study.

So, don't ignore the visages on the multitudes of posters that defile lampposts and telegraph poles during election times, and in some cases for years afterwards. Think of the torment that the poor souls are suffering. When you are accosted by a pamphlet-waving besuited male – and they mostly are besuited males – as you shop in the supermarket or collect the children at school, try to see beyond the brash exterior. Inside every Ian Paisley is a little boy aiming to please. The rest of us are the same. It's not really our fault you see. Big boys make us do it. And your votes encourage us.

MARCH 30 2007

The strange case of the Met chief and the IRA siege

IAN KATZ

At the time it seemed the perfect antidote to the Metropolitan police commissioner's image as a soft-skinned bureaucrat more comfortable discussing strategy with Home Office mandarins than rounding up villains on the mean streets of the capital. In an interview with the *Guardian* published last year Sir Ian Blair described the most dramatic experience of his early police career: after responding to a radio call about a 'bandit car' being used by a group of IRA men fleeing the scene of an attack, he and a sergeant had found themselves confronted with the terrorists.

'We turned the corner, and there is the car,' he recalled. 'It was a very defining moment. I think I spent the next half an hour pretending to be a bush. They got out of the car and started firing at us. It is an interesting experience being fired at when you have absolutely nothing to fire back with ... I loved it. I loved the job.'

The men had just carried out a drive-by shooting attack on a West End restaurant and were headed for Balcombe Street where they would take a couple hostage in their flat for six days in what would become one of the most famous episodes of the IRA's mainland campaign. It was a tale of old-fashioned derring-do told with appealing self-deprecation.

Sir Ian's account of his role in the incident attracted little attention until Steve Moysey, a US-based British academic, read the interview earlier this month, while researching a book about the siege. Moysey, who has a PhD in organisational psychology, was puzzled by a number of apparent inconsistencies between the commissioner's account and what he had learned during a year spent investigating the events leading up to it.

'They made me sit up and say that doesn't look right,' he said. He was particularly bemused by one detail of Sir Ian's story: 'The statement that as they [the IRA men] got out of the car "they started shooting at us" is just inconsistent with what I know to have occurred. It just didn't add up.'

Moysey contacted John Purnell – who with his partner Phil McVeigh were the first policemen to confront the Balcombe Street gang – who was equally puzzled. 'Steve Moysey said: "I've never heard this before, it's the first time it's ever been mentioned" and I said, "Snap",' recalled Mr Purnell. 'I've never for one second associated Ian Blair with Balcombe Street in any shape or form and his account of seeing [the terrorists] get out of the car and being shot at as they got out of the car is totally impossible.'

Yesterday Sir Ian said that in the original interview he had been trying to discuss 'what the excitement and thrill of the job was as a young cop. This is me with less than a year's service, so it's 31 years ago.' He acknowledged that he had not personally seen the

IRA men getting out of their car and opening fire, but had become aware that they had done so after arriving in the Balcombe Street area on the night of December 6 1975. 'Wherever it is we arrive [in the Balcombe Street area], I am aware from what I'm hearing that it must be that they are out of the car and they are firing, because I heard the firing ... I didn't see it and I didn't say I saw it.'

Though he says he is not completely sure where he first arrived, he insists he was present while shots were being fired. But he says he was never 'in the thick of it' and did not imply that he was.

The most intriguing aspect of Sir Ian's fuller account of his involvement concerns his part in the pursuit of the stolen Ford Cortina driven by the IRA gang before they abandoned it near Regent's Park. It is well known that Mr Purnell and Mr McVeigh followed the IRA car in a commandeered taxi. But yesterday Sir Ian said he too had briefly joined the chase after encountering the IRA car in Park Street near the original shooting.

'We turned into Park Street and there were two or three vehicles in front of us going extremely fast.' He believed one was the 'bandit car' and another may have been a taxi, but Sir Ian and his sergeant were not able to keep up, 'because we were driving a Hillman Hunter, which has a top speed of 25mph minus'. The top speed of the least powerful Hillman Hunter in 1975 was 83mph and the top speed of a 1970s-era taxi was 60mph.

These details may be academic, according to Mr Purnell. Asked about Sir Ian's latest account of the pursuit last night he said: 'There was no chase. It was just going along at a normal speed. [The IRA men] actually said later they didn't know they were being followed.'

Representing Ukraine ...

MICHAEL HANN

When I was in my teens, the Wedding Present were my band – the one of whom I could bear to hear no evil spoken. A mutual interest in matters Ukrainian led me to befriend their then guitarist, Peter Solowka (I had an unrequited crush on a girl with Ukrainian parents; he actually had Ukrainian parents) and when I discovered his passion for the music of his forefathers I supplied him with a couple of the Ukrainian songs that the band eventually recorded.

Come autumn 1988 and I was working as an intern in the House of Representatives in Washington DC for a congressman named Robert Matsui. The work was, at best, tedious: clipping newspapers, answering phones, running off to right-wing firebrand Newt Gingrich's office to get free cans of pop from a woman I knew who worked there (the Coke bottling plant was in Gingrich's district – he had a whole room full of complimentary cans). To perk things up, I started visiting the congressional research service, which I milked ruthlessly for its files on Ukraine. Why I thought this would impress either the girl of my dreams or my favourite band, God only knows. In my defence, I was only 19. I know better now.

But what to do with this wealth of material? Then, a stunning idea! The US version of Hansard, Congressional Record, has a section called Extension of Remarks, which consists of undelivered speeches, printed under the congressmen's names, to show some moaning special-interest group that, yes, we feel your pain and we take your problems seriously. So, I put it to my lackadaisical supervisor (a Republican who had somehow found himself in the office of a liberal Democrat), why not let me write some Extensions of Remarks about Ukrainian matters? Nothing too heavy, just praising the indomitable spirit of the Ukrainian people under the Soviet yoke in this, the 1,000th anniversary of Christianity in Ukraine. The kind of thing that the near non-existent Ukrainian community of Sacramento (Matsui's district) would surely cheer. He agreed. And my deathless prose on matters Ukrainian duly appeared in Congressional Record.

But was this enough to prove myself the Wedding Present's most devoted fan? Perhaps not. And so I hatched a plan to get a piece of legislation through Congress. I would persuade the world's most powerful legislative body to designate one day of the year as National Ukrainian-American Day. All right, it wasn't the introduction of a universal healthcare plan, but I refer you again to my age.

Getting Congress to approve a day of commemoration isn't that hard. You don't need a bill to pass both houses, you don't need a gruelling committee stage, you don't need presidential approval (leastways, you certainly didn't in 1988). All that was required was a small number of congressional signatories to get the proposal before the relevant committee, which would then wave it through (no one would bother questioning something that might win them a couple of votes).

Gingrich was on board early, making it truly bipartisan. (He thought I worked for him – I was in his office so often picking up pop. 'How you doing?' he'd say, clapping me on the shoulder as he strode through his foyer. 'Doing a great job here.') Though when I say 'on board', what I mean is one of his assistants forged his signature on my sheet. For weeks, I traipsed the corridors of the Rayburn, Longworth, and Cannon buildings, where the representatives' staffs work, getting friendly interns to persuade their supervisors to add their bosses' names to my list. Slowly, we were getting there – until disaster struck.

National Ukrainian-American Day was a couple of signatories short of going to committee when the house rose for the 1988 presidential and congressional elections – and anything not already passed was scrapped. My legislative triumph, the one that would have put the Wedding Present on the US political map, was lost for ever.

Six months later the Wedding Present released their album of Ukrainian folk songs, featuring the ones I'd sent them. And guess what? I didn't even get a thanks in the sleevenotes.

APRIL 4 2007

The man who said no to MI5

VIKRAM DODD

The British resident Jamil el-Banna, 44, knew Abu Qatada, a cleric accused of being al-Qaida's spiritual leader in Europe. In 2002 Mr Banna, a father of five from London, was seized by the CIA and secretly flown to Guantánamo Bay, after MI5 wrongly told the Americans that his travelling companion was carrying bomb parts on a business trip to Gambia. On Friday, his companion, Bisher al-Rawi, was released without charge after four years in the US detention camp, after it emerged that he had helped MI5 keep track of Qatada. But Mr Banna's incarceration in Cuba continues.

It has now emerged that only days before Mr Banna's arrest MI5 visited him at his home and attempted to recruit him as an informer, with the lure of a new identity, relocation and money.

The *Guardian* has obtained this MI5 document in which the intelligence officer details, in his own words, that encounter.

Note For File
Date: 31 October 2002
Subject: Meeting with Abu Anas [an Arabic version of Jamil el-Banna's name][1]

Summary
Unannounced visit to Anas at home by ****** [blacked-out name of MI5 agent] and MPSB D/Sgt ****** [name of Metropolitan police special branch detective sergeant]. Anas welcoming and apparently friendly denies any involvement in extremist activity; concerned about being arrested or turned back when leaving for Gambia or being excluded once outside the country; asks about progress of application for British nationality and possibility of a return of personal items seized during police raid last year; shows no interest in resettlement package in return for cooperation.

Detail
2. On 31 October at 0845hrs, I and ****** of MPSB called at Anas's home. This is a reasonably well-maintained 1930s semi, probably worth around £300,000 if the local estate agent's window is anything to go by. Parked on the drive at the front was a small, silver-coloured car, displaying a green L-plate.

3. Anas opened the door himself. In Arabic, I introduced us as Michael from the British government and Andy from Scotland Yard and asked if we could have a brief chat with

---

1 Explanations in square brackets are the *Guardian*'s own words.

him. He immediately invited us in and took us into the living room at the back of the house; his wife, dressed in traditional full-length hijab, but with the face uncovered, and three young children were already in there, so we waited in the corridor in case either Anas or his wife were sensitive about us being in the same room as her, but they beckoned us in and then said that they were in the middle of checking Anas's blood-sugar level – for the last five days he had been suffering health problems and had just been diagnosed by the doctor as having diabetes. Eventually the wife shooed the children out, but hovered around the door to listen to the conversation. The meeting was conducted in Arabic throughout.

4. Anas asked me to repeat who we were and I said that I was from the Security Service – Scotland Yard? he queried, so I explained that Andy was from Scotland Yard and that I was from the *mukhaberaat* [Arabic for secret police], although it was important for him to understand that we were not like the *mukhaberaat* in most Arab countries. He immediately agreed with this comment.

5. I then said that, with the arrest of Abu Qatada, we would be able to focus more attention on other members and groups in the extremist community. Anas immediately said that he was not a member of such a group, although he conceded in response to my naming names that he was a friend of Abu Qatada.

He explained that as a youth he had led a dissolute life, but had then rediscovered Islam and had been to Afghanistan. It was there that he had met Qatada, whom he considered to be a friend. There was no way that he would allow Qatada's family to go without food or assistance during Qatada's detention.

5. [*sic*] I told him that in addition to increased focus on UK-based extremists, we were investigating reports of terrorists based abroad who were keen to mount attacks in the UK, possibly using biological or chemical weapons. He agreed that such people were correctly labelled terrorist.

I told him that the use of such techniques would pose a threat to all residents of the UK, as biological weapons would not differentiate between Muslims and Christians, and that as the father of young children he should be concerned by such a possibility. Both Anas and his wife, who was standing by the door, agreed with this. She then left to look after the children.

6. I continued saying that in the event of a successful attack in the UK, it was not possible to predict the government's reaction. It was quite possible that he could find himself swept up in a further round of detentions. He did, however, have a choice – he could continue with his current life or ... at this point he interrupted to ask what I meant by his current life. I told him that I meant his association with members of the extremist community and also his involvement in criminal activity, like his recent arrest and caution for petty shoplifting in an Asda supermarket.

He laughed and shook my hand saying that I knew everything. He went on to say that he was not involved in any extremist activity and he did not believe that some people he knew could be considered a threat to the UK and, indeed, there was a fatwa saying that Muslims should respect UK laws. I pointed out that there was also a fatwa which declared that Muslims in the UK could consider themselves to be in a state of jihad and could therefore take *ghaneema* (spoils of war) from non-Muslims. He again laughed, but did not deny this

7. He then went on to say that he was not a well man: in addition to diabetes he had trouble with his back due to beatings at the hands of the Jordanian authorities. He was only interested in providing for his children the opportunities that he himself had not had as a child.

He assumed we knew about his business venture in Gambia with Wahaab [al-Rawi, brother of Bisher], which he hoped would prove profitable. He said he would be travelling the next day and asked whether he would be arrested or turned back at the airport. I said that if he had a valid travel document he should be able to travel without a problem. He then asked whether he would be able to get back into the country. I repeated the travel document point.

8. I returned to the choice which he could make: he could either continue as at present, with the risks that entailed, or he could start a new life with a new identity, new nationality, money to set himself up in business and to provide for his family, and an opportunity to move to a Muslim country where his children could be brought up away from the bad influences in western society.

He asked if I wanted him to leave the UK. I told him that that would be for him to decide, but that I could help him if that was what he wanted. He said that his children were being brought up as British nationals, going to normal English schools, his life was now in [the] UK.

He then asked about progress on his application for UK nationality, as he had completed the required years of residency. I told him that this was a decision for the home secretary. He queried whether the home secretary decided all cases or only his. I told him that the home secretary decided all cases.

I added that I was in a position to make recommendations to the home secretary, but that the final decision rested with the home secretary. Anas asked if the home secretary intended to grant his application. I said I did not know, but that, if we were asked for a view, we would be obliged to report Anas's previous involvement in Afghanistan and his association with persons currently detained for extremist activities.

9. I again returned to the choice he had: if he chose to help us by providing details of all his activities and contacts, we would assist him to create a new life for himself and his family. I told him that I did not expect him to give me an immediate answer, it was an important decision and he needed to think carefully about it.

10. Anas then asked when he could expect the return of the items seized during a police raid on his house some time ago he explained that his computer, videos, address books had all been taken and not returned. He was particularly keen to get family photographs back. I told him that I would try to find out what was happening and would let him know.

11. Anas's wife had come back in by this time and asked whether we wanted some tea We declined, saying that we were ready to leave. Abu Anas saw us to the door and waved us off cheerfully

Comment

12. Anas appeared cheerful and relaxed throughout, although always ready to learn what we knew about him. He maintained that he was not involved in any extremist activity and was focused on his family's welfare. He did not give any hint of willingness to cooperate with us. His desire for British nationality and the security that this would provide may be worth exploring further with him, should he return to the UK. ****** will make enquiries of SO13

[Scotland Yard's anti-terrorism branch] to establish the status of Anas's possessions. It may be possible to arrange for the return of some of these items, even in Anas's absence, to generate some goodwill.

Last night supporters said Mr Banna should be released immediately. Brent Mickum, a US-based lawyer who has visited him in Guantánamo Bay, said the US had repeatedly questioned his client about Qatada and had offered money and resettlement in the United States for him to testify against the cleric, who is currently in Britain and the subject of a control order.

Concern about Mr Banna's health while in captivity in Guantánamo has grown, with a deterioration in his mental well-being and his eyesight worsening due to his diabetes.

Mr Banna's wife's local MP, the Liberal Democrat Sarah Teather, has remained in close touch with her and her five children. Ms Teather said: 'Jamil el-Banna and Bisher al-Rawi were picked up and handed over to the CIA on the basis of the same faulty intelligence passed by British security services. Both men had been approached by MI5 to work with them. These cases reflect very badly on the British government, who have used these men and their families as expendable pawns.'

Last year, the *Guardian* reported that documents in the case showed that wrong information had been passed by the UK security services to the United States before Mr Banna and his business partners were arrested in Gambia. Those documents and the one published today were obtained by lawyers for the men detained in Guantánamo in a court case brought against the UK government.

A spokesman for the Foreign Office said Britain would not press the United States for the release of Mr Banna, because he was not a UK national. They take the same view about eight other British residents still in held in Guantánamo. An exception was made for

Mr Rawi after it was alleged he had helped MI5 monitor a suspected Islamist extremist.

Mr Banna was granted refugee status after arriving in Britain in 1994, alleging he had been tortured in Jordan.

APRIL 5 2007

Weep for the ghosts of calypsos past

MIKE SELVEY

I am writing this sitting on a bum-numbing wooden bench 12 rows back in the lower tier of the Double Decker stand at the Antigua Recreation Ground and, if I shut my eyes, I can still sense the spirit of Caribbean cricket that existed here before the International Cricket Council got hold of it, ran it out of town, then sanitised it out of existence.

Of all the cricket grounds around the world at which I have seen international matches none has given me the joy that this place has. In front of me, protruding from the stand so that it almost hovers over the boundary, is the platform on which Chickie Baptiste would stand his giant disco speakers and girls would gyrate along with Labon Benjamin, the clown Gravy, who cavorted in the rafters, defying health and safety, risking life and limb. When Chickie cranked it up and the Double Decker crowd jumped to the rhythm, the whole stand oscillated.

I have a pal who came to watch here and sat in this very seat for all five days of a Test. On the opening morning he knew no one:

inside half an hour he had been assimilated into the posse. So each day he arrived to meet the Professor (a professor, oddly enough) and his gang, a case of beer under one arm and a bottle of brandy in his hand. The brandy was gone before play began, they lunched royally on stew from the large pot the Professor brought and they became firm friends.

All the while, despite the distractions, the cricket took centre stage. The noise was an enhancement rather than an intrusion, as was the constant competing percussive brilliance of the iron band, musicians whose rhythm came from beating metal pipes or hubcaps, brake drums, door panels.

It is a bit tumbledown, is the ARG. The paint peels, but then it always did. No one minded. The crowd flocked to the ground on a whim, cricket-watching an act of spontaneity. Across the field the scoreboard, manual and informative, is devoid of names now. But once, 13 years ago, it clicked round to unprecedented figures as Brian Lara pulled Chris Lewis towards the Anglican cathedral of St John a block beyond the square-leg boundary, kissed the turf on which he had been batting and precipitated celebrations. Sitting in the intimate open press box, I watched as a grey-haired figure, Mandela-like from a distance, made an unmistakable measured tread through the rumpus to the middle to join the celebration of Lara's then world-record Test score of 375. Sir Garfield Sobers had seen his own batting record humbled and gloried in it. A decade later and on this same pitch, Lara's single-minded determination saw him recover the record he had lost to Matthew Hayden's 380 only months earlier with a score of 400 not out.

This is the spiritual home of Sir Vivian Richards. He grew up within a spit (and still lives close) and went to school at the Antiguan Boys school over the way. Long before he marked the ground's elevation to Test status with a stunning century, he clambered up trees outside to perch and watch matches. Across the road is the prison where his father was an officer and it was from there that the ground staff came. (A true conversation with a man rolling the pitch by hand: 'How long are you going to do that for?' 'Another 10 years, man.') Here it was that the master batsman caned England exuberantly for the fastest-ever Test hundred.

I never saw that, but I witnessed Gordon Greenidge and Desmond Haynes construct an opening stand of almost 300 against England; Courtney Walsh cruelly batter Robin Smith; and he and Curtly Ambrose wreck England in the final session of a game they had already drawn in their mind. I have seen Carl Hooper bat sublimely against Pakistan and in the same match Dickie Bird dumbfounded during a drinks break by the sight of Gravy, his beard plaited and dressed in a cerise ball gown, advancing rapidly towards him pursued by Mayfield, a fellow in a green frock coat, yellow trousers and frogman's flippers. In 2000 Gravy announced his retirement by attending the match in full bridal dress. You don't get that at Lord's – not in the pavilion at any rate.

It has gone now. Rather than plough strong investment into upgrading the ARG sympathetically to preserve cricket's integrity here, Chinese money, grabbed eagerly, has produced the new stadium out of town. Of its kind it is a fine facility and a fitting monument to the greatest batsman of the modern era. But what of the other heroes? It has a north end and a south end, as bland as that. Where is the character? Where is the recognition of Antigua's cricket heritage immortalised in calypso: Richie Richardson ('Who is dat man flashin' blade in de han'?'), Ambrose ('He mek de batsman shiver when he run up to deliver') and Andy Roberts? The stands named after Richardson and Roberts still look down on the field set up for net practice.

This still should be their epitaph. Instead Antigua has a white elephant that will see, if it is lucky, one Test match a year and little else. There is talk of enticing baseball teams down from the States. That is the legacy that the World Cup could leave on the island. Baseball. I shut my eyes once more, feel the vibes and want to weep.

APRIL 7 2007

Letter to the editor: Novels are not all about you, Natasha

IAN McEWAN

I smiled a little wryly when I read Natasha Walter's review of my novel *On Chesil Beach* (*Review*, March 31). In a generally favourable notice, she reported that my views about the peace movement stuck in her throat. She managed to extract these views from the brief musings of one of my characters, a CND member who, in 1961, thought that the Soviet Union, for all its many failings, was still a force for good in the world. Historically, such a position was perfectly possible; I knew of people who thought this even in the 1980s. Ms Walter regarded it as a smear against peace activists as 'hopeless naifs'. But she was prepared to forgive me because, as a mature reader, she knew not to let an author's political opinions, however vile or rightwing, get in the way of her judgment.

I accept that being forgiven by critics is an occupational hazard, but just for the record and Ms Walter's throat, perhaps I could set this matter straight. When she was still at her primary school I was campaigning, writing and speaking against nuclear weapons. I was a member of European Nuclear Disarmament and travelled to the Soviet Union with Mary Kaldor and Jonathan Steele of the *Guardian* to make contact and common cause with the unofficial and harassed peace movement there. With the composer Michael Berkeley I wrote an oratorio against the nuclear arms race. I am proud to have appeared in public with EP Thompson. My views have not changed substantially; the renovation or replacement of Trident is a waste and a folly; I am sceptical about the proposal to build a new generation of nuclear power stations in the cause of limiting CO_2 emissions when we have an adequate, safe, untapped nuclear facility 93 miles away.

As for *Saturday* – a character in a novel who expresses hostility towards novels in general should not be seen as an entirely trustworthy mouthpiece of his novelist creator. For example, the pro-Iraq-war views Henry Perowne expresses in an argument with his daughter are not mine and nor, for that matter, are her anti-war opinions. On the other hand, I would agree with Perowne that some – not all – peace protesters are naive. Who can forget those daft and earnest English folk parading through central London last summer with placards that read, 'We are all Hizbullah now'?

I sometimes wonder whether these common critical confusions arise unconsciously from a prevailing atmosphere of empowering consumerism – the exaltation of the subjective, the 'not-in-my-name' syndrome. It certainly seems odd to me that such simple precepts need pointing up: your not 'liking' the characters is not the same as your not liking the book; you don't have to think the central character is nice; the views of the characters don't have to be yours, and are not necessarily those of the author; a novel is not always all about you.

'I am plotting a new Russian revolution'

IAN COBAIN, MATTHEW TAYLOR AND LUKE HARDING

The Russian tycoon Boris Berezovsky has told the *Guardian* he is plotting the violent overthrow of President Vladimir Putin from his base in Britain after forging close contacts with members of Russia's ruling elite.

In comments that appear calculated to enrage the Kremlin – and that will further inflame relations between London and Moscow – the multi-millionaire claimed he was already bankrolling people close to the president who are conspiring to mount a palace coup.

'We need to use force to change this regime,' he said. 'It isn't possible to change this regime through democratic means. There can be no change without force, pressure.' Asked if he was, in effect, fomenting a revolution, he said: 'You are absolutely correct.'

Although Mr Berezovsky, with an estimated fortune of £850m, may have the means to finance such a plot, and although he enjoyed enormous political influence in Russia before being forced into exile, he said he could not provide details to back up his claims, because the information was too sensitive.

Last night the Kremlin denounced Mr Berezovsky's comments as a criminal offence, which it believed should undermine his refugee status in the United Kingdom.

'In accordance with our legislation [his remarks are] being treated as a crime,' said Dmitry Peskov, the Kremlin's chief spokesman. 'It will cause some questions from the British authorities to Mr Berezovsky. We want to believe that official London will never grant asylum to someone who wants to use force to change the regime in Russia.'

It will not be the first time the British government has faced accusations from the Kremlin that it is providing a safe haven for Mr Berezovsky. When he told a Moscow radio station last year that he wanted to see Mr Putin overthrown by force, Jack Straw, then foreign secretary, told the Commons that 'advocating the violent overthrow of a sovereign state is unacceptable' and warned the tycoon he could be stripped of his refugee status. Russian authorities subsequently sent an extradition request to London. That failed when a district judge ruled Mr Berezovsky could not be extradited as long as he has asylum status.

In an interview with the *Guardian*, however, Mr Berezovsky goes much further than before, claiming to be in close contact with members of Russia's political elite who, he says, share his view that Mr Putin is damaging Russia by rolling back democratic reforms, smothering opposition, centralising power and flouting the country's constitution.

'There is no chance of regime change through democratic elections,' he says. 'If one part of the political elite disagrees with another part of the political elite – that is the only way in Russia to change the regime. I try to move that.' While declining to describe these contacts – and alleging that they would be murdered if they were identified – he maintained that he was offering his 'experience and ideology' to members of the country's political elite, as well as 'my understanding of how it could be done'. He added: 'There are also practical steps which I am doing now, and mostly it is financial.' Mr Berezovsky said he was unconcerned by any threat to strip him of his refugee status. 'Straw wasn't in a position to take that decision. A judge in court said it wasn't in the jurisdiction of

Straw.' He added that there was even less chance of such a decision being taken following the polonium-210 poisoning last November of his former employee, Alexander Litvinenko. 'Today the reality is different because of the Litvinenko case.'

Mr Berezovsky, 61, a former mathematician, turned to business during the Yeltsin years and made his fortune by capturing state assets at knockdown prices during Russia's rush towards privatisation. Although he played a key role in ensuring Mr Putin's victory in the 2000 presidential elections, the two men fell out as the newly elected leader successfully wrested control of Russia back from the so-called oligarchy, the small group of tycoons who had come to dominate the country's economy.

A few months after the election Mr Berezovsky fled Russia and applied successfully for asylum in the United Kingdom after Mr Litvinenko, an officer with the KGB's successor, the FSB, came forward to say he had been ordered to murder the tycoon. Mr Berezovsky changed his name to Platon Elenin – Platon being the name of a character in a Russian film based loosely upon his life. He was subsequently given a British passport in this name.

As well as claiming to be financing and encouraging coup plotters in Moscow, Mr Berezovsky said he had dedicated much of the last six years to 'trying to destroy the positive image of Putin' that many in the west held, portraying him whenever possible as a dangerously anti-democratic figure. He said he had also opposed the Russian president through *Kommersant*, the influential Russian newspaper he controlled until last year.

Last month Mr Berezovsky was questioned by two detectives from the Russian prosecutor general's office who were in London to investigate the death of Mr Litvinenko. He has denied claims that he refused to answer many of their questions.

Last night the Kremlin said Russian authorities might want to question him again in the light of his interview with the *Guardian*.

'I now believe our prosecutor general's office has got lots of questions for Mr Berezovsky,' said Mr Peskov. He added: 'His words are very interesting. This is a very sensitive issue.'

The Foreign Office said it had nothing to add to Mr Straw's comments of last year.

APRIL 20 2007

Review: Menopause the Musical

LYN GARDNER

Offering less of a rosy glow and more of a long cold douche of the soul, *Menopause the Musical* is the least competent and most cynical piece of theatre to hit London since the Blue Man Group. It makes me think quite fondly of *The Vagina Monologues*, a show so ghastly that it made my vagina try and leave the theatre entirely unaided by my legs in protest at the drivel inflicted on women in the name of empowerment.

Like *Mum's the Word* and *Bernadette the Musical* before it, *Menopause* has very little to do with theatre and everything to do with canny special-interest marketing and merchandising. Anyone for a *Menopause the Musical* mug? *Mum's the Word* realised there might be a ready-made audience of women who would apparently like nothing better than to spend their evening away from the kids hearing about other women's leaking breasts and sleepless nights. Back in the 1980s *Bernadette* miraculously kept going for months – despite stinking notices – thanks to coach parties of church groups, although in the end even God couldn't save the show from itself.

Menopause the Musical (the title is trademarked, which says it all) taps into a ready-made market of affluent baby-boomers. The show's creator, Jeanie Linden, describes it thus: 'It includes fun parodies of 25 songs from the 60s, 70s and 80s and culminates with a high-spirited invitation for audience members to celebrate on stage.'

What this means is that Linden has taken songs such as 'I Heard it on the Grapevine', 'A Sign of the Times' and 'Puff the Magic Dragon' and changed the lyrics to include the maximum number of references to hot flushes. She then puts the songs in the mouths of four fiftysomething women who are apparently spending the day at Marks & Spencer in Marble Arch. The product placement is shamelessly blatant, and a gift voucher is available to win each night. I cancelled my M&S More card immediately.

Some of this might just be forgiven if the show had any flair at all, but it is dire in construction and execution and quite offensive and reactionary in the way it reduces all women over 50 to their hormones and portrays them as a bunch of chocolate-craving, weight-obsessed neurotics. '*Menopause the Musical* is about women ... not theatre,' gushes Linden in the programme. Wrong. It's about making money. I refuse to be somebody else's cash cow, and so should you.

APRIL 23 2007

Jacqui breaks glass ceiling

MARTIN KELNER

It has been a long hard struggle, what with those plucky Pankhurst girls defying the establishment, risking arrest and imprisonment, Emily Wilding Davison throwing herself in front of the king's horse in the 1913 Derby, then all the bra-burning in the 1970s and feeling obliged to read those Germaine Greer and Marilyn French books. But it has all been worth it.

Finally a woman gets to commentate on a Premiership football match on *Match of the Day*. All right, it was only Fulham v Blackburn Rovers, but what a triumph for female emancipation as Jacqui Oatley got to say things like 'Jason Roberts found himself in acres of space there', 'Fulham caught totally square at the back' and 'What a crucial goal that could be', all statements previously thought – and still thought by Dave Bassett and the *Daily Mail*'s Steve Curry – impossible to utter without being in possession of a penis.

I ought to say that I am not an entirely impartial observer at this milestone in the history of women's difficult journey. I worked with Jacqui in Leeds, where she produced my local radio programme a few times. What with that and following Wolverhampton Wanderers, she clearly has not had an easy ride. She certainly has not been plucked from the chorus line by the BBC as some sort of gimmick and probably does not need me or anyone else to patronise her by saying she is sharp, intelligent and witty and loves the game of football – and as it happens has quite a capacity for dealing with arsy presenters.

Whether she wants faint praise or not, though, she was destined to get a little of it on *Match of the Day* – you would expect nothing else – when Gary Lineker pointed out that 'even the presence of our first female commentator could not inspire Fulham to victory' and the pundit Lee Dixon said, 'She did well, though, didn't she?' to murmured assent.

The view from the rehearsal room – where my local women's theatre collective is preparing for a new sparse production of *The Vagina Monologues* – is that only when Jonathan Pearce is patted on the head in this fashion by the panel will any kind of equality have been achieved, and for the time being Dixon and all other men remain potential rapists. They added: 'Mike Newell, Dave Bassett, Jim Davidson, the late Benny Hill, your boys took one hell of a beating.'

The Vagina Monologues, you may recall, was considered too rude a title to appear on a theatre marquee in Florida, so the play was renamed *The Hoohaa Monologues*, which struck me as an apt way to describe some of the coverage last week previewing Jacqui's TV debut. She was, after all, merely following in the tradition whereby the six or seven minutes of highlights of one of the Premiership's less interesting matches are allocated to one of Radio Five Live's people.

Like most of her predecessors in this slot, Jacqui talked too much. Radio commentators always do when they start in TV, what with dead air being anathema more or less on the radio. The added pressure brought on by the shards of glass as she smashed through the ceiling probably did not help either. But once Jacqui has the confidence to let the pictures do more of the work, we may wonder what all the fuss was about.

APRIL 24 2007

The strange story of milk

FELICITY LAWRENCE

As cow 777 passes from the herd, nudged by an automated gate into the milking parlour at Kemble Farms, the signal from the transponder in the bracelet on her foreleg is read by the Cotswold estate's computer. The cow is identified and logged in while she files down the stalls. When 777 enters the empty berth at the end of the line the bar opens for the cow behind, so the stalls fill up without the need for human intervention. In the pit below, three eastern European workers move quietly up the lines attaching automatic milking teats to 36 sets of udders at a time.

As the vacuum begins to suck, 777's milk flows down the pipes and through an underground meter, which measures and records her output, while information from the pedometer also attached to her foreleg is analysed by the latest software to calculate how far she has moved inside the adjoining cowshed since her last milking. When 777 comes into season she will walk more than usual and the computer will mark her down for her next insemination. If she has not walked as much as usual she may have an udder infection or the lameness to which cows bred for intensive dairy production are prone, and the computer will filter her out for treatment.

As 777's udders empty and the milk stops pumping, sensors in the machine detect the interruption to the flow and water is forced automatically back up the pipes to clean cow and equipment. Then the teats pop off by themselves, leaving 777 to exit back to the shed.

Kemble Farms is one of the most efficient dairy operations in the country. The cows give so much milk they are emptied three times a day. Yields are typically 9,000 litres per cow per year – not the highest known, as some farms have now broken the 10,000-litre barrier, but a long way above average and spectacular compared with a decade ago, when average yields were nearer 5,000 litres per cow. Thirty years earlier, average yields were 3,500 litres.

The herd size here, usually around 700 cows, puts Kemble in the super-efficient league too. The average number of cows in a dairy herd in the United Kingdom is now 100; in 1994 it was 79. A £2m investment in a light and airy, aircraft-hangar-sized shed – where the cows can be kept indoors seven months of the year and fed the concentrated feed they need to maintain such levels of production – has enabled the family business that owns the farm to achieve economies of scale and cut labour costs. And yet Kemble

Farms has been selling milk at less than the cost of production. Its costs – fuel, fertiliser, water and feed – have gone up 8 per cent in the past 12 months, but the price it is paid for its milk by Dairy Crest, which processes and packs it for Sainsbury's, has fallen by 8 per cent over the same period. Like most of the British dairy industry it is struggling to make money.

Today the National Federation of Women's Institutes is launching a Great Milk Debate with a conference in London and meetings around the country to address the crisis in dairy farming. The WI's 211,000 members voted the plight of milk producers their top priority last year and they want farmers to get a fairer share of the money spent on milk in the shops.

The price of milk in the shops has risen roughly 20 per cent in five years, from just over 44p a litre in 2002 to just over 53p in 2007. Yet the price paid to farmers has fallen. In 1995, producers got 24.5p a litre for their milk; the average today is 18p a litre, which represents a loss of more than 3p on every litre. Kemble Farms has been getting 19p a litre. The result has been a huge rise in supermarket profits from milk, but an exodus from dairy farming that is still accelerating. On average, three dairy farmers leave the industry every day. There were 35,000 dairy farms in the UK in 1995 and there are now only about 19,000. A further 3,000 dairy farmers told the Milk Development Council in a survey earlier this month that they plan to leave in the next two years.

Tesco, which sells about a quarter of the country's fresh milk, promised at the beginning of this month to pay more to farmers. Its move follows schemes by other retailers to support farmers. Kemble Farms heard last week that it will get a rise of roughly 1p a litre, but that will move it only from loss to break-even. Few believe the dairy industry's problems are solved.

'We either pack up or intensify further,' says David Ball, one of the directors of Kemble Farms. 'We've already increased output 15 per cent in the last year. We could keep more cows, and get a further 25 per cent. We're aiming for 10,000 litres a year per cow in the next few months. We would be driving everything – the animals, the plant – to the maximum. In a factory we are used to that idea of 24/7, but with animals and land there are other considerations. We resist treating animals like machines.'

Kemble Farms has high standards of animal welfare – it is audited by RSPCA Freedom Foods – but as Mr Ball explains: 'From the consumer point of view, dairy equals cows in nice pasture – and we're being driven away from that, until we follow the poultry world.'

The irony for Colin Rank – one of the family that owns Kemble Farms – is that his cows drink water from a Cotswold spring that he could bottle and sell for 80p a litre. 'We're giving it to cows and devaluing it by turning it into milk. Like all dairy farmers we could pack up tomorrow and do something better with our capital, but we do it because we have an emotional investment in the land and the animals. And we know there's a market for our product, if only the market worked.'

April 24 2007 – guardian unlimited

Bullying for England

Dave Hill

I was eating a salt beef sandwich in a cafe yesterday when in came an Englishman of a particular variety – a performing cockney. White, 60-odd and buzzing with a slightly over-acted bonhomie, he was making a food delivery of some kind and also had a message to convey. He announced for all to hear that he'd just been in west London and on the street he'd spotted Tony Blair. 'I shouted to him, "Where are all the flags?" He just shrugged!'

His point was, of course, that we English weren't making enough of St George's Day and that the government was partly to blame. This has become a commonplace complaint – at least, it has in some newspapers and elements within society. Most of the moaners have nothing new to say. In the Sunday Telegraph Damian Thompson used the Christian thinktank Ekklesia's ideas for reviving St George's Day as an excuse to lambast – surprise everyone! – 'the PC brigade', blah-de-blah, white poppies, dum-de-dum, and even government immigration policy. Yesterday, the bold Sir Dickie of the *Mail* had one of his routine hissyfits, bitching on about 'the revisionists' from whom 'nothing is safe'. Bleat, bleat, bleat, meet the Columnist As Sheep, seeing any deviation from bland Georgeist orthodoxy as turning the dragon-slayer into the 'patron saint of the Guardianistas'. Oooh, vicious! And you thought Elizabeth was a queen.

My eyelids droop as I report these tired cliches. And yet they are instructive in a way. Running through them is a strand of deep contempt for English culture and ignorance of the nation's past. The now ritual finger-pointing at a 'liberal elite' accused of loathing its own homeland and all who feel differently is just a big, bullying noise to conceal such commentators' bitter resentment of the ways in which English people feel and demonstrate affection for their homeland; ways that have long been immune to grandstanding nationalists and are as various and paradoxical as the nation itself. Orwell understood this in his own way just as I understand it in mine.

The English don't do patriotism like some other nations do, mostly because we've had less reason to. Those who hate it that we don't hang off flagpoles like the Americans or French conveniently forget that those were nations shaped by struggles that nourished such expressions of unity. Endlessly repeated gripes that 'the politically correct' are more keen on Ramadan and St Patrick's Day than 'our own' festivals and traditions are rooted in a blank refusal to acknowledge why it might be that minorities have sometimes felt a need to close ranks around a common heritage anchored elsewhere. Their reasons have included a need, sometimes urgent, to defend themselves against the very aspects of Englishness (and Britishness) that the gripers themselves cultivate: a rigid, suspicious and dimwitted definition of national character and culture whose borders its neurotic champions patrol with an authoritarian zeal quite at odds with our long-standing love of freedom.

Yesterday David Cox conjectured that the establishment discourages expressions of pride in Englishness because it fears and despises the English working class. A few finer distinctions were needed here: yes, the establishment despises those now marooned at the social margins, but not only those who are white and define themselves as English – it despises those in every other category too. Also, some such expressions have needed to be resisted, English football hooliganism being the prime example. Has it not dawned on the St Georgists that some of its ugliest examples coincided with the reign of Margaret Thatcher, the British prime minister who aligned herself with belligerent patriotism more closely than any other in modern times?

How times have changed and for the better, in this respect at least. Gordon Brown's promotion of a re-branded 'Britishness' is looking like a damp squib, and a good thing too: it fails to recognise that good citizenship and adherence to a prescribed national identity need not be the same thing; it fails to appreciate that in these globalising, post-deference days, allegiance to a nation is less easily ordained from on high. Meanwhile, the Scottish Nationalists' appeal has grown. If Britishness is to be a binding idea for modern times it will emerge untidily from below.

As for popular Englishness, well, our travelling fans have evolved considerably. Old failings still lurk but the majority who travelled to last year's World Cup in Germany displayed a new spirit and maturity. Meanwhile, those at home sparked a valuable debate about what all their flag-flying might mean.

Was it a defensive response to multiculturalism and devolution or a sign of a national mood that was more warm and generous than that which the Union Jack had come to imply? The answer was probably a blend of both. But the phenomenon should silence the St Georgeists' relentless whine that some cringeing conspiracy of metropolitan liberals has made the English feel ashamed of Englishness – whatever that elusive thing may be. Maybe the reason we didn't make much of a display yesterday was that April 23 just doesn't turn most of us on. And if it ever it does, we'll make it known – in our different, distinctive and often rather un-St Georgeist ways.

APRIL 27 2007

How do I come out to my colleagues?

BETH DITTO

The truth is, there are so many pressures on the outside that push us to stay in the closet, and so many pressures on the inside that push us to come out. The closet can be a safe, comfortable place and, at the same time, lonely and miserable. Eventually the inside starts to look like a Rubik's cube – only you know the right pattern that will match up all the colours.

Think of all the people you work with. Who do you think would handle the news best? Is there someone you talk to more than others? Is there any watercooler conversationalist you are particularly fond of? If there is, then start with them. There is no rule in The Pink Triangle Guide to Coming Out that you must wear a rainbow flag cap and organise a full band parade. These are my no-fail steps to coming out:

1. Make the decision. Tell yourself that you will come out. This means becoming comfortable with the thought of your co-workers knowing about your sexuality. Be prepared for any reaction, including the good ones (when my mom hugged me and said, 'Six, one, half a dozen, the other' – Arkansas-speak for 'It's all the same to me'), the awkward (the time my aunt asked me, 'How y'all do it?' in the middle of Thanksgiving dinner) and the ugly ('I feel so sorry for all my gay friends who are going to hell,' which was said to my best friend by a mutual friend).

2. Pick that one person you like the most at work – that one person who always asks you to go for a smoke or to get a coffee with them at breaktime. Use your instincts. Getting the cat out of the bag is the hardest part and once you've overcome the initial fear of getting it through your teeth, it will get easier and easier.

3. Don't get too down on yourself for having told lies about your sexuality. If you find yourself having to untell some of those lies, just know that, even if it doesn't make sense to others, it was all you could do to feel safe at the time. That being said, now is a good time to learn how to tell the truth. Like I say, start small.

4. Don't be discouraged by any close-minded reactions. My mother has the best advice of all in these situations. It goes like this:

they can't kill you and eat you, no matter what and, if they do, you're probably not the one people need to be worried about ... What would you rather be: a cannibal or a lesbian? A lesbian? Yeah, that's what I thought!

APRIL 28 2007

In praise of ...
Mstislav Rostropovich

LEADER

What is it about the cello that makes its very finest practitioners into moral exemplars for mankind? All that can be said is that through the many miseries of 20th-century Europe, first Pau Casals and then Mstislav Rostropovich stood out as towering musical personalities who made their instrument sing of loss, hope and freedom. It was Casals who brought the cello literature, particularly that of Bach, in from the neglected margins of classical music. It was Rostropovich who ensured it would remain there, inspiring compositions from Britten, Prokofiev, Shostakovich, Gubaidulina and many more. Both gave epochal performances of the greatest of all cello concertos in the most testing of circumstances: Casals was airlifted from besieged Barcelona in 1937 to Prague to make a defining recording of the Dvorak concerto, while a weeping Rostropovich gave an emotionally charged London performance of the same work as the Soviet tanks rolled into Prague in 1968. Casals did not live to see Catalonia and Spain emerge from the tyranny of Franco. But Rostropovich did not merely live to see Russia throw off the tyranny of communism, he also played a decisive part in making it happen. Rostropovich , who died yesterday aged 80, was a life force. His energy and generosity were irresistible. He was always ready to do something new, in life or in music. If ever a man lived every minute that was allotted to him, it was he. When comes such another, either as cellist or human being?

MAY 1 2007

Free – the man accused of being an al-Qaida leader

IAN COBAIN AND JEEVAN VASAGAR

A man who was accused of being one of al-Qaida's leaders in Britain and who is alleged to have sent one of the July 7 suicide bombers to a terrorism training camp in Pakistan is living freely in the Home Counties and is not facing any charges.

According to evidence brought before the Old Bailey jury in the fertiliser bomb plot trial, Mohammed Quayyum Khan, a part-time taxi driver from Luton, is in direct contact with one of Osama bin Laden's most senior lieutenants.

Quayyum, known as 'Q' to his alleged al-Qaida associates, is also accused of being the leader of a group of would-be terrorists whose plot to bomb London was foiled 18 months before the 7/7 attacks.

Among the allegations against Q during the year-long trial were that he was:

- the *emir* (leader), of a group planning to use a massive fertiliser bomb to attack the Bluewater shopping centre in Kent, the

Ministry of Sound nightclub in London, or high-pressure gas pipelines around the south-east
- instrumental in arranging for Mohammad Sidique Khan to travel to Pakistan, where he attended a terrorism training camp, in 2003
- a provider of funds and equipment for jihadi militants fighting American forces in Afghanistan

The counter-terrorism operation that culminated in yesterday's court case is understood to have begun with an MI5 investigation into Q in 2003. Despite the number of serious allegations levelled against him at the Old Bailey, police and MI5 say they have never found sufficient evidence to arrest or charge him.

His home has been searched at least once; neighbours have said police tore up floorboards and dug up his garden. However, there appears to be no plan to question him about his alleged link with the men who killed 52 people and injured more than 700 in the London bombings.

Q is in his 40s and married with several children. In recent years he has also used at least three other names similar to Quayyum. He is said to be a former associate of the fundamentalist clerics Omar Bakri Mohammed and Abu Hamza, and is said to have arranged for Bakri to speak in Luton before the preacher was banned from re-entering the UK after the 7/7 attacks.

Haji Sulaiman, a former president of Luton Central mosque, said Q had 'brought Omar Bakri [Mohammed] to Luton'. He added: 'I didn't let him [Omar Bakri] come in our mosque. I didn't like those guys.'

Today Q lives in a rented semi-detached house in Luton. Until recently he was working as a part-time taxi driver, and a *Guardian* journalist has also seen him working as a chef in a small cafe. When approached, he denied he was Q. He is thought to have since disappeared.

He is thought to have been born in Pakistan, a country he has visited often in recent years. The Old Bailey heard that during one trip in 2003 he was followed by the Pakistani intelligence agency, the ISI. The agents are said to have tracked him overtly to let him know they were aware of his presence there.

He was said in court to be taking orders from a senior al-Qaida figure in Pakistan called Abdul Hadi. This man is understood to be Abdul Hadi al-Iraqi who, according to reports in the US, is a Kurd who served as an officer in Saddam Hussein's army. He is said to be a confidant of Bin Laden, and to have acted as an emissary to Abu Musab al-Zarqawi, al-Qaida's leader in Iraq. Iraqi was named by the US state department as a terror suspect shortly after the 9/11 attacks. The US government revealed last Friday that he had been captured several months ago and sent to Guantánamo Bay.

Q's alleged relationship with a senior al-Qaida figure was claimed by Mohammed Junaid Babar, a member of the fertiliser bomb gang who turned informant after being arrested by the FBI in New York.

Babar told the Old Bailey jury: 'Hadi is just giving orders, but underneath Hadi there would be different, I guess you would call it cells, and this was a particular cell. The ultimate emir on top was Hadi. But underneath him there were multiple emirs, three or four emirs, before you reached Abdul Hadi, and Q was one of those emirs.'

Babar told the court he had met one of the defendants in the fertiliser plot trial, Salahuddin Amin, at Islamabad airport, where Amin was waiting to meet two British jihadists who had been sent to Pakistan by Q on a 'fact-finding' mission. Babar said he knew the pair by their noms de guerre, Ibrahim and Zubair. The trial judge ruled that the jury should not be allowed to learn that Ibrahim was actually Sidique Khan, as that fact could prejudice them against the defendants.

Babar said that he, 'Ibrahim', and others had driven to a terror training camp, collecting chemicals to make explosives en route, and spent a month learning how to assemble bombs and fire weapons. The court also heard that two young associates of Q from Luton were killed while fighting for the Taliban in Aghanistan in 2001.

While a number of the fertiliser bomb gang admitted knowing Q, his role was disputed during the trial. Amin told the court he had met Q when they were working as taxi drivers in Luton, and that Q was a family friend. He told police Q had sent money and equipment to jihadists in Pakistan, but claimed in court that he made this admission only because he had earlier been tortured for 10 months by the ISI.

He denied that Babar had been present when he met Sidique Khan and denied taking him to a terrorism training camp. The man who was to go on to lead the 7/7 bombers had been sent to him by 'brothers in Luton', he told the court, but could not say who they were.

Amin also denied Babar's claim that Q was his emir. Several defence lawyers condemned Babar's account as a concoction of 'elaborate lies', saying he was an FBI double agent or that he invented the plot to get a reduced sentence in the US, where he has admitted terrorist offences.

Prosecution lawyers, on the other hand, said that Babar had been an 'impressive, truthful and accurate' witness.

The court also heard that a number of meetings in the UK between Q and one of the defendants, Omar Khyam, had been secretly filmed by MI5, who gave Q the codename Bashful Dwarf.

During cross-examination, Khyam admitted meeting Q shortly before he was about to leave the country. 'He gave me money,' he told the court. 'He said, 'It's better for both of us if we don't meet each other.' Because the security services may be monitoring me.' Khyam refused to say how he first met Q, or discuss his role.

Scotland Yard and the security service maintain that there is insufficient evidence to bring charges against Q. The *Guardian* has repeatedly tried to speak to Mohammed Quayyum Khan about the allegations that were made in court. He has declined to comment.

MAY 1 2007 – GUARDIAN UNLIMITED

This is England

ROB SMYTH

Anyone with a rudimentary knowledge of mixing colours knows that when you put red and blue together you get purple, but there was nothing deep about the match between Liverpool and Chelsea at Anfield tonight. While it was inevitably infused with the highest drama, it was lowest-common-denominator football and, to reverse a cliche, a shocking advert for the English game. This is England.

It was perversely just that such a cowardly, risk-free game should be decided by penalties and hugely ironic that a contest between two erudite, thoughtful managers should be so staggeringly witless. If it had been a boxing match it would have been stopped because it was too boring. The freedom of trade in football over the past 15 years has, theoretically, homogenised club sides and stripped them of their national identity, yet this was as excruciatingly English as fish and chips and weekend punch-ups, full of primitive football and barely suppressed ill-will. The ball was given more air than a load of wet washing and football's soul was certainly hung out to dry. Indeed, the match could have been taken from any episode of *Match of the Day* in the late 1980s. Who says retro is cool?

Liverpool pride themselves on the pass-and-move traditions developed in the Boot Room, yet this was more like kick-and-chase developed in the Hoof Room. The intellect of their goal – for which, perversely, the ball barely left the floor – could not absolve the gibberish that sandwiched it. The end may well justify the means; that depends on the individual's view of the balance between success and glory. But it is hard to legitimately argue that it was an edifying spectacle. How must Ronaldinho, Francesco Totti, Lionel Messi and their fellow *fantasistas* have felt watching 19 *pragmatistas* (the cheeky-chappy class of Joe Cole makes him a worthy exception) serve up this fare? It was like showing an episode of *EastEnders* at the Cannes film festival.

Liverpool were always likely to bomb Chelsea, given the success of the tactic in the league game between the sides in January, and it was notable that there were only two relatively minor changes from that side: Boudewijn Zenden for Fabio Aurelio and Javier Mascherano for Xabi Alonso. But the omission of an aesthete like Alonso spoke volumes about the contest ahead, as did Chelsea's transparent plan to blag a 0-0 draw. In the end, Liverpool were able to lean on their most reliable matchwinner: penalties. With their record in shootouts – 10 wins in 11 now – they will probably become the first team to win a league title on penalties.

In amongst the mediocrity there were, inevitably, some wonderful demonstrations of the human spirit: Michael Essien – asked to play out of position at centre-half again – was majestic; Steven Gerrard's all-action heroism enabled him to wipe the floor with Frank Lampard once more; Jamie Carragher and John Terry put their backs against the wall and valiantly took whatever hits were coming; and Claude Makelele reminded us why his name will forever define a position.

Yet the football remained loveless, full of sour faces and dour tactics. It is, of course, hard to enjoy playing under this pressure

– gravity always wins – but the likes of Ronaldinho manage to show their teeth from time to time. The only teeth on show here were those being pulled by unfortunate neutrals. It all evoked the famous headline after the dire draw between Ireland and England at Italia 90: NO FOOTBALL PLEASE, WE'RE BRITISH. While there was glory and spoils for the victors, anyone with a knowledge of football knows that this rudimentary nonsense is spoiling the game.

MAY 1 2007

With the Brits in Helmand

DECLAN WALSH

I have just spent two weeks embedded with British troops and it was, at times, an intense experience. I curled into a ball as an Afghan fighter tried to blast open the jeep I was travelling in with a rocket-propelled grenade. I interviewed a corporal from Newcastle as he soaped himself in an outdoor shower. I played touch rugby on a helicopter landing zone. And I watched life ebb from the chalky limbs of a wounded young British soldier as sweating medics desperately tried to save him.

Life in the military, though, is mostly boredom. 'Hurry up and wait' is the order of the day in Helmand where helicopters don't show up, generals change their mind and the enemy is never quite where you expect. The main British base, Camp Bastion, boasts a British-style pub complete with widescreen TVs, wooden furniture and east European barmaids. All that's missing is beer – the camp is entirely dry. A small shop sells copious quantities of glossy lad mags. Don't bother asking for the *Economist*. Sitting outside the beerless bar in the searing heat, sucking on a can of warm Pepsi, is a good time to learn the military lingo. 'Scoff' is food, 'brew' is tea and 'remf' can be used to disparage any soldier not involved in fighting: it stands for 'rear echelon motherfucker'.

Beyond 'the wire' – outside the camp – lies a very different world. I travelled across the desert to Sangin, the cockpit of insurgent activity in Helmand, with the Royal Grenadier Guards. The regiment has a 351-year history and a reputation for stuffiness, but the commander and his men were thoughtful and welcoming. After a gut-wrenching seven-hour drive – during which we came under Taliban fire – we arrived in Forward Operating Base Robinson ('Fob Rob'), four miles south of Sangin.

Fob Rob looked like something out of *Apocalypse Now*. Against the setting sun, heavy vehicles churned through the sand, kicking up clouds of fine dust. The ground shuddered as Canadian and American artillery pounded Taliban positions five miles away. Fob Rob was also testament to the international make-up of the Nato force in Afghanistan. British squaddies escaped the heat in a small bunker watching war movies starring Steven Seagal. Others walked around bare-chested, getting sunburned within minutes. Americans were forbidden from removing their clothes, but christened their vehicles with names such as 'Napalm Death'. Young Afghan soldiers smoked *charras* (hashish) in a small enclosure near the front gate. Danish explosives officers offered polite advice on skirting landmines. In between dropping 155mm howitzer shells on the Taliban, the two Canadian artillery teams bitched about each other. 'Those guys over there are making fun of us!' wailed one soldier.

The Taliban are not the only danger. Tarantulas, scorpions, camel spiders and malaria are among Afghanistan's many risks. The British and Americans grudgingly respect one another. 'Fucking Americans,' muttered one Grenadier officer after our convoy was left stranded in the middle of Sangin when our swaggering American Special Forces escort suddenly disappeared for two hours without explanation. An American officer shocked his British counterparts by suggesting that Afghan soldiers should be used to clear an area after a mine strike – effectively using them as human minesweepers. 'Their country, their war,' he declared. He may have just been feeling bitter; one of his comrades had just been injured by the Taliban.

The Grenadiers are trying to knock the rag-tag Afghan National Army (ANA) into shape. It's no easy job. In public, officers praise the Afghans' zest for the fight – 'All they want to do is kill the Taliban,' said one – but privately they lament their lack of enthusiasm for soldierly discipline. At evening meals officers swap tales of desertions, unkempt barracks and brutal disciplinary tactics, with a mix of chortles and rolled eyes.

For a time the chance to embed was a rare jewel for British journalists. As John Reid's prediction that Helmand could be won 'without a shot being fired' came crashing down around him, access to the military was highly limited. Now it is more open, but there are still compromises – most notably the stipulation that all stories must first be filtered through headquarters to make sure no 'op-sec' (operational security) is compromised. The officers managing this process were reasonable, yet still it felt uncomfortable.

But for all the bravado, the business of war is about shooting and being shot, and a spell with the 'immediate response team' – a British helicopter medical rescue team – was as sobering as a slap round the face. Racing across the desert to collect critically wounded soldiers (of all nationalities), we picked up soldiers hit by bullets, mines and shrapnel.

Can Britain win in Helmand? During one briefing officers made a 3-D map of the province with household objects – engineering tape for the roads, electrical cord for the rivers and red poker chips for enemy positions. The gambling link was apt: all bets are still on.

MAY 2 2007

Could you live with a man who keeps six owls in the front room?

LUCY MANGAN

It is probably a good general rule of thumb that if you have more than 70 of something in your house – except, perhaps, teabags – it might be time to ask yourself whether you are a little bit odd. If your nickname is Barn Owl Bill, however, and your 70 things are – and you might have seen this coming – barn owls, you may consider yourself to have already arrived safely at Weirdsville and set up camp.

Bill Hyam – one of the participants in Channel 4's documentary *Animal Addicts* – keeps six of the owls (and most of their excretions) in his front room. The rest are in cages at the back of his terraced council house in Preston, Lancashire. We didn't hear from the neighbours, but the prospect was tantalising. Would it have been a series of Les Dawson-a-likes, hitching up outraged bosoms and pouring forth a volley of complaints? Or do they follow the lead of Carol – Barn Owl Bill's impressively phlegmatic partner of five years – who keeps smiling as she chops up another of the 200 chicks defrosting on the living-room floor.

'It's just one of them things,' she says. 'You just get on wi' it, don't you?'

Beware thinking you can change a man. There is always a chance that you will end up poking bits of dismembered pullets through wire-cage doors, three times a day, for the rest of your life.

Helen Hinde, who is 79, lives in Surrey with 16 german shepherds. That's one more than her licence allows since she was convicted of cruelty to animals 10 years ago ('I can criticise myself very hard, and I do') – and that's only if you don't count the seven puppies she has bred in secret. Helen doesn't count them, because they are going to be sold to help her pay some bills. Just as soon as she can find good enough homes for them.

In Norfolk, Beryl and Elizabeth are awaiting the outcome of an appeal against their joint conviction for cruelty to animals. They racked up a total of 350 dogs, cats, rabbits and guinea pigs in squalid kennels and outhouses at their farm before the RSPCA tired of giving them warnings to shape up and shipped the pair off to court. The women do not accept that they did anything wrong ('We didn't bother anyone and really no one had any reason to bother us'), but the judge disagreed and has banned them from keeping animals for the next 15 years.

Such programmes always risk amounting to nothing more than the 21st-century equivalent of the travelling freak show, but the trap was avoided here by letting the stories of the sad, thwarted human lives that resulted in such extreme devotion to and obses-sion with animals gradually take shape amid the flurry of fur and feathers. Barn Owl Bill was brutally assaulted 27 years ago, an attack he blames for the MS and bone disease that now keep him in bodybraces and almost constant pain. He took refuge in alcohol and pills, until someone at the pub gave him a barn owl to look after. It turned out to be salvation in saucer-eyed form.

'I think this is the job I was supposed to do,' he says, simply and without sentimentality. 'I think this is the reason I was mugged.'

We watch him release back into the wild one of his rescued birds, whose returns to health are obviously a source of joy as Bill's own body deteriorates.

'It feels fantastic,' he says, and clearly means it, as he starts to cry.

The first sign that Beryl's addiction to animals is born of some-thing more than innate eccentricity came as she explained why the minuscule dog tucked under her arm is so beloved.

'This one would kill for me. It's been dragged along the floor, hanging on to a man's trousers more than once, with them kicking out, trying to get her off them.'

Suddenly the air was thick with shadowy men against whom her tiny dog has offered the only protection and defence. Later on, she relates how her father murdered her brother and sister. You suspect that both Beryl and her dogs spend a lot of time growling at ghosts.

Helen was a woman born out of her time. She always preferred work and books to socialising, and putting her career first after she qualified as a vet in 1957 meant that she never got married ('I do wish I had an other half, I wish there were children going on ahead of me') and her natural introversion gradually calcified into total reclusivity. It was not a life as clearly marked with tragedy as Beryl's, but one that seems to have comprised a series of subtle punishments for being a strong-willed, intelligent and independent woman before it was socially acceptable to be so. In many ways this was a film about individuals caged as effectively as any unfortunate animal, and with rather fewer people around to care about their welfare.

MAY 3 2007

Lord Browne: a sad departure

LEADER

The heart sinks at the casuistry of all those who have professed indifference to Lord Browne's private life, but have, with sad sighs, deplored the small but stupid lie to court that brought about the former BP chief executive's resignation on Tuesday afternoon. For the head of any company – let alone one of Britain's biggest and most respected – to attempt to mislead a court, even on a detail that would not have swayed the outcome and that hardly reduced his personal embarrassment, was foolish at the very minimum. But Lord Browne's lie – a 'white lie', said Mr Justice Eady – was surely fuelled by vanity, humiliation and a wish for privacy. It was not in the category of Lord Archer or Jonathan Aitken's efforts to subvert justice (and seek damages) in libel cases. Browne's downfall was the consequence of a paper's determination to intrude into his personal life on the grounds that doing so would be in the public interest. Everything that has happened since flows from that.

Lord Browne is a public figure whose business activities are a proper area for media investigation. There has been no shortage of commentary about his stewardship of BP, both positive and negative, especially in the light of an explosion at one of the company's oil refineries in Texas in 2005, which killed 15 people, and the huge sums he has been paid. The *Mail on Sunday*, like any newspaper, has always been free to publish stories about this or other aspects of BP's activities, not least the close links between the company and the government. It could have done so already on the basis of conversations with Lord Browne's former partner, Jeff Chevalier, without naming him. But the evidence points to the fact that the paper's original focus was not simply a business story. It also wanted (as is clear from court documents) to write about the relationship between a powerful business leader at the margins of celebrity and a young Canadian man.

In a happier world this should not have been enough to interest a newspaper. Homosexuality, it is comforting to think, is now no sort of scandal. Prejudice has become rarer. Last Monday, regulations came into force banning discrimination in services from hotels to the health service. But it is difficult to avoid concluding that at the heart of this case is the fact that Lord Browne was gay. He chose not to discuss the matter for reasons that may have involved both personal reticence and his business dealings with countries less tolerant than Britain. This left him vulnerable after his four-year relationship ended, even though – as is apparent from BP's own investigations – there was no scandal to expose. The intrusion involved dragging a failed relationship into print – no matter that the European Convention on Human Rights offers the assurance that 'everyone has the right to respect for his private and family life, his home and his correspondence'.

Whether Lord Browne would have suffered similar intrusion if he had not been gay is an open question; straight celebrities suffer at the hands of an overly intrusive press too. But the fact is that he was and the consequences of this cost him his job. Discrimination against women and minority groups persists in many areas of life. This episode is a reminder of its impact. Lord Browne will have many regrets, not least over his mistake in trusting someone who then asked for money shortly before contacting a paper (which, as the judge came close to implying, sounds like a sort of black-mail), which then paid his expenses. It might have been easier if he had mentioned earlier that he was gay – but there was no compulsion on him to do so. It might have been better not to have sought an injunction; absolutely better to have stuck to the truth. But beyond all this, Britain, a liberal land, has seen a man forced from his job primarily as a result of a paper deciding it was a sensation that he was gay.

MAY 5 2007

They write you up, your mum and dad

LUCY ETHERINGTON

When I was a teenager my mother and stepfather wrote a sitcom about our family. It was called *Second Thoughts* and first aired on Radio 4. ITV snapped it up and it ran for five series from 1991 to 1994. It also spawned three series of a spin-off called *Faith in the Future*. Lynda Bellingham played my mother, Jan; James Bolam was my stepfather, Gavin; my brother, Tom, was played by a gawky child actor called Mark Denham; and Julia Sawalha played me.

It was about a divorcee (Bolam) dithering over whether to marry another divorcee (Bellingham), the mother of two demanding teenagers and a dog – played by our family pet, Levi, even though he was crippled by arthritis and had to be lifted on set. The dogs in our family got all the breaks.

I went along to the first recording reluctantly, out of duty, not expecting much – it was a sitcom after all. I was reading English and drama at university and therefore only liked plays written by eastern Europeans where peasants revolted and middle-class people shot themselves. My parents, like many parents before them, had paid to have me educated to the point where I would look down on their work. I also brought along my new boyfriend – an art student called Nigel, who only watched films with subtitles. He had been easily tempted by the offer of the free bar.

The studio was hot and uncomfortable. The recording went on for two hours. A row of my aunts sat in front of us and kept turning around to snigger at me whenever Sawalha stropped about like a horrible moody teenager – which, of course, put pressure on one to be gracious and not moody at all – or when the actors playing my parents simulated some kind of sex act (mainly, thankfully, of the moving duvet variety favoured by prime-time comedy). In the row behind, my brother was having one of his manic episodes, the result of a brief but comprehensive breakdown (I should add that he's been vehemently sane now for 15 years), and was laughing loudly at bits that weren't supposed to be funny.

In the LWT bar afterwards, as Nigel and I sunk as many free pints as we could, my naturally gregarious mother insisted on introducing us to everyone – the cast, the crew, the families of the cast and crew – and finally to Julia Sawalha. She seemed really nice.

'I've never played a real person before,' she said.

'Oh,' I replied. What was I supposed to say? 'Thank you for reducing me to such a perfect teenage stereotype?'

Clearly I was having an adverse reaction to meeting my light-entertainment alter ego, becoming more cynical and twisted by the second. Of course, it wasn't Sawalha's fault. She was just reading the lines written by my mother, who had clearly decided that giving birth to me automatically gave her copyright on my life.

I don't know why I kept going to the recordings – it can't just have been the free bar. To sit on unyielding plastic seats under burning lights, to watch your personal family drama played out on old studio sets borrowed from other forgotten sitcoms, to witness your parents' love life (the pre-watershed version) enacted by the bloke from *Only When I Laugh* and The Oxo Mum, to see myself – who I had always assumed to be richly complex and deep – portrayed as a series of scowls and door-slams. Of course, in some ways it was oddly flattering. Something like that makes you feel interesting. You rise for a moment above the crowd. Never mind that you haven't done anything important or creative.

I was also learning that the media can be very seductive. People ply you with drinks and constantly tell you you're wonderful – a bit like a religious cult, but with crudités.

Second Thoughts achieved an average of 8 million viewers and was recommissioned. As the plots extended, the net widened to include more characters lifted from our lives – often unwittingly. There was Liza, based on my stepfather's ex-wife, portrayed as an interfering bitch. The ex-husband character had moved rather conveniently to California, so didn't have to appear at all, when in reality my father was simply ignoring us in New Malden. I suppose my mother probably felt she had put him through enough already.

My friend Caroline was extremely put out by a character called Caroline, who was Sawalha's single and slightly overweight best friend.

'It's not you!' my mother protested, even though both Carolines had a boyfriend who turned out to be gay and had unrequited crushes on their hairdressers. My friend Joel – a gawky musician – deliberately didn't notice his part in the *Second Thoughts* spin-off *Faith in the Future*. Probably because the thinly disguised Jools – a gawky musician – was pathetically in love with his friend Hannah (Julia Sawalha).

My brother's extremely witty friend, Chris, refused to speak when he came round to our house, fearing that anything he said would end up as a poor one-liner in *Second Thoughts*.

Meanwhile, I was still with Nigel, who for his degree show had made 40 ceramic rhinos for a piece called *Untitled*. My parents took us to dinner – one obvious upside of their success was that they were suddenly well off – and throughout the meal showed a suspiciously inordinate interest in Nigel's work, getting him to explain it in detail. At the end, they asked if they could hire the 40 rhinos for a scene in their show. Nigel took the money gratefully and didn't ask questions. The fool.

We went along to the recording. In the episode, Hannah gets an art student boyfriend. When asked about his work he repeats word for word what Nigel told my parents over dinner and comes across as an absurdly pretentious prat. The 40 rhinos appear at the end, when a drunk Bolam returns home to find them scattered around his room (you had to be there). When it was over, Nigel turned to me, aghast.

'They totally took the piss out of me!' he said, in shock. 'How could they do that?'

I shrugged. 'Now you know how it feels.'

'I feel as though I've been mugged!' he spluttered.

I knew what he meant – for me it had been like thinking you're as deep and complex as Hamlet, being shown a mirror and instead of the Dane, you see David Brent. But after years of being written about, I was perhaps less shockable.

My mother wrote personal columns about her life for *She* and *Cosmopolitan*. She wrote about us – my brother's love for his BMX, how boring it was helping kids with homework, and later about my driving lessons, my boyfriends, my first (and last) house party. (I have no idea how my father felt when she wrote about their marriage and sex life. I imagine he refused to read it.) Literally everything was copy. It was quite normal for us to have the minutiae of our very ordinary suburban lives considered worthy for print.

Second Thoughts, however, was more disturbing because the sitcom gag-a-minute format trivialised something that was essentially traumatic and disruptive. Yes, our family break-up was occasionally blackly hilarious too, because life is like that, but my brother and I didn't exactly find it ITV prime-time funny.

When they announced their divorce, our parents stoically tried to protect us in the usual way – by completely concealing their emotions and pretending everything was fine. (To find out what really happened, I had to read about it years later in a *TV Times* feature called *The Real Second Thoughts*). My reaction at the time was fairly textbook: I went completely off the rails, got expelled from school, developed an eating disorder (which I preferred to call my very effective and simple diet plan, and which also featured in an episode of *Second Thoughts*), started drinking and clashed endlessly with all figures of authority.

When I'd finished, my brother had his freak-out, which was totally out of character and lasted – perhaps coincidentally – until *Second Thoughts* ended, and then completely and miraculously ceased.

Tragedy hit again, when my dear friend Joel killed himself – not because of *Faith in the Future*, I hasten to add, although his problems did begin around the same time it first aired.

I always felt it was strange, to have one light-entertainment version of our family and the other, darker reality playing simultaneously – one on a set, the other in a real room. And in my more metaphysical moments I suspected that the existence of the sitcom was creating an adverse reaction in real life – all the comedy being sucked out of it. That wasn't true, of course. Life was carrying on being complex, horrible, ridiculous, wonderful, painful and funny in all the wrong places.

But there was a good side, mainly financial, although my mother and stepfather's impressively solid marriage was clearly cemented through their working partnership. My brother got a car, Nigel and I got our wedding.

Now that I have children of my own, I am not sure I could do the same thing to my family. Recently I've written a novel that was lifted almost directly from life – but I deliberately massaged it until the real people have become unrecognisable. In all honesty, I would have preferred to use the real version, because reality can be so ingeniously inventive, but I couldn't do it. Not only would I risk destroying relationships, but also the *Second Thoughts* experience has made me more wary.

And as for my parents and what they did to us? Well, I've got kids – I understand how hard it is to be a working mother, and how when you write, real life is sometimes too much of a gift. All life is potential copy, almost irresistibly so. And there is no richer source of inspiration than your own family.

MAY 8 2007

Obituary: Isabella Blow

EMINE SANER

'A cross between a Billingsgate fishwife and Lucretia Borgia.' That was how the fashion designer Alexander McQueen once described Isabella Blow, at various times fashion supremo of *Tatler*, *Vogue* and the *Sunday Times*, who has died in hospital aged 48 after having cancer and depression.

She was most famous as a talent-spotter and benefactor to young British designers. She championed McQueen after buying his entire graduate collection in 1992, and discovered and nurtured the milliner Philip Treacy, whose elaborate hats became her trademark. She also discovered the models Sophie Dahl and Stella Tennant.

From 1997 to 2001 she was fashion director of the *Sunday Times Style* magazine, where I was her assistant. Her distinctive tuberose scent heralded her arrival at News International's drab offices in east London – if you didn't spot one of her Treacy hats on the horizon first. This was the signal to apply lipstick and high heels – according to Isabella, wearing jeans and trainers was a sackable offence. Often, because of the rush, lipstick would end up on my teeth or halfway down my chin, but this was fine because that was Isabella's look, too.

When her expenses became too inflated she agreed to use the underground instead of taxis, and found that she enjoyed it. I would meet her at the station to show her the back route to the office. It was a daily worry that the sight of her – in stilettos, furs, perhaps her one-legged trouser suit and hat – would cause a road accident on the main dual carriageway.

Isabella – or Izzie, as she was known – said that her love of fashion came from her grandmother, Lady Vera Delves Broughton, a photographer, explorer and hunter. The family had lived at Doddington, a castle with 14,000 hectares of land in Cheshire, since the 14th century, but it was sold to pay off her grandfather's gambling debts and, as a child, Isabella could see the castle only from her family's cottage on the estate. Her parents never got over the death of their only son – a two-year-old who Isabella saw drown in the family swimming pool – and she told me they had seemed to lose interest in her and her sisters.

Born in London, she was sent to Heathfield school in Ascot, Surrey. When she was 14 her mother announced she was leaving the family, shook her hand and said goodbye; Isabella rarely saw her after that. Her father, Sir Evelyn Delves Broughton, remarried. When he died in 1993 he left her £5,000 of his £6m fortune. She was never good at holding on to money, despite lucrative advertising deals and consultancies (notably with Swarovski – she was the driving force behind the reinvention of the crystal company), because her generosity was enormous.

She became part of the avant garde New York scene and was friends with Andy Warhol, Roy Lichtenstein and Jean-Michel Basquiat. She came back to London in 1986 as assistant to the then *Tatler* fashion director, Michael Roberts. In 1993 she went to British *Vogue* and after the *Sunday Times* returned to *Tatler* as fashion director.

After A-levels and a secretarial course, she took odd jobs, such as cleaning. Even then, she would fashion a dishcloth into an elaborate hat to keep her hair out of her face. She moved to New York in 1979 to study Chinese art at Columbia University. In 1981 she married Nicholas Taylor, but they divorced two years later. Her friend the musician Bryan Ferry introduced her to Anna Wintour, editor of American *Vogue*, who hired her as her assistant.

In 1989 she met her second husband, Detmar Blow, a lawyer and later an art dealer. When they married at Gloucester Cathedral she wore a headdress commissioned by the then-unknown Treacy, which marked the start of their friendship.

Isabella's appearance – Wallis Simpson as envisaged by Salvador Dalí – at the front row of fashion shows became as eagerly awaited as the collections themselves. She once wore a jewel-encrusted lobster on her head, and on another occasion an outfit, inspired by Joan of Arc, which included a heavy, oily chain that she dragged behind her. Afterwards, she visited Karl Lagerfeld at his Paris home and dragged the dirty chain all over his plush cream carpets.

At a lunch with Nicholas Coleridge, managing director of Condé Nast, she wore a pair of antlers covered in a heavy black lace veil. When he asked how she would able to eat, she said: 'Nicholas, that is of no concern to me whatsoever.'

Towards the end of her life Isabella had become as recognisable as the designers and young artists she championed. The Design Museum held an exhibition in 2002 entitled *When Philip Met Isabella*, celebrating the relationship between Treacy and his muse. In 2004 she had a cameo appearance in the film *The Life Aquatic With Steve Zissou*.

She is survived by Detmar and a considerable hat collection.

Isabella Blow, fashion journalist, born November 19 1958; died May 7 2007. Subsequent to the publication of this piece it became clear that Isabella Blow had committed suicide.

MAY 9 2007

'A time to love, a time to hate, a time of war, a time of peace'

MICHAEL WHITE

Tony Blair once talked in Belfast about the hand of history on his shoulder. Yesterday, it appeared to be tickling his midriff. Not just his, but all of the VIPs gathered at Stormont to install the new power-sharing executive. Whenever someone cracked a joke, they all laughed frantically.

It wasn't hard to see why. The day was a bit like one of those Hugh Grant weddings where guests are tense beneath the surface jollity, braced for something to go wrong. The two families have hated each other for ever, but here were Ian and Gerry bravely trying to make a go of it. They had to wish them well.

Strictly speaking, it wasn't a wedding, more a civil partnership and Martin McGuinness, not Gerry Adams, was Ian Paisley's unblushing Sinn Féin bride. The DUP leader isn't much of a civil-partnership enthusiast, but, as he genially kept reminding people who didn't need reminding, his entering government with the Shinners was just as improbable until recently. Yesterday all his oratorical power, so long a destructive force, was gracefully directed towards the common good.

Most of it anyway. Though everyone was on their best behaviour they all managed little point-scoring digs. Mr Paisley spoke of his Unionism, Mr McGuinness of his belief in a united Ireland; Mr Paisley quoted the Bible, Mr Adams's team spoke a little Irish. But the wedding went ahead.

JULY 8 2007

The peloton make it to the top of the hill in Goudhurst, Kent during stage one of the Tour de France 2007. TOM JENKINS

JULY 22 2007

The town of Tewkesbury is surrounded by floodwaters after torrential rain hits Gloucestershire. DANIEL BEREHULAK/GETTY IMAGES

APRIL 2 2007

Presidential hopeful US Senator Hillary Rodham Clinton speaks at a barbecue in Fort Madison, Iowa, USA. KEVIN SANDERS/AP

MARCH 13 2007

Kate Middleton stands beside boyfriend Prince William
in the paddock enclosure on the first day of the
Cheltenham Festival (see page 147). CARL DE SOUZA/AFP

Quoting the Old Testament's 'To everything there is a season ... ', Mr Paisley came to King Solomon's lines 'a time to love and a time to hate / a time of war and a time of peace'. Hearing those words from that voice must have raised the hairs on the back of every Catholic neck. But he went on to affirm that 'from the depth of my heart' he believes the time for peace has come. He even sounded keen to get started. He is 81 after all, entering office just as Mr Blair, 54, is leaving it.

When his turn came to reassure anxious Protestants, Mr McGuinness quoted Seamus Heaney, the poet's warning against talking too much of Others. They must all 'get to a place through Otherness', he said. Mr McGuinness can be a menacing man, but when he wants to he can do a good twinkle. Yesterday he twinkled, so that both the ex-demagogue and the ex-gunman sounded as if they meant it.

Later, Mr Blair and his Irish counterpart, Bertie Ahern, took their bow and patted each other's backs, as members of the Amalgamated Union of Statesmen usually do. If you think Mr Blair has problems, spare a thought for Mr Ahern, facing an election on May 24. He may end up power-sharing with Sinn Féin too.

First there were the formalities in the grandiose building, built to house what – then and now – is really a county council with attitude: 108 members of the legislative assembly (MLAs), 18 of them women, elected in March, now meeting formally to vote in ministers with the much depleted Ulster Unionists' leader, Sir Reg Empey, having to nominate himself. It took just 45 minutes.

Up in the gallery sat Senator Edward Kennedy, an old volcano among the grandees and ghosts of the peace process, plus Mr McGuinness's old mum, much kissed yesterday. Shadows of the Troubles's 3,500 dead were also present, mentioned by all speakers. No Spanish civil war 'pact of forgetting' here, the wounds are too raw.

Apart from the overnight death from cancer of George Dawson, a DUP MLA, everything went according to plan. It was by turn moving and banal, inspiring and weighed down by procedural tedium, but it was normal and that is what the province wants. This is the one corner of the United Kingdom where security is being scaled down – not up. There was a small demo, but Mr Blair brought it with him: Iraq.

In the latest of his many swansongs the prime minister spoke of restoring normal politics and the need to end 'ancient hatreds and political differences', but that was his only mention of the Labour party. Mr Ahern spoke of ending centuries of 'the anger and pain of an old quarrel' in Ireland. Yet it was noticeable that when the speeches ended most of the handshakes and hugs seemed to be confined to their own sides.

Glasses were raised across Northern Ireland last night, many brimming with what Mr Paisley used to call 'the Devil's buttermilk'. But there is still a long dull slog towards normality.

MAY 11 2007

Getting Blair

STEVE BELL

I first knowingly set eyes on Tony Blair at the Labour party conference in Brighton in 1991. I remember a toothy grin and not much else, other than a speech of remarkable vagueness. He spoke of vision, but all I could see was a neat, eager suit – eager to impress but strangely empty. Grubby dungarees and workerist chanting were clearly things of the past. This party meant business.

Blair erupted into full view on the death of John Smith in May 1994, when he instantly became frontrunner in the race for the leadership. Teeth, ears, ears, teeth, thin bloke, youngish, er ... Some people were calling him Bambi, because of his youth and doe-eyed air of innocence, so I tried it for a bit, but it didn't really work. Bambi doesn't have teeth, whereas Blair has far too many.

I even tried drawing him as Andy Pandy, but much preferred Harriet Harman as Looby Loo. Draw a rounded square, put an eyeball in each top corner and bingo! It's Harriet. As I am a strip cartoonist and obliged to repeat a caricature 20 times over the course of a week, I cherish formulaic caricature. I had no formula for Blair.

Then it was his first conference as leader in late September of that year. I was on the top deck of a Blackpool tram when I bumped into George Pope, a Labour party stalwart I'd not seen for some years.

'I don't think much of your Blair,' he said. 'You haven't got him yet, have you?'

Moments like these are difficult for the sensitive professional. While I have no right to expect the world to fall at my feet, chortling gratefully at each new offering, this was impugning my professional integrity, which is like laughing at my penis, only worse.

The trouble was he was right. Cartooning is a kind of perform-ance art for furtive exhibitionists and you're only ever as good as your last performance. I had to perform every day that week and there was no way I could avoid drawing Tony Blair.

I fudged the first day and drew a large tram with a very small Blair in the driving seat. Day two at the Labour conference is always the leader's speech. I wandered around the Winter Gardens like a hungover fart in a trance, clutching my tiny little hardback sketchbook. Being a large person I am naturally discreet. Since my earliest years I have always resented the idea of some git breathing down my neck while I draw. All they ever say is: 'Let's have a look' and 'I don't think much of that', or worse 'Who's that supposed to be?' So I deploy my sketchbook in such a way that a casual observer might think that I am scratching my armpit, or possibly my testicles.

All around the conference centre there are TV monitors relaying whatever is going on on the conference floor, as well as normal TV. I remember watching Blair on screen and detecting a momentary flash in his left eye. I jotted down what I saw. I'd seen something similar while studying Thatcher on screen many years before, but thought nothing more of it until later in the day, during his actual speech, sitting at the foot of his garish turquoise podium, among the photographers, staring up at him. Of course! Thatcher had a staring left eyeball. Blair has a staring left eyeball too.

Thatcher was mad.

Maybe Blair was mad as well.

I had no particular reason to think that Blair was mad. He had just become leader of the opposition and hadn't actually done anything. But the eyeball was trying to tell me something.

My dad would say about Tony Benn: 'The bugger's mad!' I used to disagree with this analysis, as it's hardly Benn's fault he has two staring eyes. One could certainly attribute steely determination to Blair, and Thatcher had that in spades. As for madness, we'd have to wait and see. It was worth a punt and as usual the deadline was approaching. I drew Blair morphing into Thatcher.

It seemed to fit.

What Blair has – as seen in that first sketch – is one angry (left) eye and one smiley, twinkly (right) eye. Once I'd established that, everything else fell into place. Big ears, loadsa teeth, weak chin, projecting lower lip, conical head and weird top knot (a small echo of Thatcher's resplendent quiff). At last I had a formula that I could use in the strip, with the added bonus that, because Blair's features are distinctive, they could be applied to any object or animal existing or yet to be discovered.

Since then, only details have changed. He's aged, his hair has greyed and thinned, his widow's peak has become more pronounced and the eye has definitely got madder. The other eye has gone a bit wild as well. It's as if the eyeballs can no longer make up their mind. His expanding forehead bears the vivid imprint of the ravages of power. Sometime in 2004 – after the invasion of Iraq (a mad act if ever there was one) and various uncomfortable inquiries – I noticed that it had taken on a kind of Klingon quality. Yet by the time of the general election campaign in spring 2005, his forehead had become like a cross between a baby's bum and a snare drum. I'd be prepared to bet that he'd had Botox.

Now as power drains away from him in these, his final days, he seems more relaxed, just slightly plumper, and apparently concerned about who he should get to do his portrait bust for the members' lobby in the House of Commons, to sit underneath the 8ft monster Thatcher statue. This is an interesting proposition and I would be happy to accept the challenge. It's not as if I haven't done the preparation and I stoutly maintain that a cartoonist has every bit as much commitment to truth and accuracy as any portraitist. But Blair is said to be unwilling to undertake formal sittings for a portrait.

He's not always been this shy. I once met someone who had painted him in the nude when they were both students at Oxford. Could it be that, having been the subject of so much intensive scrutiny for so long, he already knows the worst about what he looks like, so what's the point of some bland official daubing? If he's had steak for years, why would he suddenly want hamburger?

MAY 11 2007

A strange occasion to play 'Things Can Only Get Better'

SIMON HOGGART

'I ask you to accept one thing. Hand on heart, I did what I thought was right.'

Tony Blair was speaking in the familiar auditorium of Trimdon Labour Club, possibly the last place in the world where everybody loves him. But the message was for the world: for Britain, for America, for Europe – and anyone who might be listening in Basra. And just in case there was anyone present who didn't want to join in the praise for himself, he had praise for us. We were 'the blessed nation ... in our innermost thoughts, we know: this is the greatest nation on earth,' he said, almost moist-eyed. Possibly that line was cut from the feed to Washington.

Trimdon, a neat and spruce community in County Durham, had become a media village. Ten satellite trucks were parked on the well-mown green. Inside the Labour Club, where in 1983 an agent called John Burton spotted the young lawyer's potential and employed sleight of rulebook to give him the last Labour seat going. It has been the chosen setting for all the great events of his political life.

And the audience proved some of what he said. I've been going to Trimdon on and off for 10 years and people have become notice-ably more prosperous – better-dressed, better-fed, the skin glossier. It's only the old men, the former miners, who look pinched and stooped, their faces lined as if they had never quite been able to scrub the last of the coal dust away.

We waited. Vaguely inspirational pop music boomed out. 'Search For The Hero Inside Yourself', 'Higher And Higher'. People appeared with placards, some in suspiciously similar styles: '10 Years, 3 Elections, 1 Great Britain', 'Britain Says Thanks', 'Tony Rocks'. Without evident irony, they put on 'Things Can Only Get Better' at top volume. A woman tried to get everybody dancing and clapping to this (which may soon be retitled 'Still Some Room For Improvement'). Quite a few people did join in, but most didn't, so it looked as if a happy-clappy congregation had been infiltrated by Anglicans.

Then he arrived. He began folksy, thanking Maureen and, er, Maureen's friends. 'She said to me "four more years" and I said, "Maureen, that's not on-message for today."' He thanked John Burton. He thanked Cherie and their children ('who never let me forget my failings' – surely he had enough people to do that?). After that, he was away.

Most prime ministers are actors, and this was a thunderous performance. He was revealing about why he had stayed so long: 'Sometimes the only way you can conquer the pull of power is to set it down.' He made it sound like getting out of bed on a cold morning. He went back through the failed politics of the past, but we soon realised that this was not a description of Blairism it was a description of Blair. No cabinet colleague, no MP, nobody else was mentioned. Even the word 'government' was banned. It was him, him, him!

He recited again his achievements – more jobs, shorter waiting times – the list we've heard a thousand times. Now we had a country 'confident in the 21st century, a country comfortable in its own skin' – a faintly disturbing image, as if we were one gigantic sausage.

Some thought he had been messianic. But he had suffered doubts, hesitation, reflection and reconsideration. Changes had been 'hellish hard to do'. Suddenly we were on to Iraq and 'the blowback from global terrorism'. Had he been wrong there? No. 'It is a test of will and of belief and we can't fail it.'

So no apology there, but he did say that in 1997 expectations had been high – 'perhaps too high'. And he added, 'apologies to you for the times I have fallen short'. Apologies for what? He admits to getting things wrong, but won't tell us what they were.

'But good luck,' he said to us, and was away, passing through a guard of honour mounted by Trimdon's Labour supporters, to cries of 'Thank you!' from them and 'Move out the fucking way!' from the photographers. And I did see one woman dabbing her eyes.

MAY 12 2007

The town that banned plastic bags

PATRICK BARKHAM

Sandra Beard didn't stand a chance. Net curtains twitched. Shoppers tutted. The holidaymaker had advanced a mere 50 yards down Modbury High Street before Helen Pickles burst out of her shop looking askance.

'Madam,' the joint proprietor of R&H Pickles Hardware trilled at Mrs Beard, 'is that a plastic bag you're carrying?'

Two weeks after becoming the first town in Europe to ban plastic bags from its shops, an extraordinary transformation has taken place in the south Devon community. Carrying a plastic bag has become antisocial behaviour. Wicker baskets, rucksacks and reusable bags of every shape and size swing from the arms of shoppers in the bustling town of 1,500 people. But if you're spotted with a plastic one you risk becoming a social pariah.

'I had to rescue one lady because she was walking down the road with a plastic bag and her friends were saying, "You can't be seen in Modbury with a plastic bag,"' said Rebecca Hosking, 33, a wildlife camerawoman who came up with the idea.

'I ran out of my flat and said, "It's OK, she's reusing it. She's allowed to bring it into the town."'

From the butchers to the Co-op supermarket, none of the town's 43 traders uses plastic bags. The 2,000 special edition Modbury bags made from fair-trade recycled cotton are already a collectors' item; stores also sell 5p biodegradable cornstarch bags, biodegradable bin bags and even biodegradable bags for dog mess.

There is one plastic bag left in town and it is so rare it has a name – 'The Granny's Knickers' – and has become the subject of earnest debate as it hangs from an oak tree by the car park. It won't foil the residents for long. Modburians have a talent for environmental problem solving.

Unlike fashionable Totnes nearby, Modbury is not a beacon for alternative lifestyles. 'It's a horsy, farmy town that's always been very conservative,' said Ms Hosking. 'If we've done it, it proves you don't have to be one of those "green" towns to change over.'

Their plastic bag ban was not the result of years of campaigning. Ms Hosking suggested it in the pub one evening in March shortly after filming a BBC documentary about the devastating effect of plastic bags on marine life in Hawaii. She showed the film to the town's traders. Four weeks of sleepless nights researching viable alternatives followed and plastic bag-free status began on 1 May.

Since then she has fielded thousands of calls from shoppers and traders across the world wanting to follow Modbury's lead. More than 60 towns in the United Kingdom, including 15 in Devon and Cornwall, have approached her for help. International media have swarmed there; several celebrities desperate to 'endorse' Modbury's action have been politely rebuffed.

Ms Hosking says she sometimes feels like Brian from Monty Python's *Life of Brian*. There is certainly a messianic glint in proud locals' eyes when they talk about the ban.

'It's fabulous,' said Anne Tillett, wielding a flowery blue bag. 'I popped into a supermarket in another town yesterday and because I hadn't planned ahead I didn't have my bag and I just couldn't take a plastic bag. I've become a missionary.'

Adam Searle used to hand out 200 plastic bags every day. His deli is busier than ever, but he barely uses two cornstarch bags a day.

'I don't think I'll get through my biodegradable bags before they biodegrade,' he said. 'You have a couple of awkward people who go "It's a load of rubbish" and you explain what it's about and they pat you on the back.'

It is impossible to find a cynic or contrarian even among outsiders. Terry and Gill Lodge, two holidaymakers, were oblivious to the revolution in Modbury until they went shopping. They didn't bat an eyelid about buying a reusable bag.

'Bloody marvellous,' said Mr Lodge. 'In Salisbury we always shop in Waitrose and their plastic bags are so flimsy that you put them in the boot of your car and they fall to pieces. Not satisfactory at all.'

'The sooner we get rid of plastic bags and packaging the better,' added Mrs Lodge.

Ms Hosking could easily make her fortune as a plastic-bag guru, but wants to get back to her day job – filming buzzards. Towns that keep asking her for 'a manual' on how to do it need to look closer to home. 'It has to come from residents and from the community,' she said.

Billed as a six-month experiment, townsfolk are adamant there will be no turning back. It received no funding or council intervention, but Modbury was helped by its preponderance of independent traders. Only the Co-op supermarket was part of a chain and it has been an enthusiastic supporter. But Ms Hosking reckons it is still possible for towns with big chain stores.

'The supermarkets have two options: they can come with you and all the town looks good or they look bad when the whole town bans bags and they don't.'

Back on the high street, Mrs Beard and her friend, Rose Rogers, were expecting that tap on the shoulder.

'Before we went on holiday, my son said, "Plastic bags are banned in Modbury. Mind you don't get arrested walking down the street with one,"' said Mrs Rogers. But Mrs Beard was not offended by her interrogation.

'My plastic bag is recycled,' she said. 'I always carry one around in my handbag.'

MAY 18 2007

The British media does not do responsibility

SIMON JENKINS

The media coverage of the missing McCann child has largely escaped censure. This is because it concerns an ongoing tragedy and because the grief of those directly involved is so real. Neither justifies freedom from comment. The coverage has been absurdly over the top and cannot have served the interests of the family or the eventual cause of justice.

I was astonished to see the BBC news department sending its star presenter, Huw Edwards, to southern Portugal to handle what was essentially a single-thread story with at least two other on-screen reporters in place. The corporation must be stiff with under-employed staff. Presumably as a result of this decision, the McCanns regularly led the *Six O'Clock News*, ahead of Gordon Brown's leadership bid – even when there was nothing new to report from the Algarve.

In this voracious feeding frenzy the media presence in Portimao was reduced to extremes of invention to justify the prominence the story was getting back home. We learned of false sightings, car chases, child traffickers, barren women, beach paedophiles and dark dungeons. A 'suspect' was enveloped in private detective work way beyond any consideration for natural justice. The sympathy a reader or viewer was bound to feel for the McCanns was overwhelmed in an exploitative swarm. Star foot-ballers were signed up, as were Hell's Angels, MPs wearing yellow ribbons and ministers meeting deputations. It was as if a missing child were this year's Make Poverty History campaign.

Madeleine has become Maddy, an angel face in the clutches of a monster. The reasonable attempts of the McCanns to avoid publicity and be seen to cooperate with the much-battered Portuguese police were as broken sticks in a tornado of coverage. No aspect of the case was left intact by invading armies of counsellors, paediatricians, psychologists, criminologists and trauma consultants. 'Every parent's nightmare' became the nation's nightmare. Families closed their doors to the world, hugged their children close and cursed Portugal.

To suggest that this might not be a good way of finding a miss-ing child is clearly spitting in the wind. It is possible that publicity in the McCann case might have induced witnesses to come forward in the immediate aftermath of the girl's disappearance.

It is equally possible that media hysteria could drive a cornered criminal to desperate measures to cover his or her tracks. Is it worth the risk?

There were 798 child abductions in Britain in the last period for which figures are available (2003-4), of which most were intra-family, but 68 were 'by strangers'. Of these, a majority were quickly and quietly resolved, by information being available and acted on before the captor realised. Twenty-five of them took longer, in addition to dozens from preceding years. Since the disappearance of Madeleine on May 3 another 450 young people have gone missing in Britain. While many are teenagers, none has received anything like the attention given to the McCanns.

So what made this case so special as to merit the trans-shipment of Fleet Street's finest and the BBC's chief newsreader? The answer is that a 'Big News Story' is not a systematic concept. It does not emerge on to the page according to some calculus of merit, as satirically suggested by Michael Frayn in his novel *Towards the End of Morning*. It does not claim its place on the front page via a table stipulating five dead Englishmen (or one Londoner), 50 dead Europeans and 1,000 dead Chinese.

To acquire front-page status, a story must compete with dozens of similar human-interest stories on a particular day, boosted by happenings over the light news period, such as a bank holiday. Hence the phenomenon that alsatians only attack children at Easter and there is a 'road carnage horror' every Christmas, though statistics on both are constant throughout the year. The story should relate the ordinary lives of readers, as did the Soham murders, but not the deaths of the Morecambe Bay Chinese cockle-pickers. It must contain tears, suspense and mystery.

Such features are not cynical or strange. A newspaper story strives to attain the quality of a novel, if only because it knows that readers like novels, as television viewers like soap operas. The human imagination is attuned to narratives that have beginnings, middles and ends, preferably ends that carry some moral message. Under this pressure what is extraordinary is not that newspapers sometimes make things up (and get them wrong), but that they make up so little.

The McCann story ticked all these boxes. It was not another runaway teenager or the death abroad of another 'promising gap-year student'. It was a heartbreaking and open-ended mystery. Any parent could relate to it. Any reader could, by expressing sympathy and showing vigilance, participate in relieving pain and possibly solving the case. This might involve intrusion into private grief and blatant xenophobia, but that is hardly a media novelty. Britons travelling abroad seem to feel entitled to the same consideration by the authorities as they would get at home and journalists feed that unreasonable expectation.

I have found the coverage of the McCann story prurient and tedious beyond belief. That the BBC should regard it as more important than Brown's ascension to national leadership crumbles my faith in that great organisation. Tabloid values have come to British public-service broadcasting with a vengeance and without even the commercial pressure of the private sector. It is like the daily attention given to the kidnapping of the BBC's brave Gaza correspondent, Alan Johnston, when dozens of other kidnappings – including of journalists – go unreported.

In this spirit I must constantly remind myself that the British media does not do responsibility. It does stories. And stories tell better when they are about individuals, not collectives. The media is unconcerned with what people like me find decorous or important. It kicks down doors and exposes the hidden corners of the human condition. It fights competition, plays dirty and disobeys the rules. There is nothing it finds too vulgar or too prurient for its wandering, penetrating lens.

Journalists may have cooked the McCann story to a burnt crisp, but they cook many other stories that way and I say, thank goodness. There are plenty in power who feel too much was written and said on the Royal Navy hostages, on cash-for-honours, on BAE sleaze and on David Kelly. Tough luck on them.

Damilola Taylor was just one among many youngsters whose lives are ruined or lost on Britain's sink housing estates, conditions highlighted by the extraordinary publicity attached to his case. Many brave people are killed for trying to impose order on Britain's streets, but it was the teacher Philip Lawrence who captured the public's imagination. Sometimes there is no better way to alert the nation to street violence, racism or even the dangers faced by families abroad than through the tragedy visited on an individual victim.

The British press plays hard cop to the soft cop of the British constitution. It goes where politics dares not tread, certainly the present pusillanimous parliament that still cannot find a way of holding the government to account for Iraq, as Congress is finally doing in America. The press does not operate with any sense of proportion, judgment or self-restraint, because it is selling stories, not running the country. The unshackled and irresponsible press sometimes gets it wrong. But I still prefer it, warts and all, to a shackled and responsible one.

MAY 19 2007

Welcome to Tehran

GHAITH ABDUL-AHAD

On a recent overcast afternoon in Basra, two new police SUVs drove onto a dusty, rubbish-strewn football pitch where a group of children were playing. The game stopped and the kids looked on.

Three men in white *dishdashas* got out of one of the cars. One, holding a Kalashnikov, stood guard as the other two removed some metal tubes and cables from the back of a vehicle. As the two men fiddled with the wires, the man with the gun waved it at a teenager who wanted to film with his mobile phone. Then, amid cries of 'Moqtada! Moqtada!' and 'Allahu Akbar!', there were two thunderous explosions and a pair of Katyusha rockets streaked up into the sky. Their target would be the British base in Saddam Hussein's former palace compound. Their landing place could be anywhere in Basra, and was most likely to be a civilian home. The men got back in their cars and drove away, and the children resumed their match.

'Since the British started deploying the anti-rocket magnetic fields, our rockets are falling on civilians,' Abu Mujtaba, the commander of the group of Mahdi army men told me later. The 'magnetic fields' are the latest rumour doing the rounds of Basra's militias; another is that the British are shelling civilians to damage the reputation of the Mahdi army.

The scene I had just watched was an everyday incident in an area long regarded as relatively safe and stable compared with the civil war-racked regions to the north. But as the British army's decision not to deploy Prince Harry highlighted this week, Basra and the nominally British-controlled areas around it are far from secure.

During a recent nine-day visit, politicians, security officials and businessmen explained how the streets of the city were effectively under the control of rival militias competing to control territory, the fragile post-Saddam apparatus of state and revenue sources, such as oil and weapons smuggling. As in Baghdad, gunmen speed through the streets on the back of pick-ups and the city is divided between militias as mutually suspicious as rival mafia families.

'If the Prophet Muhammad would come to Basra today he would be killed, because he doesn't have a militia,' a law professor told me. 'There is no state of law, the only law is the militia law.'

The Politician

His description of life in the city was echoed by Abu Ammar,[1] once a prominent Basra politician. A secular technocrat, he had high hopes when the British first arrived more than four years ago. The city had been hit hard by Saddam's wars against Iran and Kuwait and he was optimistic that the occupation would bring democracy and prosperity. But the rise of the militias had put paid to that, he said. Now he was too scared to talk in a hotel lobby and insisted we meet in my room.

'When these religious parties say Basra is calm, that's because they control the city and they are looting it,' he said. 'It's calm not because it's under the control of the police, but because all the militias have interests and they want to maintain the status quo. The moment their interests are under threat the whole city can burn.' Like many I spoke to he said the appearance of a functioning state was largely an illusion: 'The security forces are made of militiamen. In any confrontation between political parties, the police force will splinter according to party line and fight each other.'

1 Not his real name.

The Militia Commander

The people who really control Basra are men such as Sayed Youssif. He is a mid-level militia commander, but his name and that of his militia – God's Revenge – strikes fear anywhere in Basra.

Beginning with a small group of gunmen occupying a small public building, the former religious student built up a reputation as a fearless thug, killing former Ba'athists, alcohol sellers and eventually freelancing as a hitman for anyone willing to pay the price. I went to see him in his Basra compound. Gunmen dressed in the uniforms of ministry of interior commandos stood guard outside and a sniper watched from the roof.

In the room outside his office, tribal leaders, officials and more gunmen sat, barefooted, waiting for Sayed Youssif to call them. Some wanted him to help their relatives join the army or police. Some had problems with other militias and were seeking his protection, but most were there to pay homage to a powerful man whose help they may one day need. As the official apparatus of state slides into chaos, men such as him have become the main dispensers of justice and patronage. No one in Basra can be appointed to the army, police or any official job without a letter of support from a militia or a political party.

Sitting in front of a mural of an eagle emerging from Basra and enveloping the whole of Iraq, he retained the manners of a religious student; stretching his arms on his lap, he lowered his head to listen intently as visitors addressed him. But on the desk in front of him two phones that rang constantly and a pistol with two cartridges hinted at the power he now wields.

Sayed Youssif had just made a ruling in the case of a Sunni man whose brother was accused of shooting at Shias more than 15 years ago. Relatives of the alleged victims were demanding that he pay them compensation or be killed. The man pleaded that his brother had left the country two years before and he was too poor to pay 7m dinars (£250,000) in compensation. The Sunni man shook, pleading for mercy.

'Time has changed,' said Sayed Youssif in a low but powerful voice. 'Now you Sunni come here and beg like the mice. Do you remember the days when no one of us could even talk to you? You were the tyrants then, but we are not tyrants like you – I will give you a week to go to your tribe and either convince them to hand your brother over or you will be judged in his place.'

At the moment, he explained, he was preoccupied with a power struggle against the Fadhila Party, another Shia militia that has controlled the governorship and the oil terminals for most of the past two years. Sayed Youssif and a group of other militias all with strong ties to Iran were trying to displace Fadhila.

'I have told all city council members: you have to make a choice, you either vote against the governor or you will die,' he told one of his aides. The next day, two bombs exploded outside the homes of city councillors from the Fadhila Party.

The General
One afternoon I went to meet a senior Iraqi general in the interior ministry. A dozen gunmen in military uniforms lay dozing as a junior officer led me through a maze of corridors padded with sandbags.

The general was on the phone to another officer when I entered. He was jokingly threatening the caller: 'Shut up or I will send democracy to your town.' When he finished his conversation, the general – who didn't want his name published, because he feared retribution from militias – stretched out his hand to me and said, ' Welcome to Tehran.'

I asked him about British claims that the security situation was improving. His reply was withering: 'The British came here as military tourists. They committed huge mistakes when they formed the security forces. They appointed militiamen as police officers and chose not to confront the militias. We have reached this point where the militias are a legitimate force in the street.'

He and other security officials in Basra – including a British adviser to the local police force – described a web of different security forces with allegiances to different factions or militias. 'Most of the police force is divided between Fadhila, which controls the TSU [the tactical support unit, its best-trained unit], and Moqtada, which controls the regular police,' the general said. 'Fadhila also control the oil terminals, so they control the oil-protection force and part of the navy. Moqtada controls the ports and customs, so they control the customs, police and its intelligence. Commandos are under the control of Badr Brigade.'

The relationship between militias and the security units they had infiltrated was fluid and difficult to pin down, he said. 'Even the police officer who is not part of a militia will join a militia to protect himself, and once he is affiliated with a militia then as a commander you can't change him ... because then you are confronting a political party.' More than 60 per cent of his own officers – and 'almost all' policemen – were militiamen. 'We need a major surgical operation, to clean the city,' he said.

The British army's Operation Sinbad was designed to do just that. The army has claimed it was a success, but the general saw it somewhat differently. 'The Sinbad operation failed miserably, because it didn't cleanse the police force,' he said. 'Ahead of us we have years of fighting and murder, a militia will be toppled by another militia and those will split, so day after day we are witnessing the formations of new groups. And the British withdrawal is leading to a power struggle between the different factions.'

The Intelligence Officer

In the living room of his modest Basra home, a senior military intelligence official – let's call him Samer – told me the militias could take control of the city in half an hour if they chose. Next to the sofa we sat on lay a rocket-propelled grenade launcher, a machine-gun and couple of grenades. Samer had survived two assassination attempts. As a young man with a pistol tucked into the back of his trousers brought us cans of Fanta, Samer described the economic forces behind the growth of the militias.

'The militias and the tribes are cartels,' he said. 'They control the main ports, the main oil terminal, and they have their own ports and everyone smuggles oil. When the balance of power is disrupted, they clash in the streets.'

He told me how a few weeks earlier an official in the directorate of electricity loyal to Moqtada al-Sadr had been replaced by another one loyal to the Fadhila party, triggering clashes in the streets between different police units. When there was a clash between two militias, the police force split and one police unit began fighting other units. Police cars became militia cars. (One Mahdi army commander was aghast that I found this strange: 'Of course I should travel in a police car, do you want the commander to travel by taxi?') Complicating matters further, Samer said most militiamen had multiple IDs associated with different groups. 'They switch, depending on who pays more.'

Like the general, he said much of the blame for the current situation lay with the British: 'The British officers are very careful about their image They are too scared to go into confrontation. They allowed the cancer to [take over the body]. Even if the militias burn the city tomorrow, [the British] won't go into confrontation. They know they are outnumbered and they have huge losses if they do so.'

The next day I went back to see the general. He was sitting with two other officers discussing his day. 'Our uncles, the British, flew me today to Ammara to attend the security handover ceremony,' he said.

'Give it one month and it will collapse,' one of the officers replied.

'One month?' the general laughed. 'Give it a few days.'

The Iranians

You can't move far in Basra without bumping into some evidence of the Iranian influence on the city. Even inside the British consulate compound visitors are advised not to use mobile phones because, as the security official put it, 'the Iranians next door are listening to everything'. In the Basra market Iranian produce is everywhere, from dairy products to motorcycles and electronic goods. Farsi phrase books are sold in bookshops and posters of Ayatollah Khomeini are on the walls. But Iranian influence is also found in more sinister places. Sitting in his house in one of Basra's poorest neighbourhoods, Abu Mujtaba described the level of co-operation between Iran and his units. His account echoed what several militia men in other parts of Iraq have told me.

'We need weapons and Iran is our only outlet. If the Saudis would give us weapons, we would stop bringing weapons from Iran.' He went on: 'They [the Iranians] don't give us weapons, they sell us weapons: an Iranian bomb costs us $100, nothing comes for free. We know Iran is not interested in the good of Iraq, and we know they are here to fight the Americans and the British on our land, but we need them and they are using us.'

Despite this scepticism about Tehran's motives, he said some Mahdi army units were now effectively under Iranian control. 'Some of the units are following different commanders, and Iran managed to infiltrate [them], and these units work directly for Iran.' Most of the Shia militias and parties that control politics in Basra today were formed and funded by Tehran, he said.

His assessment was shared by both the general and the intelligence official. 'Iran has not only infiltrated the government and security forces through the militias and parties they nurtured in Iran, they managed to infiltrate Moqtada's lot, by providing them with weapons,' the general told me. 'And some disgruntled and militias were overtaken by Iran and provided with money and weapons.'

In his office, littered with weapons bearing Iranian markings, Samer showed me footage his men had shot of a weapons smuggling operation after they captured six brand-new Katyushas.

'In Basra, Iran has more influence than the government in Baghdad,' he said. 'It is providing the militias with everything from socks to rockets.' But, like many, he was philosophical about Iranian interference. 'Unlike the US and the UK, Iran invested better. They knew where to pump their money, into militias and political parties. If a war happens, they can take over Basra without even sending their soldiers. They are fighting a war of attrition with the US and UK, bleeding them slowly. We arrest Iranian spies and intelligence networks, but they are not spying on the Kalashnikovs of the Iraqi army – they are here to gather intelligence on the coalition forces.'

Sayed Youssif was sceptical of the allegations against Iran. 'We Iraqis fought Iran on behalf of America for eight years, but I won't fight America on behalf of Iran,' he said. But others cite evidence of Iranian influence being used to pursue less strategic aims. A businessman in Basra, who regularly imports soft drinks from Iran, told me he once had a dispute with his supplier in Iran over price. When he refused to pay, gunmen from a pro-Iranian militia stormed his shop and kidnapped him. He was only released after paying all of what he owed to the Iranian dealer.

Nasaif Jassem, a city councillor for the Fadhila party, which controls the governorship and the oil industry in Basra, was critical of Iranian interference. Fadhila, widely seen as backed by the British, split from the main Shia alliance in Baghdad after accusing it of having a sectarian agenda.

'This British occupation will go, but the other occupation, that of Iran, will stay for a long time,' he said. 'They want to have an agent in Iraq that they can move every time they want, just like Hizbullah in Lebanon.'

Fear of the Iranians runs through the city. I saw it in the offices of the general as we sat there late one night. His two mobile phones had rung, each with someone asking for a wrong number. The general's face turned pale and he said: 'They have located me – the militia control all the transmission towers for the mobile network and now they have located my position.'

Were 'they' the Iranians or a militia? I asked.

'They are all the same.'

He called on his guards to send more men outside. 'Do you think I or the British commander can walk freely in Basra?' he asked. 'No is the answer, but the Iranian chargé d'affaires runs around freely.'

MAY 21 2007

The day Argentina knew the war was lost

JOHN SHIRLEY

Twenty-five years ago today the British won the Falklands war. Argentina did not surrender for another three weeks, but by nightfall on what the military called D-Day, 3,000 Royal Marines and paratroopers had scrambled ashore at the little farm hamlets around San Carlos Water on East Falkland and the game was up. They were still 90 miles from Stanley, but privately Argentinian commanders conceded that once the taskforce had secured the bridgehead, they could not be defeated.

Not that it seemed like that at the time. It was a perilous operation. The textbooks say that for an amphibious operation an army should have secure lifelines, air superiority and a troop advantage ratio of 3 to 1. British forces were about to mount the biggest amphibious landing since Suez, 8,000 miles from home, with limited air cover and no missile defence shield. Nor did the numbers match up: the enemy, well dug-in, was estimated at 11,000 men. As Brigadier Julian Thompson – the head of 3 Commando Brigade and the architect of the land campaign – told his unit commanders: 'This will be no picnic.'

Now, in the early morning darkness, hundreds of men, their faces black with camouflage cream, their helmets flecked with tufts of gorse, scrambled silently down into the landing craft for a hazardous hour-long journey to three beaches. Then what Brigadier Thompson called the Fanning Head Mob opened up. This was a detachment of 60 Argentinian soldiers dug-in on a headland above the bay. Rod Bell, a Spanish-speaking Royal Marine officer, had gone ashore with a loudhailer in an effort to persuade them to surrender. The sharp, excited chatter of machine-gun fire was their response.

Daybreak brought waves of Argentinian fighter jets. They screamed in off the sea in more than 60 sorties that day alone, strafing and shelling the British flotilla and knocking out three warships. Nothing seemed to deter them; they flew so low you could see their faces. Over the next few days San Carlos Water acquired a new nickname: Bomb Alley.

The best news of the day came in mid-afternoon: the 450 men

of 42 Commando – the Royal Marine unit with whom I was embedded – were going ashore. Among the commandos all was suddenly excitement and anticipation. Weapons were distributed; grenades, mortar bombs and ammunition handed out. Camouflage was adjusted and soon we were jumping into the landing craft.

The journey was quietly apprehensive. Helicopters clattered overhead carrying Rapier missile batteries and other stores ashore. Men talked lightly among themselves. Last cigarettes were handed out. I was struck by how little hostility anyone showed towards the Argentinians; they were the opposition, not the enemy. As we drew closer in, the landscape engulfed us, looking disarmingly like Dartmoor-by-the-Sea, all peaty slopes and granite outcrops. We synchronised our watches, earplugs were handed out, men instinctively cocked their rifles. Quite suddenly, the landing craft touched bottom, the ramp went down and we waded ashore, water lapping round our knees. This was not the Normandy beaches, but it was our first landfall for six weeks and it was a relief to be out of Bomb Alley.

An hour or so later I met my first Falkland islander, an elderly farm labourer stooping forward with an offering of soup in a Silver Jubilee mug.

'You a reporter?' he inquired. 'Tell me, did Leeds United get relegated?'

John Shirley covered the Falklands for the Sunday Times.

MAY 25 – JUNE 4 2007   GUARDIAN UNLIMITED

The Hay relay story: ten writers, ten chapters, one story

CHAPTER ONE
BY BERYL BAINBRIDGE

George was drumming his fingers on the tabletop. As usual, he was tired. They had been to an early mass that morning and spent the rest of the day walking round the street markets. He said, 'We really ought to go now. It's getting on for midnight,' and half rose to his feet. Maria took no notice; she had turned sideways in her chair and was scrutinising the couple seated beside the potted palm tree. The yellow-haired girl was staring sulkily down at her plate, her fork stabbing at the food as though to inflict punishment. Her escort had his elbows on the table and a gold cigarette case beside his crumpled napkin.

George leaned forward and prodded Maria on the shoulder. 'Don't stare,' he hissed. 'They deserve privacy.'

'If they didn't want to be seen,' Maria said, 'they would have stayed at home.'

Suddenly the girl pushed back her chair and left the table. The man, pocketing his cigarette case, hastily followed.

'Probably your fault,' George said.

'They didn't notice me,' Maria snapped. 'They were too busy having a row.'

When they went out into the lobby, the fair-haired girl was nowhere to be seen. Her companion was talking to a fat man in a dark-blue suit who was standing in the corridor leading to the back entrance of the hotel; he was wiping his mouth on his sleeve.

CHAPTER TWO
BY ROSE TREMAIN

'Did you see that?' said Maria, as she and George stepped out into the hotel garden. 'The fat guy was wearing a designer suit. Kenzo, I'd guess. But he was using the sleeve like a handkerchief. To wipe away what? Lipstick?'

'God knows,' said George. 'Who cares, anyway? I wish you'd leave people's lives alone.'

Maria and George walked along a decking pathway to the beach. They did this every night: they went and stared at the sea, before returning to their room. It was a moment which George savoured; it seemed to be the only time in their day when Maria stopped pointing things out to him, when she wasn't staring and commenting and criticising.

He looked at her now, in the near darkness, standing very still, with her arms folded across her breasts, wisps of her dark hair lifted by the onshore breeze. She was still beautiful. Or almost-beautiful. She was what people called a 'fine-looking woman'. But George knew how completely indifferent to her he had become. The truth was, she wearied him. Though he should have been happy to be here, in this expensive, exclusive place, he was not. He would have preferred to be in his office in London – with Maria miles away from him, on the other side of the city, writing her ridiculous books in her garish, untidy room.

CHAPTER THREE
BY THOMAS KENEALLY

But because this was such a 'special treat' hotel, George felt bound to make uxorious gestures as he and Maria returned to the hotel, taking her by the soft and still firm flesh beneath her elbow as they went up the stairs. How edgy and cowardly he felt. When they were younger a weekend in a hotel was a catalyst for hectic and unreflecting love. Now the possibility that he might be expected to make an erotic overture made him edgy. When did sleep replace sex as the ultimate currency of contentment?

'Watch the stairs,' he advised her as they entered the hotel, as if a woman of her age and vigour needed such advice.

They crossed the now familiar lobby. A poster of a couple smiling over a table laden with langouste and wine seemed almost a provocation to the satiated feeling which made his abdomen uncomfortably tight.

'Perhaps the lift,' he said, 'rather than the stairs.' If he continued to imply she was older then she was, he could avoid any expectation she might have.

'The stairs wouldn't hurt you,' she said. But she consented to the lift by approaching it. He leaned past her to press the button. They heard the whirring of the mechanism. The door opened. The fat man in the suit and the blonde girl looked out at them as if amazed to find the lift was in any way communal. The girl's features were distorted – swollen yet not bruised.

'You aren't a doctor, are you?' asked the fat man in a panic. 'My client is having an allergic attack.'

CHAPTER FOUR
BY DAVE EGGERS

George was a doctor. But not a good doctor. He was, in fact, a terrible doctor. And witnessing this girl in peril, he had the impulse, as he had in every such circumstance, to pretend he knew nothing at all about medicine.

'My husband is a doctor!' Maria said, and he hated her for it. 'George, save this girl!'

And so it began. With the girl and the fat man looking hopefully on, George fumbled, he inspected, he sweated in the most porcine way. The girl's face was puffy, turning a beautiful olive green, but she was breathing regularly and her vitals were normal. He had absolutely no idea what was wrong with her. He briefly considered telling her it was ebola and thus hopeless, when his helpful wife, God damn her, interceded again.

CHAPTER FIVE
BY LOUISA WAUGH

'You step back, darling,' she hissed, and fished something small out of her clutch bag. She wielded this thing between her cruelly manicured thumb, index and middle fingers. It was a slender yellow vial. When George didn't shift quickly enough, Maria stabbed him in his side with her elbow.

'Move.'

Snapping the top off the vial, she leaned over the olive-green girl, opened her mouth and dripped bright drops of liquid onto her tongue. No one moved. They all waited to see what was going to happen now. The fat man seemed to stop breathing. Rubbing his aching side, George found himself wondering if the fat man would inflate unless he exhaled.

'Aaah,' the girl made a long gentle whistling noise as her eyes opened. The fat man threw his arms round Maria.

'What was it?' he demanded, staring at Maria.

'Rescue Remedy,' she purred. 'You never know when you'll need it.'

George cringed. Bloody hippy juice. The fat man, who strangely hadn't looked at the girl since she came round, smiled dumbly.

'I am a very wealthy man,' he said to Maria slowly, as though English was not his first language. 'I will buy you anything you want. Anything.'

Maria's eyes glinted.

'Well, there is one small thing I'd love: but it won't be easy ... '

CHAPTER SIX
BY BLAKE MORRISON

'That was so embarrassing,' George said, unbuttoning his shirt. Next to the wardrobe hung a spectacularly inept painting of a beach at sunset. Why were hotel rooms always furnished with bad art?

'It was meant to be embarrassing,' Maria called through. 'Such an odious man. Did you notice how he referred to the poor girl? "My client," Hah!'

Waves broke gently in the distance. From the bathroom came the flurry of Maria unzipping her skirt, running water, brushing her teeth. As always, her energy exhausted him.

'But a graveyard plot – what a thing to ask for,' he said.

'He did say anything – and no one's been buried in St Botolph's for a hundred years.'

'He thought you were bonkers. You frightened him.'

'He's frightened because I've rumbled him. He knows I know he's a pimp.'

'Anyway,' George said, pretending not to hear (Maria's lurid fantasies were always best ignored), 'what do you want a grave for at your age?'

'I was always told to plan ahead,' she said, suddenly naked beside him. She stroked his hair a moment before slipping between the sheets. 'Come to bed, darling. All this talk of graves makes me feel sexy.'

He touched his brow where her fingers had been. It felt cold and clammy, like freshly turned soil.

'A man offers you the earth,' he said. 'And you ask for your own burial plot.'

'What makes you think it's for me?' she said, reaching for his hand.

CHAPTER SEVEN
BY AL KENNEDY

George has tried his best. It was so unusual for Maria to display any erotic enthusiasm that he had briefly found himself carried hotly along through the process of slipping off his comfortable suede shoes, his even more comfortable flannel shirt and his even, even more – well, his trousers were a simple admission of defeat, of being a man who had moved beyond valuing his comfort and become someone like his father – sheepish, paunchy, soft.

He hadn't, of course, assisted in the unveiling of Maria. Her underthings were disappointingly substantial these days and the way she looked at him, particularly if he was anywhere near naked, tended to end their evening before it began.

But this time he genuinely had made a valiant attempt, picturing – only for a guilty breath – the mystery, racy blonde while attempting to be satisfying, thrusting, the ghost of himself before the suede, the corduroy and the general beige had descended to wither his soul. He had murmured references to mortality in the hope that they might inflame her, 'I bet you'll have a lovely head-stone – very striking. After me, naturally. I'll die first.' He'd heard himself volunteering. 'Will you come to the funeral? Will you, er ... ' His body, stuttering to a halt, derailed his realisation that he couldn't imagine her devastated or even mildly perturbed by his loss.

Now he started bleakly at the shadowed ceiling above them, Maria's sleeping breath hissing coolly by his neck. And what was that other noise?

Sounded like weeping. Sounded like a woman weeping out in

the hallway. Sounded like the kind of distress that required a response.

CHAPTER EIGHT
BY DEBORAH MOGGACH

Maria had fallen asleep. Her leg lay heavily against his thigh. It must be exhausting work, making him look a fool. She'd had plenty of practice, over the years. George could still recall the prickling sense of recognition when he had read the manuscript of her first novel and encountered Harry, the bumbling, alcoholic GP with contemptuous teenage children and a strong, capable wife.

Maria would whip on her dressing gown and go to investigate. The sound had stopped but there was somebody out there in the corridor, he could sense them holding their breath.

Fuck it. George removed his wife's leg and climbed out of bed. He would show her! He walked across the room and opened the door.

The corridor was empty. He stepped out. His bare feet sank into the carpet. It was sopping wet.

At that moment he realised that he was not alone. At the end of the passage a man stood, gazing at the grandfather clock as if expecting it to chime. It was the man they had seen that first night, eating dinner with the girl. He looked as if he had slept in that linen suit. George walked up to him.

He turned. 'Help at last,' he said. 'You look fit.'

George was absurdly flattered. 'Think so? My wife says –'

'We'd better get started,' said the man. 'I want to get it done before the dogs arrive.'

CHAPTER NINE
BY TOBY LITT

'And which dogs, exactly, would those be?' asked George.

'You know,' said the man in the linen suit. 'Of course you know. We all do. The hounds. Now, help me move this. We don't have much time.'

Away down the corridor, the female sobbing started up again.

'What's that?'

'It's her,' said the man. 'Now, lift.'

George took one side of the grandfather clock and the man took the other. They were about to pick it up when the chimes began to strike. Somehow, although the clock was only a clock, it seemed rude to move it whilst it did what it did – a bit like trying to drag along a dog that's paused to take a crap. They waited as the clock struck 12 times.

'Now, towards me,' said the man.

They braced themselves, lifted the clock off the floor.

'But who is she?' George asked, realising only now that she – whoever she was – should have been his first priority, not furniture removal. Hippocratic oath and all that.

'The client,' said the man. 'For the hounds.'

They shifted the clock a few feet to the side – revealing, in the wall now exposed, a wide door of shiny black wood. A silver keyhole was inset, on the left hand side.

George wasn't absolutely sure, but he thought he could hear barking coming from somewhere – distant, wild barking.

Just then, a voice spoke up behind them. George knew without looking – it was the fat man with the foreign accent.

'Here is the key,' the fat man said. 'Get it open,' he said. 'Quickly.'

'Yes, Master,' said the linen-suit man, taking between his fingers a small, ornate silver key.

The fat man stepped back, wiping his mouth on the sleeve of his Kenzo suit.

The barking was getting louder, wilder. George realised, with horror, that it was coming from behind the door.

'Your meddling wife saved her earlier,' the fat man said. 'But not this time. This time we have the hounds.'

The woman's crying became screaming – perhaps she could hear the barking.

'But I don't understand,' said George.

The linen man turned the key in the door.

Hardly had he opened it before the hounds burst through, a dozen of them at least. They bounded down the hotel corridor, white, muscular, baying – but then came to an abrupt halt. Someone was blocking their way.

It was Maria, and she held in her hand what looked like another vial of the Rescue Remedy.

'Back!' she commanded, and the dogs cowered away, whimpering. 'You will not have her!'

'Shit!' said the fat man. 'How much holy water that bitch carries?'

George took this as a question for him.

'How should I know?' he said. 'I never even knew she carried any.'

The fat man walked towards Maria. 'Who you think you are,' he asked, 'Buffy?'

CHAPTER TEN
BY MARINA LEWYCKA

Maria didn't say anything. Her eyes were fixed on the dogs. She was gazing intently, making little murmuring noises from her throat. One by one, the great beasts sank onto their haunches on the sodden carpet. They stretched out their paws, panting and rolling their eyes as if surprised by their own obedience. Then, to George's amazement, the fat man seemed to buckle at the knees, flopping down beside them. This was odd, thought George. He's going to get rather wet. The linen suit, he noticed, was not linen at all, but a coarse, shaggy fabric that looked as though it had been woven from spun dogs' hair. He was licking the sleeves and whimpering as he stared up at Maria with imploring doggy eyes.

George found himself whimpering too. In the uncertain light of the corridor, she looked pale, almost ethereal. Her brows were knotted in a frown, beads of sweat glistened on her upper lip. She was trembling, George realised, from the effort of concentration as she held the vial out in front of her. He had not seen her look so vulnerable, so appealingly fragile, and yet so in command – well, not since last time.

A warm throb started up below his paunch. The sheepish softness swelled in his trousers. At last.

Without taking her eyes off the dogs, Maria murmured, 'George, darling. Turn the bath taps off. Do it now.'

In an intimate corner of the quiet coach on the 17.23, snaking back towards Paddington, Maria's head slips a little further down on George's shoulder and his hand slides a little further inside her dress. An empty vial of Rescue Remedy rolls off the seat beside them onto the floor.

'That was wonderful, darling. We should do it more often.'

'Mmm. Yes. Pity about the blonde, though.'

'Couldn't be helped.'

Summer

Living with teenagers: Eddie's girl

ANONYMOUS

Sunday morning and there's a girl in Eddie's room. Jack saw her first.

'I went in there to get the PSP and I just saw this long blond hair all over the floor,' he says in the awed voice he usually reserves for reporting football scores. 'I don't know who she is, but she's well buff.'

'She's not in his bed?' checks his father.

I can see him trying to decide what to feel. Eddie's had people in his bed before – not girlfriends exactly, just people, male and female, who drift back from parties in the small hours and doss down like so many sardines.

We don't like it very much. It's not so much that we're worried about the possibility of sex – though our children, of course, love to tell us that we are – it's more the disorganised casualness that depresses us, the fact that they never get up and when they do, they wander round the house half-dressed and unable to utter enunciated words. In some ways, it's the very sexlessness of these sleepovers that seems so odd. Do none of them want the fun and emotional satisfaction that one-on-one brings?

But this is different. This morning I noticed that a bottom sheet, duvet cover and pillowcase had disappeared from the shelf on the landing. I have never known Eddie make up a bed for someone in his life. Not even himself.

'And a towel!' exclaims Becca. 'There's a towel in the bathroom and some contact lens stuff. She must have washed her face.'

This really is rare. None of Eddie's friends wash.

'She really is quite buff,' says Jack again. 'It's weird. I mean, I just can't believe she'd go out with Eddie.'

'She probably isn't,' Becca decides. 'I mean, not "out".'

'Hey,' I say. 'Hold on a moment, guys, that's not quite fair. Eddie's very good-looking and he's lovely when he wants to be.'

'Are you his mum by any chance?' says their father.

Eddie's never really had a girlfriend. He knows plenty of girls and has girls as friends. And I think he's had sex. In fact, I'm pretty sure he has. We've found condoms in his pocket and just been glad he's using something. But he's never, to my knowledge, met up with a particular girl, for a date or anything. I'm never sure if this should bother me. At his age, I was nowhere near having sex, but I was high on the romance, the uncertainty, the sheer poetry of knowing boys. Sometimes I worry that Eddie will never have this.

'He's not a girl,' his father points out when I sporadically express this worry. 'Don't expect him to be like you were in 1978.'

At about 11.30am the girl comes downstairs, closely followed by Eddie. We all try not to stare. Eddie is never up before lunchtime on Sundays.

'Hi,' smiles the girl.

'This is Sarah,' says Eddie gruffly.

'Hi, Sarah,' we all say, trying not to speak in unison.

Sarah is nicely dressed in skinny jeans and a white smock thing. Cowboy boots. A pretty smile. Dimples. I see Becca quickly clocking the details.

Eddie is also dressed. Unheard of for a Sunday morning. He flips on the kettle.

'There's some real coffee on the stove, if you want it,' I say, trying not to sound too eager or too much as if I want to invite Sarah to move in and have my grandchildren.

'Sit down.' Their father hastily shuffles chairs to make a space for Sarah. You can see Jack wishing he wasn't wearing a dressing gown over his T-shirt and tracksuit bottoms.

'Hope you don't mind that I stayed over?' Sarah says. 'But the last bus had already gone.'

'Of course, we don't mind,' I tell her warmly. 'We wouldn't want you going home on a night bus.'

'What time did you come in?' their father asks.

Ed grunts and Sarah laughs, as if she already knows what he's like. Now I'm with Becca. She probably isn't his girlfriend. Yet. I mustn't rush things. I mustn't like her too much.

We ask her if she goes to Ed's school? She does. Year below him. What AS-levels is she doing? English, French, Drama and History. She wants to do History of Art, maybe at Edinburgh.

'Ed isn't going to university,' Becca announces and Ed shoots her a look.

'I haven't decided,' he mutters. 'I'm still thinking. I may apply this month, actually.'

His father and I try not to exchange too excited a glance.

Eddie pours out coffee for Sarah and – another first – offers us some. Then he looks at his watch. 'We need to get on,' he tells Sarah, 'if we're going to Tate Modern.'

I make sure not to look at Becca.

JUNE 6 2007

The legacy of 1967:
Israel cannot make peace alone

EHUD OLMERT
PRIME MINISTER OF ISRAEL

Six days, 40 years ago. Looking back to the weeks preceding the war, it may be difficult for you to imagine just how desperate life seemed for Israelis, ringed by peoples whose armies pointed their weapons towards us, whose leaders daily promised the imminent destruction of our state and whose newspapers carried crude cartoons of Jews being kicked off the face of the earth. As we consecrated mass graves in expectation of the worst, we were once again people facing annihilation. We had no alternative but to defend ourselves, no strategic allies to ensure our survival. We stood alone.

Our victory in those six days in June 1967 – swift, complete and totally unexpected – showed us and the world we were not going to be wiped off the map that easily. Israel fought an unwanted war to defend her very existence, and today there are still leaders who call for Israel to be wiped off the map. But there is a danger that that will be forgotten, overtaken by a re-reading of history. Our survival in 1967 is now – in the eyes of the world and, with worrying consequences in the United Kingdom – the Original Sin of the Israeli–Palestinian conflict. Our opponents argue against the ongoing 'occupation' as if it were the Gordian knot of the conflict. If only we were to leave the territories the conflict would end. And they threaten international isolation if we do not.

If only the conflict were so simple; if only the answer were so simple. Over the last 15 years successive Israeli governments have initiated talks with the Palestinians in every conceivable permutation in an attempt to reach a settlement. In the 1990s Israel withdrew from all the Palestinian cities in the West Bank, handing its affairs over to a Palestinian Authority. Nearly two years ago Israel withdrew its troops and civilians from Gaza, with no preconditions. Last year my Kadima party came to power on an agenda promising further withdrawals. In the face of concessions that have threatened our own domestic consensus, the constant refrain has been the Palestinian refusal to end its violent attacks on our citizens.

Palestinian violence is not a response to the capture of the West Bank and Gaza. Palestinian nationalism's roots are not so shallow. From the emergence of the Zionist movement over a hundred years ago, Arabs have opposed our claim to independence on our historic homeland, often violently. Our conflict is not territorial, it is national.

The only way we can resolve the conflict is by establishing secure and recognised boundaries for the peoples of the region. It was on that basis we were able to conclude a peace treaty with Egypt, exchanging land for a peace that has endured for nearly 30 years. We did the same with Jordan. It is on the same basis that we will, I hope, be able to resolve our conflict with the Palestinians, with two peoples living in two states. Jerusalem, our eternal capital, can then be a city that represents peace rather than discord, a city for all its residents that does not distinguish between race, religion or class. Those are the principles that I myself implemented as mayor of the city for 10 years.

As a young politician I voted against the return of Sinai and peace with Egypt. I was mistaken. We will not hesitate to take bold initiatives to advance peace, even if they require heavy concessions. The legacies of Menachem Begin and Anwar Sadat, of Yitzhak Rabin and King Hussein, stand as an inspiration for all who work for peace.

We need such political maturity from our Palestinian partners now if they are to stop the internecine fighting that is tearing apart their society, exposing our citizens to a daily barrage of deadly rocketfire and preventing any progress on peace talks. Israel will not tolerate violence against its citizens and my government will act decisively to protect them. But I also know that we will not resolve the crisis through military means alone. I will continue to meet Mahmoud Abbas and discuss ways in which the Palestinian Authority can fight against lawlessness and extremism, and urge him to control the violence emanating from Gaza.

In the wider Arab world there is ever greater recognition that Israel will not disappear from the map. I take the offer of full normalisation of relations between Israel and the Arab world seriously and I am ready to discuss the Arab peace initiative in an open and sincere manner. Working with our Jordanian and Egyptian partners, and hopefully other Arab states, we must pursue a comprehensive peace with energy and vision. I look forward to being able to discuss this with our other neighbours. But the talks must be a discussion, not an ultimatum.

Israel is prepared to make painful concessions to pay the price for a lasting and just peace that will allow the people of the Middle East to live in dignity and security. But as strong and resourceful as Israelis are, we cannot make peace alone.

JUNE 6 2007

The legacy of 1967:
our rights have to be recognised

ISMAIL HANIYEH
PRIME MINISTER OF THE
PALESTINIAN NATIONAL AUTHORITY[1]

When the Israeli leaders launched their expansionist war in June 1967 they never envisaged that 40 years later they would still be haunted by the consequences. At the time, they were driven by one strategic objective: to end the conflict by seizing all that remained of Palestine and complete the process of ethnic cleansing that started in 1948. They did not realise the resolution of this conflict would take much more than military superiority.

The occupation of the West Bank, the Gaza Strip, the Golan Heights and the Sinai peninsula was portrayed as the victory of David over Goliath. For the next two decades the Palestinian experience was drowned out by the clamour of Israeli hubris. The world paid little attention to the expropriation of Palestinian land, the apartheid regime established by the occupation and the systematic destruction of Palestinian livelihoods.

It was only in 1987 that the world awoke to the reality of a popular Palestinian uprising – *intifada*. A new generation had come of age, thirsty for freedom and peace with dignity in their own land. The two decades since have confirmed that my people will not repeat the mistakes of 1948. They will remain rooted in their land, whatever the price, and pursue their legitimate right to resist the

1 He was dismissed from office on June 14 2007 by President Abbas. [Ed.]

occupation. That right is supported by, for example, UN Resolutions 2955 and 3034, which affirm the 'inalienable' right of all peoples to self-determination and the legitimacy of their struggle against foreign domination and subjugation 'by all available means'.

Israel's fateful error was to underestimate the resolve of the Palestinians. Tens of thousands have been killed or wounded by the Israeli army since 1967. During 2006 the number of Palestinians killed reached 650. Since the beginning of the Israeli occupation in 1967 more than 650,000 Palestinians have been detained by Israel – about 40 per cent of the male population. Today three-quarters of the Palestinian people are displaced: there are 5 million Palestinian refugees throughout the world.

With the signing of the Oslo accords in 1993 we were told that things would get better. But life became more hellish as Israel accelerated settlement building and seizures of our land. Meanwhile, the world was fed the fallacy that Israel was defending its 'threatened existence'. In reality, it is Israel, through the prosecution of colonial war, that has threatened the Palestinians' right to live in their land. And when they were most needed, the world's most powerful states refused to ensure respect for the international law that 'the acquisition of territory by force is inadmissible'.

In contempt of the will of the international community, Israel continues to build its annexationist apartheid wall across the West Bank. Which western state would, in the 21st century, accept that its citizens be literally caged and locked into cantons?

Undaunted by repression, my people have embraced democracy as a means of struggle and governance. Yet in response, the world's most powerful democracies have imposed an economic blockade against my people, while Israel continues to kill, expropriate and destroy with impunity. The humanitarian catastrophe in the occupied West Bank and Gaza is clearly designed to subvert the elected government and create a client authority that concedes every wish of the occupier. There can be no exit from the impasse without sanctions being lifted and Israel's release of the hundreds of millions of dollars of our money it has seized.

In the 1967 war Israel conquered the land of Palestine, but it did not conquer the people. And in its attempt to debase and dehumanise my people, Israel has debased and degraded itself before the family of nations. The 1967 war has over 40 years engendered successive wars and destabilisation of the Middle East. The increasing mistrust between the Arab-Muslim peoples and the western world is rooted in the conflict in Palestine.

The first step to change this catastrophic climate is for the west to engage with the Palestinian National Unity government, which envisages the establishment of an independent state on all the Palestinian land occupied by Israel in 1967, the dismantling of all the settlements in the West Bank, the release of all 11,000 Palestinian prisoners in Israeli jails and the recognition of the right of all Palestinian refugees to return to their homes. If Israel is serious about peace, it has to recognise these basic rights of our people. The 1967 war remains an unfinished chapter. Nothing will stop our struggle for freedom and to have all our children reunited in a fully sovereign state of Palestine, with Jerusalem as its capital.

JUNE 7 2007

BAE accused

DAVID LEIGH AND ROB EVANS

The arms company BAE secretly paid Prince Bandar of Saudi Arabia more than £1bn in connection with Britain's biggest-ever weapons contract, it is alleged today. A series of payments from the British firm was allegedly channelled through a US bank in Washington to an account controlled by one of the most colourful members of the Saudi ruling clan, who spent 20 years as their ambassador in the United States.

It is claimed that payments of £30m were paid to Prince Bandar every quarter for at least 10 years. It is alleged by insider legal sources that the money was paid to Prince Bandar with the knowledge and authorisation of Ministry of Defence officials under the Blair government and its predecessors. For more than 20 years ministers have claimed they knew nothing of secret commissions, which were outlawed by Britain in 2002. An inquiry by the Serious Fraud Office (SFO) into the transactions behind the £43bn Al-Yamamah arms deal, which was signed in 1985, is understood to have uncovered details of the payments to Prince Bandar. But the investigation was halted last December by the SFO after a review by the attorney general, Lord Goldsmith.

He said it was in Britain's national interest to halt the investigation, and that there was little prospect of achieving convictions. Tony Blair said he took 'full responsibility' for the decision. However, according to those familiar with the discussions at the time, Lord Goldsmith had warned colleagues that British 'government complicity' was in danger of being revealed unless the SFO's corruption inquiries were stopped.

The abandonment of the investigation provoked an outcry from anti-corruption campaigners and led to the world's official bribery watchdog, the Organisation for Economic Cooperation and Development, launching its own investigation. The fresh allegations may also cause BAE problems in America, where corrupt payments to foreign politicians have been outlawed since 1977.

The allegations of payments to Prince Bandar is bound to ignite fresh controversy over the original deal and the aborted

SFO investigation. The Saudi diplomat is known to have played a key role with Mrs Thatcher in setting up Britain's largest series of weapons deals. For more than 20 years Al-Yamamah – Arabic for 'dove' – has involved the sale of 120 Tornado aircraft, Hawk warplanes and other military equipment. According to legal sources familiar with the records, BAE Systems made cash transfers to Prince Bandar every three months for 10 years or more.

BAE drew the money from a confidential account held at the Bank of England that had been set up to facilitate the Al-Yamamah deal. Up to £2bn a year was deposited in the accounts as part of a complex arrangement allowing Saudi oil to be sold in return for shipments of Tornado aircraft and other arms. Both BAE and the government's arms sales department – the Defence Export Services Organisation (Deso) – allegedly had drawing rights on the funds, which were held in a special Ministry of Defence account run by the government banker, the paymaster general.

Those close to Deso say regular payments were drawn down by BAE and despatched to Prince Bandar's account at Riggs bank in Washington DC. Under the terms of a previously unknown MoD instruction from the department's permanent secretary, Sir Frank Cooper, the payment deal would have required Deso authorisation. The money was not characterised as commission, but as quasi-official fees for marketing services. The payments are alleged to have continued for at least 10 years and beyond 2002, when Britain outlawed corrupt payments to overseas officials.

SFO investigators led by the assistant director Helen Garlick first stumbled on the alleged payments, according to legal sources, when they unearthed highly classified documents at the MoD during their three-year investigation. Before the investigation was abandoned, the SFO interviewed Alan Garwood, head of Deso. Sources close to the arms sales unit say that he and Stephen Pollard, the commercial director of the Saudi project, were questioned about the reasons for authorising the payments.

Prince Bandar, currently head of the country's national security council, was asked about the alleged payments by the *Guardian* this week.

He did not respond.

BAE Systems also would not explain the alleged payments. The company said: 'Your approach is in common with that of the least responsible elements of the media – that is to assume BAE Systems's guilt in complete ignorance of the facts.' Its spokesman, John Neilson, added: 'We have little doubt that among the reasons the attorney general considered the case was doomed was the fact that we acted in accordance with ... the relevant contracts, with the approval of the government of Saudi Arabia, together with, where relevant, that of the UK MoD.'

The attorney general's office would not discuss claims about Lord Goldsmith's concerns of 'government complicity' in the payments. A spokesman said the SFO inquiry had been halted because of the 'real and serious threat to national security'. 'There were major legal difficulties ... given BAE's claim that the payments were made in accordance with the agreed contractual arrangements.' The spokesman added: 'None of this is altered by the *Guardian* story.'

The MoD – where the minister Paul Drayson runs Britain's government arms sales unit – also refused to elaborate. 'The MoD is unable to respond to the points made,' said a spokesman, 'since to do so would involve disclosing confidential information about Al-Yamamah, and that would cause the damage that ending the investigation was designed to prevent.'

The Liberal Democrat deputy leader, Vince Cable, called for an urgent inquiry into the new disclosures last night. 'This is potentially more significant and damaging than anything previously revealed,' he said. 'It is unforgivable if the British government has been actively conniving in under-the-counter payments to a major figure in the Saudi government. There must be a full parliamentary inquiry into whether the government has deceived the public and undermined the anti-corruption legislation which it itself passed through parliament.' He added: 'It increasingly looks as if the motives behind the decision to pull the SFO inquiry were less to do with UK national interests, but more to do with the personal interests of one or two powerful Saudi ministers ... Tony Blair's claims that the government has been motivated by national security considerations look increasingly hollow.'

Last month, Dr Cable raised the issue of BAE in the Commons and accused Prince Bandar of benefiting personally from the Al-Yamamah deal. The new disclosures may also make BAE's attempted takeover of the US-based Armor Holdings more difficult. The deal requires approval from US regulators. Separately, the state department has protested to the Foreign Office about the ending of the SFO inquiry, saying it undermines global efforts to stamp out corruption by exporters.

JUNE 11 2007

The first sparks of greatness

RICHARD WILLIAMS

Lewis Hamilton may not be the youngest driver to win a formula one race, but his victory in yesterday's Canadian Grand Prix will take its place among the most remarkable achievements in the history of the sport. As the first driver whose approach to the job comes close to matching the sophistication of his machine, he has single-handedly raised the stakes for his own generation and those to come.

No one has ever made the business of driving a formula one car look so easy. Yesterday he gave a performance of flawless composure in the most demanding of circumstances, controlling an afternoon in which the disruption caused by four safety-car interludes in effect meant that he had to win the race five times over. Like such great champions as Juan Manuel Fangio and Jim Clark, in whose tyre tracks he appears destined to follow, he has clearly decided that the least problematic way to win a race is from the front.

Yet although the word 'robotic' has been used more than once to describe the qualities of a young man who made his Grand Prix debut after a training period that included thousands of hours in the McLaren team's unique and highly secret simulator, the remarkable thing about Hamilton is that, like all his truly great predecessors, he drives with emotion. And that, more than his natural eloquence, his good looks or the colour of his skin is what makes him such a compelling figure.

In an era when bored onlookers often comment that the cars seem to be going around as if on rails, Hamilton has already proved he is capable of getting the spectator's pulse racing. He is not afraid to let his car slip and slide around corners, because he knows how to do it in a way that makes him go faster. And he is willing to take what looks to the outside world like a risk, although so fine are his calculations that it will not have resembled much of a risk to him.

He knows, for instance, that the opening seconds of a race offer the best chance to make up a precious place or two. The start is always a chaotic, complicated affair, emotions rising along with the engine revs. He profits from the momentary mistakes and hesitations of others as they head for the first corner, because he has run through every possible permutation of incident in advance and his calmness allows him to take advantage of rivals who are nearing boiling point.

Hamilton has been prepared for this and other aspects of the job with all the seriousness and some of the specific training techniques brought to bear on astronauts and fighter pilots. But however scientific the approach may be, nothing has managed to diminish the competitive aggression and the sheer enjoyment apparent each time he leaves the pits and goes to work.

All formula one drivers operate from a basic level of competence that few can comprehend, never mind reach. At any given time, after all, there are only 22 of them in the whole world. Within that gifted circle, however, what differentiates the very best from the also-rans is an ability to understand the complexity of what they are doing and to maximise the improvement of every tiny detail. These days what they need to know about tyre behaviour alone, and its effects on the rest of the car, would fill a book.

Hamilton is one of the very few who have mastered the technical side of the game without allowing it to compromise the qualities that illuminated the driving of the greatest champions. In this respect, as in one or two others, he resembles Tiger Woods, whose ferocious appetite for technical improvement in the hugely sophisticated environment of contemporary sport has not turned him into a soulless machine.

And the rewards, too, could one day be measured alongside those enjoyed by Woods. Hamilton may be earning no more than £600,000 this season (compared to Kimi Raikkonen's £20m), but already it is being suggested that he will become the first £50m-a-year driver, not including the endorsements that his looks and his personality will inevitably attract. His father, Anthony, who manages his affairs, has been taking his time over selecting an agent to make the most of such possibilities, another indication of the measured wisdom with which Hamilton's career is being conducted.

Was he lucky when he caught the attention of Ron Dennis, the McLaren team's boss, at such an early age? If there was ever an example of making your own luck, this was it. Hamilton's self-confidence in making the first approach was matched by Dennis's recognition of some quality that made the Stevenage schoolboy stand out from among the countless numbers of would-be formula one stars. As Grand Prix racing is not a philanthropic endeavour, Dennis is unlikely to have been influenced solely by the possibility of nurturing the sport's first driver of mixed race.

Their relationship has been among the keys to Hamilton's success. Dennis is a cautious, conservative, emotionally contained man who values hard work, intellectual rigour and loyalty, so his protege had to prove with every step that he was worthy of further promotion, demonstrating his diligence and commitment throughout a relationship that is coming up to its 10th year.

In return Dennis put at Hamilton's disposal the greatest learning tool that any driver has ever been given. McLaren's simulator – developed over the past eight years at a cost estimated to be above £20m – has been Hamilton's schoolroom, where he sits in a full-size formula one car, minus wheels and a functioning engine, in a darkened room in front of a large, curved plasma screen. The chassis is suspended on a multi-point hydraulic rig which moves in response to his touches on the steering wheel and pedals as he watches a circuit unfold on the screen, with appropriate sound effects.

Everything in this grown-up video game is programmed via the simulator's software: the minutest details of the circuit, the response of the engine under different conditions, the type and wear-rate of the tyres, as well as the noise of the engine. No wonder that when Hamilton arrived in Melbourne at the start of the season, on his first visit to Australia, he took to the Albert

Park track as if he had been driving there for half his life. In a sense, he had.

Dennis also introduced him to Dr Kerry Spackman, the New Zealand-born neuroscientist who has worked with him in and out of the simulator on developing his psychological responses and increasing his brain's ability to absorb, analyse, store and recall information. The brain is an instrument whose properties are only just being understood – scientists studying the effects of strokes, for example, are discovering that the right exercises can enable it to develop new circuits to replace those damaged or destroyed – and Spackman's use of virtual-reality techniques has enabled Hamilton to exploit his natural talent even further by expanding his mental capacity. In a way, it is like adding an extra litre to his Mercedes engine.

Hamilton's predecessors in the McLaren team could have availed themselves of the same opportunities, but saw little point in it. Raikkonen, for instance, clearly felt that there was little to be learnt. Having seen the results, however, those who make fortunes from managing young drivers will be quick to copy the formula.

But Hamilton has something extra, and it is the quality that puts a shine in the eyes of men such as Niki Lauda, Sir Jackie Stewart and Sir Stirling Moss. Each of them welcomed his arrival with the kind of effusive and unguarded praise that is rare in an often cynical sport, and yesterday they were rewarded for their willingness to put their judgment on the line. From their privileged perspective they had perceived the essence of the matter, in all its glorious simplicity. His talent may have been refined by science, but Lewis Hamilton has the soul of a racer.

JUNE 16 2007

Down and dirty

AM HOMES

In order to talk about Jack Kerouac's unproduced play *Beat Generation* you have to put it into some sort of a cultural context – it was 1957, Eisenhower was president, Nixon vice-president, the Pulitzer prize in drama went to Eugene O'Neill's *Long Day's Journey into Night* and no fiction award was given. *West Side Story* opened on Broadway, the sitcom *Leave it to Beaver* premiered on television, and if you were going to the movies, chances are it was to see *The Bridge on the River Kwai, Twelve Angry Men* or *Peyton Place*. On the home front there was the struggle for racial integration in schools, while the Russians launched Sputnik I and the space age began. It was 1957, and Kerouac's *On the Road* was published – other books that year included Bernard Malamud's *The Assistant*, James Agee's *A Death in the Family* and Noam Chomsky's *Syntactic Structures*.

At this point, Kerouac and his band of scribes were all about embracing and celebrating the 'beat' life. Kerouac himself had coined the term, according to some accounts as early as 1948, suggesting societal conventions that were 'beat', 'tired', 'worn out'. Many have argued that the term 'beat generation' evolved from a post-war reference to Hemingway's 'Lost Generation' to become a more positive label: the Beats were enlightened, 'beatific' ones – a confluence of the Buddhist and Catholic philosophies that were so important to Kerouac.

In 1957 Kerouac wasn't yet what he is today – a figure as dominant in contemporary culture as the faces on Mount Rushmore. In 1957 he had the benefit of a certain anonymity – he was still, for the moment, the purest version of Jack Kerouac, not a personality, not a celebrity.

Unlike the Second World War vets who came home, got married, moved to suburbia and fully embraced the American dream and the blossoming culture of more, more, more, the beat life was lived on the edges. Beats had nothing to love and not far to fall. Holy men, meditators, anti-materialists, they were the exact opposites of 'company men'. Kerouac said his experimental fraternity aspired to something else – a kind of freedom. They wanted to soar, to fly, to move through time and space unfettered. They wanted to find spirituality and deliverance among the dispossessed. And they wanted to have a good time, win a few bucks on the horses, have some drinks and get laid. Compared with the average Joe they were wild – awe-inspiring and threatening.

Kerouac's style was not just philosophically bold; it was linguistic guerrilla warfare – a literary atom bomb smashing everything. On one side of him were the hyper-intellectual Beckett and Joyce. On the other, the anti-academic: Hemingway, Anderson and Dos Passos. Kerouac absorbed it all and went beyond.

In 2005 a line of Jack Kerouac clothing was about to be released and the manuscript of *On the Road* was on tour across America when, in a New Jersey warehouse, a 'new' play by Kerouac was discovered – three acts, written in 1957 and typed up by Kerouac's ever-loving mother, Gabrielle, also known as 'Memère'. The play had never been produced – at the time there was a lot of interest, but no action. In a letter, Kerouac described his interest in theatre and film in this way:

'What I want to do is re-do the theatre and the cinema in America, give it a spontaneous dash, remove preconceptions of "situation" and let people rave on as they do in real life. That's what the play is: no plot in particular, no "meaning" in particular, just the way people are. Everything I write I do in the spirit where

I imagine myself an Angel returned to earth seeing it with sad eyes as it is.'

The play is a wonderful addition to the Kerouac oeuvre. It will be great fun to see what happens with it – I can easily imagine it being performed and each staging being incredibly different from the last – it's all about what you bring to it. It is a play of its time – which is why context is important. In bits and pieces it is reminiscent of Tennessee Williams, Clifford Odets and a bit of Arthur Miller. But by comparison to those playwrights, whose work is formal and well defined, this play is loose, unfettered. It is about juxtaposition, relation, words and ideas bouncing off one another, riffing in a bebop scatter.

Beat Generation opens in the early morning in an apartment near the Bowery in New York, with drinking – the reverie of the first glass. It is a man's world: these working men, brakemen for the railroad, drinking men, whose day off is spent betting on horses, men who swear by saying 'durnit', men who have a girl waiting on them, warming their coffee – women's liberation never made it into Kerouac's world. It is set in a disappeared New York City with the smoky scent of cigarettes hanging over all, men playing chess, the racket of the elevated subways, the feel of life lived underground, everything a little bit beat. And *Beat Generation* is pervaded by the music of conversation.

Working in spurts, Kerouac spewed this 'spontaneous bop prosody' or 'jazz poetry'. The play (like the novels) is everything and the kitchen sink too. It is a kind of demolition derby pile-up, a jazzy musical of words picking up speed and hurling themselves forward in a bumper-car version of dialogue. *Beat Generation* is about talking and friendship and shooting the shit, it is about the biggest question of all – existence. Kerouac and his rough-hewn characters – just this side of hobos – want to know how and why we exist and then in some spontaneous combustion they come to know that, in the end, there are no answers, there is just the moment we are in and the people around us.

Here is the romance of the road, rebirth and karma – Kerouac's peculiar and deeply personal combination of the working man discussing astral bodies, karmic debt, past lives and the selling of Jesus. Here is the power of ideas and the difficulty of escaping belief. And here is the love of God and the fear of God – despite Kerouac's interest in the alternative, his exploration of Buddhism and eastern philosophies, he could never escape his Catholic upbringing.

Yet the play has a masculine swagger, a brand of bravado. Language and characters career off each other, in a kind of doped deliciousness, in which one feels the heat of an afternoon, the smell of hay and shit and beer at the racetrack, the greasy squeal of brakes and the kind of down-and-dirty that never really washes off.

Kerouac was the man who allowed writers to enter the world of flow: different from stream-of-consciousness, his philosophy was about being in the current, open to possibility, allowing creativity to move through you and you to be one with both process and content. It was about embracing experience rather than resisting; it was in fact the very Roman candle Kerouac writes about in *On the Road*.

On a more personal note – without Kerouac, without Jimi Hendrix, without Mark Rothko, there would be no one. I used to think Jack Kerouac was my father (sometimes literally) and Susan Sontag was my mother. I could draw one hell of a family tree, with Henry Miller and Eugene O'Neill as my uncles and so on. Kerouac raised me spiritually, psychologically, creatively – he gave me permission to exist.

Beat Generation is a treat, a sweet found under a sofa cushion. For those of us who never had enough Kerouac, now there is more.

JUNE 22 2007

Team Gordon

MICHAEL WHITE

Personally, I'm not sure how hard Gordon Brown had thought about it before he offered Paddy Ashdown that job as Northern Ireland secretary in the new cabinet. Admirable public servant though he is, Lord Ashdown can be quite exhausting. 'Action Man' was one nickname he acquired as an MP, but 'Tigger' was another. It is not true that he used to abseil into Lib Dem meetings through a closed window, three policy bullet points between his gritted teeth, but he was certainly in the habit of ringing up senior colleagues at all hours. Pre-dawn telephone raids were a favourite technique, probably drawn from his time in the Special Boat Service. The man is a trained killer. No wonder Charlie Kennedy took to drink.

But even allowing for all that, it is hard to imagine such an energetic 66-year-old, a former viceroy of Bosnia, too, confining himself to the Northern Ireland brief, especially now that Messrs Paisley, Adams and Co have taken an oath not to remember the past. With luck they won't leave much for Posh Paddy to do there. In which case, would Gordon have put up with his Northern Ireland secretary saying, 'Are you sure about staying out of the euro, prime minister?' or 'Before you announce your budget in half an hour, chancellor, may I suggest a few changes?' I think not.

But Brown is clearly on to something: a cabinet of all the talents. Let us help him out by providing a *Guardian* fantasy Brown cabinet to take on the rest of the world. What is more, let us not confine our attention to the Lib Dem talent pool, wide and deep though it is. After all, there has not been a Liberal cabinet since 1915 and no Liberal cabinet minister since Sir Archibald Sinclair was secretary for air in Churchill's 1940-45 coalition. Sir Archie – who famously said of sluggish Spitfire production, 'The problem is there are too many square pegs in round holes. I intend to reverse that policy' – was not a huge success. But he had crawled around in the Flanders mud with Churchill during the first world war – a bonding experience.

It so happens that Sir Archie's grandson, the 3rd Viscount Thurso, sits nowadays as one of Sir Ming Campbell's Lib Dem MPs. But the *Guardian*'s fantasy Brown cabinet rejects both heredity and nepotism as principles for inclusion. There will be no cronyism here. If Sarah Brown wishes to become minister for women (we are sure she doesn't), she must get elected first – just like Ed Balls and Yvette Cooper.

In fact, the *Guardian*'s fantasy Brown cabinet of all the talents will not actually include any of the eligible Labour politicians available. That would be presumptuous and only serve to blight their chances with Gordon next Wednesday. He can be tetchy about that sort of thing.

We will even refrain from promoting the claims to high office of Ming's all-but-designated successor, Mr X: you don't need any publicity, do you, Nick? As for Boris Johnson's star qualities, they would obviously add lustre to any cabinet. Minister for communities and local government (with special responsibility for Liverpool) would be the obvious choice, more suitable even than minister for women. Feelers have been put out. But David Cameron will not even consider releasing this talented player on to the transfer market.

So here goes:

Deputy prime minister: With all this talk of Gordon needing a southern woman to lighten him up a bit, an answer exists that is even more obvious than Harriet Harman: Germaine Greer. She's from the south (Melbourne, wasn't it?), she's a leftie and she's intellectually self-confident as well as being an aesthete, both of which are what philistine New Labour needs. What's more, Dr Greer wouldn't let Gordon take himself too seriously, if necessary by pinching his bum.

Chancellor of the exchequer: Roman Abramovich. He's the perfect man to understand the balance between the entrepreneurial side of the economy and the role of the state. As the entrepeneur who trousered large quantities of Soviet oil and gas resources when it was privatised, he knows his stuff. He's also a Russian regional governor and owns Chelsea FC. Chancellor Abramovich would be tough enough and wealthy enough to stand up to the former chancellor, which may prove necessary. As a bonus he might be able to help Labour out on the fundraising side (lots of catching up to do) and could even slip a few over-the-hill players in the direction of Raith Rovers, the PM's favourite team.

Foreign secretary: A tough one, this. The *Guardian* panel briefly considered Shilpa Shetty, whom Brown praised so lavishly during the *Celebrity Big Brother* row that overshadowed his trip to India. She is graceful and smart and, if Margaret Beckett is to step down, the cabinet will need new women.

But in the end we settled on Bill Clinton. He's very well known and experienced, women voters like him, despite everything, and so do people in the developing world, despite occasionally being bombed at his instigation. Brown has a lot of friends among US Democrats. It would also be really handy if Hillary Clinton becomes US president – Bill has probably got her private telephone number.

Home secretary: This is obviously a challenging appointment now that John Reid has re-tooled the department to meet the global terrorist threat. Would it be smart to appoint an Israeli general?

No, they're tough, but their strategies never seem to work. Fidel Castro, on the other hand, has run a tight ship for years without suffering any domestic terrorism ... But could Gordon put up with his long speeches in cabinet on days when he has a dinner appointment? Probably not.

In the end the panel felt it would nominate Nelson Mandela, even though it's asking a lot of him to come out of retirement and live in a cold, wet country. His mixture of steel and grace enabled South Africa to make the transition from apartheid without the kind of bloodshed that is de rigueur in Gaza. The Mandela magic might even persuade inner-city teen gangs to drop their guns and knives down the drain. It's worth a try.

Health secretary: Ségolène Royal. The left's defeated candidate for president of France needs a break from all that domestic grief (what a pig, that chap of hers, eh?) and squabbling with those old 'elephants' in the smoke-filled corridors of the French Socialist party. What could be nicer than a sabbatical in London, which is full of French people escaping from her policies. Ségo could spend our NHS budget, quite possibly better than we do because the French NHS is, by general consent, the best in Europe. As for glamour, she sure beats Alan Milburn.

Education secretary: George Clooney. This is not as stupid as it sounds. Obviously he couldn't get health because he's a private-sector TV doctor. But he's a Democrat, virtually New Labour, he takes his politics seriously and he would certainly get some of those hard-to-reach mothers concentrating a bit harder outside the school gates. Americans are better than we are at doing egalitarian education, so George could teach us something. Andrew Adonis could stay on as his No 2 – the perfect foil in so many ways.

Defence secretary: He's 90 in a few weeks' time, but he's still got all his marbles and talks more sense than most. Denis Healey was a Labour defence secretary in the 1960s and stormed the Anzio beaches in the second world war, where he failed to meet Lee Marvin, who was there too. Never mind: he's box office. He likes Gordon, too.

Minister for justice: Aung San Suu Kyi, Burma's most famous prisoner of conscience and one of Gordon Brown's eight heroes in his new book, *Courage*, is the obvious choice for a post that requires wisdom, insight and courage. Detained under house arrest and worse by the Burmese military regime for nearly 20 years, she has had much time to reflect on the nature of prison, its effect and its limitations.

Transport secretary: Ken Livingstone. OK, they're not mates, Ken and Gordon, and it was the Brown blueprint for public/private modernisation of London's tube system that has made it one of the best-lit but not-so-rapid transit schemes in the world. But Ken had the bottle to introduce the congestion charge and spend so much of Gordon's money on buses, and the Red Ken of old has modified his leftie ways so as not to frighten the City with Hugo Chávez outbursts more than once a month. He and Dr Greer could combine to lighten up the Brown study.

Trade and industry secretary: It's got to be a man with global experience in this kind of work, a man who has handled this huge portfolio at national, European and World Trade Organisation level. Come on now, don't be bashful – step forward Peter Mandelson, the EU's British trade commissioner. Now, now, you two, give each other a hug and make up.

Work and pensions: Polly Toynbee, the Tory grassroots pin-up, is perfect for the job. Pol has written about poverty all her working life and cleaned a few hospital loos to broaden her experience, too. That may be a first in a Labour cabinet, unless Ernie Bevin's CV contained a stint on the wards. Toynbee needs no introduction to *Guardian* readers and would certainly keep Ken and Germaine in order round the cabinet table.

International development: Jennifer Lopez cares about the developing world and she is younger than Madonna. Just right to follow where Clare Short, Lynda Chalker, Judith Hart and the great Barbara Castle once trod. All formidable women. Go for it, J-Lo, you can do it!

Culture, media and sport: What a plum job! All those free tickets to the opera. Think Big Tent here. Who knows more about culture, media and sport around the world than Rupert Murdoch? Well, media and sport anyway. He's got a lot to offer and needs to pay off his debt to society before heading to the big *Match of the Day* in the sky – the celestial sky, not BSkyB. It would put Gordon's *Daily Mail* mate Paul Dacre's nose out of joint. But Paul's all heart beneath his gruff exterior. And we would all sleep better for knowing there would be no favours or rule-bending on media ownership with the Digger in charge and that nice wife of his reading the old boy's red boxes for him while he has his Ovaltine.

Leader of the House of Commons: Davina McCall. She's a nice woman and she's got plenty of experience running unruly houses. Under Davina's reforming zeal, MPs might like to experiment with voting each other out for bad behaviour. They tried it in the 18th century with impeachment and acts of attainder – it didn't all start with *Big Brother*, you know.

Leader of the House of Lords: What House of Lords?

Welsh secretary: A cultured people needs artists to lead the flock into the 21st century, not machine-like politicians. Sir Tom Jones is a possibility, and Dame Shirley Bassey hails from what is now a very smart part of Cardiff. There is Sir Anthony Hopkins, but the panel felt he might frighten younger voters who need to be encouraged. At the end of the day, there was a unanimous vote for Catherine Zeta-Jones, as long as she promises that that husband of hers won't become a burden on social services in Wales. They're quite busy enough.

Scottish secretary: Hey, let's bite the bullet here and invite Sir Sean home from Spain to keep the Welsh secretary happy discussing *Hullo!* magazine. He might even end up contributing to the funds of the Scottish exchequer, independent or not. And Dr Greer might find him easy on the eye during Chancellor Abramovich's more tedious presentations on the new stiffer tax regime for private equity firms.

Northern Ireland secretary: Look, it's almost lunchtime and the panel has had a hard morning. Paddy Ashdown by unanimous consent. If he gives Gordon any trouble, the chancellor knows a bloke who'll put the frighteners on him.

Well, that's it. Ah, not quite. Of course, every cabinet needs an enforcer and communications director in the ultra-successful Campbell mould. Can Gordon afford Jeremy Paxman to put the fear of God into the feral beasts?

JUNE 23 2007

Flowered up

PETER ROBINSON

Looking for a nice frock for today's photo shoot, Lily Allen walked into one shop in Ladbroke Grove and saw the assistant virtually dive across the room in an attempt to stop the Amy Winehouse CD playing in the background. She arrives back at the shoot and immediately starts discussing the possibility of gastric bypass surgery due to being 'fat', then announces that it is all 'off the record', even though she will post the whole thing on her MySpace blog within 48 hours. Mark Ronson, enjoying unexpectedly huge success with his *Version* album, seems less besieged by life, chatting happily about Prince parties and meeting Mani. She is the sort-of demure English rose. He is the smart-talking New Yorker. They are the Dempsey and Makepeace of pop and today, on the eve of this weekend's Glastonbury festival, Lily Allen and Mark Ronson seem like the best of friends ...

To kick things off, please introduce each other to the Guide.

LILY: This is Mark Ronson and he is an overrated, overhyped pop producer from New York City. He's basically a DJ.

MARK: I think Lily Allen is one of the most gifted pop melody writers of her generation.

LILY: 'ONE OF'? Who are the others? (*Guffaws*)

MARK: Anyway, Lily and I are friends, even though I've never done anything nice for her.

When and where did you first meet?

LILY: It was at [Notting Hill club night] YoYo.

MARK: Yes, you put that smiley-face pin badge on my really expensive leather jacket. I was almost crying.

LILY: I told Mark I was a singer and he went, 'Oh, give me a CD then.'

What was on the CD?

LILY: 'Smile', and a couple of demos from when I was signed to Warners.

MARK: I actually had to ask you twice for the CD.

LILY: Oh come on – you were not interested at ALL!

MARK: But then I listened to it on the plane, and ...

LILY: No you didn't! You listened to it about six months later!

MARK: BUT I WAS ON A PLANE. So anyway, I asked Lily if I could play it on my radio show, and then I asked her to come out to my studio [in New York] and sing 'Oh My God' for my album.

LILY: NO! You asked me to suggest some songs for your album, then you gave all the good ones to other people! Then you went,

'Oh, you can have the Kaiser Chiefs.' THANKS! And then I said, 'Oh, can you do some stuff for my album?' And you said, 'Yeah, for $200,000.' Ha-ha-ha-ha!

Busta Rhymes is on the new version of 'Oh My God'. Was he expensive?

MARK: Well, as soon as I knew it'd be a single I called him up ... I thought he might not get it, but he understood it immediately. He gets about $60,000 every time he rhymes on a record!

LILY: $60,000 isn't much.

MARK: It's kind of a lot, Lily.

How much did you pay him?

MARK: Erm, something in the neighbourhood of a nice car.

LILY: Bentley or Golf?

MARK: Let's say a second-hand Bentley. He got arrested half an hour after he left the studio ... (*Distracted by a mark on Lily's arm*) Are you self-harming? What's this?

LILY: Yeah, I'm self-harming – I just want to be Amy Winehouse.

MARK: AHEM! You see THAT'S why you walk into a shop and the people behind the counter turn Amy's music off! You've got beef Tourette's!

Who's the worst drunk?

LILY: Me.

MARK: Yes.

LILY: I get really aggressive when I'm drunk. None of my label bosses will take me out any more, because after one glass of champagne I'm standing up going: 'And another fucking thing! People like you are ruining music! You're ruining our country! Let me do it and I'll fix it!'

Would either of you say that you had normal childhoods?

MARK: I'll never say I had a normal childhood. My dad would manage bands – I'd come down in the middle of the night and Keith Moon was there playing air drums. That's not a normal childhood.

LILY: For the first 11 or so years of my life things were, well, not so nice and we lived on a council estate. The thing is, I'm proud of being middle class now – my mum was working class, as was my dad, and they worked really fucking hard to provide me with what I had. Well, my mum did. It's funny when Lady Sovereign said that thing about me, 'She doesn't have to work as hard as me, because her dad's Keith Allen.' Do you know what, Lady Sovereign? HAVE my dad. Go on! I'd love to see how many people buy your records. Go on! Take him!

Having said that, your first deal did come about because of your dad ...

LILY: Yeah, and it didn't work. It was rubbish folk music – my dad and another guy wrote it all. Then it didn't happen. Things only worked for me when I worked really, really hard myself.

Well done, Lily. Do you think the two of you would ever have met without having come from privileged backgrounds?

LILY: Probably not. You bump into people in LA and they go, 'Oh, it's such a small world' and really, it's not – it's just that you all go to the same places where you spend £7 on a drink. We're bumping into each other in the middle of Ghana.

MARK: At the same time the reason we met is that I was DJing at YoYo. And so we could easily have met anyway. While I shouldn't care, those exaggerated myths do just make me cringe. It's all stuff like, 'You hung out with Stella McCartney and had picnics with Michael Jackson.'

Did you have picnics with Michael Jackson?

MARK: No. I did have a sleepover once ...

LILY: WHAT?

MARK: Er, yeah, I did. It was at Sean Lennon's house ... And ...

LILY: YOU DIDN'T! Did he do anything to you?

MARK: Oh, this is just going to get ridiculous. Thing is, Sean was friends with Michael Jackson when he was growing up and when we were about 12 years old he was like, 'Michael Jackson's coming over tonight.' I remember turning on Channel J, which is the public access channel, and ...

LILY: ... and Michael Jackson unzipped your trousers and ...

MARK: No, and so Channel J had this picture of this girl with her top off and Michael went (*handbag action*) 'OOOH! Turn it OFF!' And me and Sean were like, 'Why? This is great!'

What time did you go to bed?

MARK: We went to bed at one o'clock and we closed the window, because there was a draught and he didn't want it to interfere with his voice. He slept on the floor.

LILY: FUCKING HELL! (*Clapping like an excited seal*) Ronson! I can't believe you slept with Michael Jackson!

MARK: Nothing happened!

Mark, is 'Stop Me' [2] *still attracting hate mail from Smiths fans?*

MARK: Not recently. I got two things from this little 15-year-old boy, going, 'I want to stab you in the eye ... '

LILY: He phoned me up asking about what to do! I get things like 'Give me a grand and I won't slit your mum's throat.' So, cheers for that. I've got five mobile phones, because of all the hate phonecalls. 'I'm going to kidnap your dog.' Please.

What don't you like about each other?

MARK: Lily's one of the few people I'm naturally intimidated by.

LILY: Why?

MARK: Not in a bad way ... But you're a bit 'cult of personality' ...

LILY: No I'm not! People say I'm a complete bitch and I'm not, I'm just really insecure and when people meet me I'm just ... not very good at it. But I'm a nice person. I bought Mark a kebab only today.

What has Mark done for you, Lily?

LILY: He definitely needs to do more. It was my birthday the

---

2 A reworking of the Smiths's track, with vocal from Daniel Merriweather, it was the first full single from Mark Ronson's album *Version*. [Ed.]

other week and I still don't have a present from him. One time I was on the fire escape of Mark's studio in New York, crying because I'd split up with my boyfriend. He came out, saw me crying, and went back inside! Ha-ha-ha-ha!

MARK: I'm not Joan Collins!

LILY: What?

MARK: Hang on. I'm still trying to think of something nice I've done for you. There must be something.

LILY: Mark, there's nothing.

JUNE 27 2007

Blair's day of triumph

JONATHAN FREEDLAND

The moment has been anticipated so long, it's easy to lose sight of its strangeness. The handover at Downing Street that will come today was formally promised six weeks ago, trailed last September and implied two years before that, when Tony Blair first announced that he would not fight a fourth election. This has been a slow-motion transition, three years in the making. Even longer, if you buy the Granita legend, which holds that the baton that passes today first left Blair's hand over an Islington dinner table in 1994.

We've had so much time to accustom ourselves to it that when the change comes, shortly after 12.30pm today, it will seem entirely normal. Yet it is anything but. Both the departure of Tony Blair and the arrival of Gordon Brown are events with no comparable precedent.

Start with the man who bids farewell. Those who saw the

Channel 4 retrospective, *The Rise and Fall of Tony Blair*, will have marvelled at the near-consensus, even among Blair's closest colleagues and supporters, that his reputation is forever tainted by the invasion of 2003. Margaret Jay ruefully reflected that all of Blair's considerable achievements would be 'terribly undermined, and probably fatally undermined, by what I think of as the tragedy of going into Iraq'. Neither she nor the others interviewed are slogan-shouting members of the Stop the War Coalition, waving their BLIAR placards. Yet even they can see no shelter from this glowering cloud, believing it will cast gloom over Blair for evermore. Which only makes today's graceful exit so puzzling.

For Tony Blair will leave today not with his head bowed or drummed out of office, but on a day and in a manner of his choosing. He has choreographed his exit with a thousand send-offs: cheers at Sedgefield, a last hug at the White House, a final round of backslapping from European leaders last week and yet another ovation from a Labour conference on Sunday. No hint of a leader made to dip his head for a fateful, lethal mistake.

Is there a precedent for this? Anthony Eden erred mightily over Suez in 1956 – until Iraq, the byword for a foreign-policy calamity. Britain lost an estimated 56 soldiers in that conflict, from an overall death toll of 900. Eden's reputation and his health were shattered by Suez and he was forced out of Downing Street by the first month of 1957.

Lyndon Johnson had recorded mighty achievements with his Great Society assault on poverty and his civil-rights legislation. Yet all that was overwhelmed by his escalation of the Vietnam war. As he sat in the Oval Office at the end of 1968, the United States had lost 30,000 men in battle; eventually that figure would exceed 58,000, alongside the estimated 5 million Vietnamese dead. At the first sign of a serious political challenge within his own Democratic party, Johnson announced he would not seek re-election, instead retreating from public life in 1969 and dying just four years later. Vietnam had broken him.

The Lebanon war of 1982 had a similar effect on Menachem Begin. Taunted by anti-war protesters – as LBJ had been – Begin grew ever more depressed, quitting a year after the disastrous invasion. He was said to be particularly haunted by the loss of more than 600 Israeli servicemen in a war that also claimed the lives of thousands of Lebanese and Palestinians. After his resignation he became a virtual recluse, rarely leaving his apartment until his death in 1992.

There is a pattern here, and Blair does not fit it. Each of these men understood that they had made grievous errors that had cost very many human lives, especially the lives of their own young men and women in uniform. That realisation weighed heavily on them, sending them into a kind of penitential, self-imposed exile. Anthony Eden did not spend his final weeks on a farewell tour, squeezing out one last round of applause. Lyndon Johnson did not angle for another big, international job. Menachem Begin did not insist on going 'with the crowds wanting more'. They all had the decency to withdraw from office quietly, carrying a heavy burden of guilt on their shoulders.

I have written before that it is an indictment of our system of government that Tony Blair was able to remain in office despite Iraq. Even if he was not culpable of deception – as he insists he was not – even if he only ever did what he thought was right, he was guilty of the grossest misjudgment – one that has led to the deaths of at least 118 British service personnel, along with as many as 655,000 Iraqis. For that mistake alone – even if it was an honest one – he should have paid with his job. It is a badge of shame for the parliamentary Labour party and the cabinet (and indeed his successor), who between them could have driven Blair from office, that they did not do so earlier. But it also reflects a moral failure by Blair that he leaves today believing himself to be a star, going out on a high.

His expected appointment as the Middle East envoy of the international community suggests he's pulled it off, winning instant rehabilitation, at least from the club of world leaders. The likeliest outcome is that he will not succeed in the job, if only because the circumstances are so utterly unconducive to progress. Indeed, the role could be a painful reminder of the most unhappy aspects of his premiership, as he encounters Arab suspicion that he is merely a lackey of George Bush, and Arab anger over Iraq and the Lebanon war of 2006. If he was to defy those odds and achieve success, providing the dogged, daily application of pressure and pursuit of detail that the Israel–Palestine conflict requires (and which he demonstrated in Northern Ireland), then he will deserve enormous credit. Indeed, he will have gone a large way towards redeeming his reputation. Maybe that's why he's so keen to do it.

But Blair's elegant exit will not be today's only novelty. Brown will also make some history. F Scott Fitzgerald once quipped that 'there are no second acts in American lives' and the same could be said of British politics, traditionally inhospitable to the second chance. Yet today sees Gordon Brown grab the mother of second chances – if it isn't a third, fourth or fifth chance.

Some hardcore Blairites believe Brown's real moment was in 1992, when he should have challenged John Smith for the leadership. That was his opportunity, they say, and he blew it. He fumbled it again in 1994, making way for Blair. You could easily add the spring of 2004, when Blair reached his lowest ebb and was ripe for ousting. Or last September, when Brown could have turned a minor revolt into a full-blown coup.

Yet Brown missed all those chances – and he has succeeded anyway. It's hard to think of an equivalent achievement: it is as if Michael Portillo were about to step into Downing Street. What's more, and for a decade, Brown has seen off a series of talked-up rivals. Jack Straw, David Blunkett, Charles Clarke, Alan Milburn, David Miliband – all of them were, at some point, pushed as alternatives to Gordon. He saw each of them off, holding on to the most unstable title in politics – heir apparent – for a full 13 years.

So, two remarkable men will see the Queen today, each staging something of a political first. Brown will arrive in office as a man determined, he says, to show no pride – and Blair will leave it just as determined to show no shame.

JUNE 28 2007

Brown's first 100 minutes

TIM DOWLING

After years of waiting, Gordon Brown has finally acceded to the premiership. Those of us who watched the drama unfold live from our sofas can now assess the prime minister's performance so far. Did he deliver on his promises during his crucial first 100 minutes as PM?

2.47pm We start the clock at the moment Gordon Brown steps out of Buckingham Palace and into his new armoured Daimler, even though he has been gassing on with the Queen for nearly an hour, when he could have been getting on with things. Just so he knows – the extra minutes come off the end of his honeymoon period.

2.50pm The BBC reports that Brown's car is making 'slow progress' towards Downing Street. Does this send out the right message?

2.53pm Brown finally arrives at No 10 and delivers a speech in which he calls out to 'men and women of goodwill to contribute their energies'. Nevertheless, he seems a bit tenuous, as if he is aware that he is competing with the tennis on the other side.

2.56pm Brown concludes his first public statement as prime minister with the words, 'Now let the work of change begin.' Yes, and about time, too.

3.07pm The PM's been inside No 10 for 11 minutes. Meanwhile, in the *Big Brother* house, unaware of the momentous changes about to take place, a woman in a bathrobe looks into a mirror and says, 'My skin looks awful.'

3.18pm As parliament debates the tribunals, courts and enforcements bill, the woman directly behind the justice minister Vera Baird suddenly jumps up and leaves the chamber. Has she been called? Is she of good will? Who is she? Somebody should tell her she left her bag behind.

3.47pm With so little happening, we may as well take the 61st minute of Brown's premiership to look back and assess his first hour in office. It was clever of him to invoke his old school motto, 'I Will Try My Utmost', in his speech, because pundits are already pointing out that David Cameron's school motto is '*Floreat Etona* (May Eton Flourish)'. But so far Brown has failed to find a means to heal a nation that is, at press time, largely underwater.

4.17pm The Downing Street website lists the chancellor of the exchequer as 'to be confirmed'. Ditto the home secretary. Ditto every other cabinet post. So far Brown appears content to rest on his modest laurels, ie the car ride and the speech.

4.27pm As Brown's first 100 minutes draw to a close, the younger generation arrives home, declares politics in general – and BBC *News 24* in particular – to be 'boring', and demands to watch the last bit of *Tracy Beaker*. With the aloof, backroom style he has adopted so far, how can Brown hope to change their minds?

JUNE 28 2007

The accession

MICHAEL WHITE

By the time Tony and Cherie Blair emerged from Buckingham Palace at 1.40pm yesterday, an ex-prime ministerial couple at last, BLAIR HAS RESIGNED was hardly the breaking news that the rolling-news channels immediately declared it. We have had some inkling of it for months now. But the moment ushered in a rare hiatus in the long and generally revolution-free history of the British nation.

For the next 57 minutes – until a smiling Gordon Brown came through the same door with the Queen's commission – the country went ungoverned. In political theory this should have been a Merrie England time of liberty or licence. But no one rioted and the burglary rate remained stable. Order was restored as easily as anarchy had earlier been unleashed when Mr Brown climbed out of his new armour-plated car at 2.52pm. Stepping gingerly to the microphone in front of No 10, he began: 'I have just accepted the invitation of Her Majesty the Queen ... '

From this formality he moved easily to an echo of the informality of the Blair regime, and once inside Downing Street he addressed the staff between calls from various foreign leaders. Telling staff to call him 'Gordon', he acknowledged that it had been an emotional day for them: saying goodbye to a great leader and a great family. He thanked them for the welcome and said it had been an interesting day for him.

'It's not every day you meet the Queen at 1.30pm, become the prime minister at 2pm, speak to the president at 3pm, and get told by Sarah to put the kids to bed at 7pm,' he told them.

At Westminster a holiday mood prevailed, the Commons chamber noisier than usual. Now that he is going, Conservative MPs quietly acknowledged Mr Blair's skills and personal charisma, even his achievements. Some ruefully recalled how Margaret Thatcher had left amid such bitterness in 1990 that it took them 15 years to recover.

To its own surprise, despite a decade of the TB-GB friction, Labour's promised orderly transition has proved just that. They can't believe their luck. As backbenchers plotted in the tearoom – first moves to embarrass Mr Brown surfaced by mid-afternoon – ministers and wannabee ministers made sure their mobile phone and pager batteries were in order: ready for the call from No 10. Inevitably, for most it will never come.

For those in exit mode it was different. John Prescott could be seen wandering the Westminster corridors, a little aimless, but smiling. John Reid went tieless to mark his release. Was he demob happy? 'I'm always happy,' he beamed. Hilary Benn, still in contention, lunched quietly in a cafeteria with his wife and daughter.

Throughout the day there had been unexpected echoes of that other new beginning – 10 years and 55 days ago – when the Blairs first arrived. Once again there were crowds and cheers, some tears, too, as democracy's removal van rumbled into view. But not everything was the same.

The weather was suitably darker and Mr Blair no longer looks absurdly young; he looks his age. When Labour MPs abandoned tradition to give him a standing ovation at the end of his stylish final session of question time yesterday – and the opposition surprised itself by joining in – the speaker, Michael Martin, indulged them. In May 1997 Speaker Boothroyd had reproached new MPs for clapping him into the Commons. But that was all before Britain experienced its 'Diana moment', when emotion was first permitted to overwhelm restraint. Mr Blair rode that change well, as he did many others, but not all. Yesterday's exchanges required him to acknowledge fresh military casualties in Iraq and to face the taunts of anti-war demonstrators on the day's short car journeys.

When did the Blairs finally realise that it was all over? Perhaps when the prime minister waved his P45 at the dispatch box and Cherie, in the visitors' gallery, looked so glum. Perhaps when he formally resigned as an MP or when he carried his own case to the King's Cross train – a private citizen again – for a last trip to Sedgefield.

If commuters feel as generously as many bloggers yesterday they will have hoped to see him spend last night in a flooded siding in Doncaster. But MPs are different – members of the same noble calling, as Mr Blair acknowledged in his final utterance.

'Labour is a very sentimental party,' more than one admitted after their startling display of affection. 'The mood has softened,' Dennis Skinner confided.

Yet, as if in denial, Mr Blair has worked frantically to the last. He had a frosty phone call with Russia's president, Vladimir Putin, on Tuesday – unaware that Tory MPs were busy plotting an ambush to defeat him on the off-road vehicles (registration) bill, the last vote of his administration. Labour whips got wind of it just in time and pulled back enough MPs to win by 197 to 165.

Yesterday had started normally enough with ministers under pressure on Radio 4's *Today* programme and blamed in the newspapers for the floods. Rolling news TV was already in business on College Green across the road from Big Ben, where Blairites busily polished their Brownite loyalty badges and Tories such as Michael Portillo – worsted by Mr Blair – settled scores. So did George Galloway, who savaged Mr Blair and called his successor Bertrand Russell to Blair's Bob Monkhouse.

The outgoing No 10 spokesman – who can now be revealed as Tom Kelly – told reporters at his morning briefing that Mr Blair was, as usual, preparing his answers for Question Time, then going to the palace. 'The rest of the page is blank,' he said.

But it was the dour Scot who was steadily moving to the spotlight and yesterday afternoon's media briefing was conducted by his man, Michael Ellam. Even as Mr Blair drove back down the Mall from Britain's ugliest royal residence, Mr Brown could be seen on television shaking hands with cheering Treasury staff as he prepared to drive the other way. This was the moment Mr Brown had 'waited so long for' – something of an understatement. Less was said of the fact that Mr Blair is going a year before he planned to when he won in 2005.

Several MPs, left and right, tried to confront him with Iraq yesterday. As so often, he stood his ground. It was not the day for that, most later agreed, though many remain astonished that he is plunging straight into the maelstrom of Middle East negotiation. Good luck, said Ian Paisley in the day's most telling tribute.

In this most symbolic day of ritual transfer of power the Queen's role is pivotal, but anonymous. None of her 11 prime ministers has breathed a word of what they talk about.

JUNE 28 2007

Go to Australia or use your own judgment

RICHARD NORTON-TAYLOR

After the pomp and ceremony of his departure from Buckingham

Palace, his speech on the doorstep at No 10 and a partial reshuffle, Gordon Brown's role as prime minister began with an onerous and somewhat sobering task. Tony Blair, when faced with the duty, immediately went white in the face, said onlookers. John Major couldn't face it: he went home for the weekend.

As prime minister, with ultimate responsibility for Britain's nuclear deterrent, Mr Brown has to write a letter, in his own hand, giving instructions detailing what the United Kingdom's response should be in the event of a pre-emptive nuclear attack. The letter will be opened only by the commander of a British Trident submarine, who would have to assume that the prime minister was no longer in a position to take 'live' command of the situation. The options are said to include the orders: 'Put yourself under the command of the United States, if it is still there', 'go to Australia', 'retaliate' or 'use your own judgment'. Each new prime minister writes the letter as soon as he or she takes office, after being 'indoctrinated' by the chief of the defence staff, who explains precisely what damage a Trident missile could cause. The letter is destroyed when they leave office.

According to Peter Hennessy, professor of contemporary history at Queen Mary, London University, Mr Blair 'went white' on receiving his briefing. 'The nuclear bit shakes them all,' he said. 'Then you realise you are prime minister, at a deeper level.'

Though nothing is known of Mr Blair's written instruction, James Callaghan is said to have authorised retaliation. When John Major had to make the decision, he cancelled a weekend at Chequers and went home to Huntingdon.

Mr Brown's orders would be sent by special low-frequency or satellite communications to the submarine commander. They would first be verified by two officials in the Cabinet Office and then two at the armed forces' permanent joint headquarters in Northwood, north-west London.

Mr Brown's new job allows him to summon, whenever he wants, the heads of MI5 and MI6, the chair of the joint intelligence committee, and the chief of the defence staff, Sir Jock Stirrup. They, in turn, now have direct access to Britain's new leader.

JULY 7 2007

Smeaton: exemplar of Glaswegian pride

IAN JACK

Until this week, the most famous John Smeaton in British history was the 18th-century civil engineer who built the Eddystone light-house and the Forth and Clyde canal, but now he has been overtaken – gloriously, though probably briefly – by the baggage handler who last Saturday ran to a policeman's aid and helped fell the burning driver of the flaming Jeep Cherokee at Glasgow airport. 'Smeatomania' arrived: his tribute website received 500,000 hits in 48 hours, the Scottish edition of the *Sun* quickly devised a 'Give John a Gong' campaign; he is a hero not only to his own people but also to Fox News.

Smeaton was brave. He thought quickly and selflessly. His popu-larity, however, owes more to the word than the deed – to an edited television interview that lasts one minute and 39 seconds, in which the key words as reported in newspapers are: 'This is Glasgow. We'll just set aboot ye.'

In fact, in his ITV interview Smeaton didn't quite say this. He said 'about' as the English 'abowt', and 'yuh' rather than the more Biblical, Knoxian 'ye'. Phonetic transcription of a west of Scotland accent is a tricky thing. What is interesting is that so many news outlets felt they had to try to capture his Glasgowness, a quality that in these circumstances turns out to be loveable.

When I saw this interview, I felt (and as it turned out, shared) a small spasm of delight. Some of this may have been an injudicious revenge, the same feeling that warmed the cockles of so many New York hearts when Bernard Goetz shot four muggers – or what he claimed were would-be muggers – on a subway train in Manhattan in 1984; the same feeling that so many Americans and American troops shared – wrongly, ignorantly, disastrously – when they imagined invading Iraq was payback for 9/11. But I don't think that was the main source of the interview's pleasure.

'Now John ... has a message for any would-be terrorist,' says the interviewer in a voice-over. And John says: 'You come to Glasgow ... Glasgow doesn't accept this, d'you know what I mean? This is Glasgow you know ... so we'll set about you. You know? That's it.'

Other cities in Britain toil to reinvent civic pride with new art galleries and marathon runs. The citizens of Glasgow possess a kind of civic chauvinism that puts many nationalisms, including Scottish nationalism, in the shade. It can be tiresome: 'See this city? Friendliest in the world,' as every second taxi driver used to say, aggressively, on the way from the airport. But given all that has happened to Glasgow in the past 50 years – the collapse of its old industries, its neighbourhood demolitions, its shrinking population (in 20 years Edinburgh will be bigger), the motorways pushed so rashly through its centre – given all this, the persistence of Glaswegian pride is a remarkable thing.

Cities often depend for their self-image on myth or well-advertised but only partial truths. In the face of bombing campaigns, London's is stoicism. London 'can take it', London will 'carry on'. Myths can be useful. People may behave better with an historic ideal in mind. But quiet endurance is hardly a London specialism

– see the people of Beirut or Baghdad – and the idea of London as a peculiarly stoic city was born only in the last century, in the last months of 1940, when Humphrey Jennings shot a 10-minute Blitz documentary, *London Can Take It*.

Glasgow's is a more complicated story. When, in the 18th century, it began to intrude on the British imagination, its reputation was for commercial pragmatism. The industrial revolution, which it helped invent, turned it from a cathedral and warehouse town into the fourth-biggest city in Europe after London, Paris and Berlin. In the space of 100 years, its population multiplied by 16, swollen by immigration from Ireland, the Highlands and islands, and (less noticed) England. Its prosperity gave it painters, architects, tea rooms, yachts, gentlemen's clubs. Its reputation was one of energetic enterprise.

An early characterisation of the qualities we now think of as typically Glaswegian appeared in *Glasgow in 1901*, a book published to coincide with the city's international exhibition of that year. It's one of the best books ever written about the city. Here the authors – one of whom, James Bone, later became London editor of the *Guardian* – prefigure the new Glaswegian archetype: the working man. The working man cares more about drink than about food. In public, he isn't nice to his wife. He is humorous, but sardonic.

> But according to his lights he is a reasonable man. He stauns up for himsel', not only against the common enemy, his employer, but also against his comrades in allied trades if they invade his frontiers. He is gruff, intractable, and independent, and his latent irritability takes fire if his rights are infringed. Of servility he has not a trace. 'Sir' is an unknown word to him, 'thank you' an unknown phrase. He is the perfect 'Wha daur meddle wi' me'.

But the book that gave it the most vivid effect, and in a way stands to Glasgow as Jennings's film does to London, was written by a Gorbals baker, Alexander McArthur, and then knocked into sexier shape by a London rewrite man, H Kingsley Long. The title comes from Paul's words, Acts 21:39: 'I am a Jew, of Tarsus in Cicilia, a citizen of no mean city.'

No Mean City, first published in 1935, was originally intended as a shocking indictment of violence and poverty, but what its millions of readers mainly remember is razor-slashing and its Gorbals location. It made the Gorbals – hitherto a slum quarter no worse than several others – a byword for Glasgow, and therefore Glasgow a byword for standing up for yourself and knocking other people down.

Of course, there are limits that have still to be put to the test. Glasgow has almost no experience of terrorism. After the first night of the Clydebank blitz in March 1941, the people of Clydebank took to the hills – very sensibly, because a second night of bombing brought the total of dead to more than 500, with only seven houses out of a total stock of 12,000 – mainly tenement flats – left intact. The social spirit of Clydebank is said never to have recovered. Certainly, nobody made a film called *Clydebank Can Take It*. Still, what Smeaton said captured something of what a city thought of itself, prided itself in, which very few cities now do. Similar words spoken at the airports of Birmingham, Edinburgh, even Liverpool are hard to imagine, even though the human resource and bravery are probably distributed equally through all of them.

JULY 13 2007

Land of the free kick

MARINA HYDE

In an instance of almost unbearable poetry, the LA Galaxy ground is called the Home Depot Center. Approach it from the 110 freeway and it rises up at you at the end of a wide, palm tree-lined boulevard, where a small army of liveried gardeners are using leaf-blowers to vacuum azalea petals from the sidewalks. Crikey, you think. Could it be any more like White Hart Lane?

When he signed for LA Galaxy back in January, David Beckham drew the facile condemnation of those bewildered that he should choose a move to Hollywood as opposed to, say, Tottenham. But as so often with the Beckham story, resistance is futile. Later today he will be formally unveiled at the team's ground – it's pronounced the Home Dee-po Center – as the all-new, £128m spokesmodel for Major League soccer. His first game will be against a touring Chelsea next Saturday.

At the Galaxy's HQ his advent has sparked fevered activity. Acres of parking lots are dotted with cars belonging to the retinue of support staff preparing for perhaps the biggest press conference in the club's history. Several of the vehicles sport Christian fishes, with one bumper sticker reading JESUS SAVES. Here, adding the words AND BECKHAM SCORES OFF THE REBOUND would not be an instantly recognisable cultural reference. This is not a heritage site.

Meanwhile, across town, the August issue of W magazine is hitting the shelves, carrying an exclusive photoshoot with the Beckhams that might delicately be described as 'lively'. We see David wandering through a rocky desert in ecosystem-inappropriate clothing (tightly laced leather trousers). We see David easing Victoria into a corset. We see a heavily tattooed David sprawled across a bed in his underwear. We see Victoria, also lingerie-clad, spreadeagled in a chair. The entire shoot may as well be captioned: 'This is your future, Major League soccer! It'll hurt less if you bite down on that leather strap.' In reality, the cover-line runs: 'When the soccer star married the pop singer, it was a match made in British tabloid heaven. Now David and Victoria Beckham are determined to become the new American idols.'

And as always with the Beckhams, it is the determination that's so hypnotic. You could power small countries off their extraordinary drive. It might be a strategem, it might be unconscious, but their most brilliant way of short-circuiting the sneerers has been never to hide how much they want it – whatever 'it' might be. Breaking LA may be the couple's greatest challenge yet, but truly, how could their story not end up in the town where the movies get made?

The municipal motto of Carson City – the south-eastern suburb in which the Home Depot Center is located – is 'Future Unlimited'. It could double as a statement of Major League soccer's hopes. Yet shifting one's gaze from the cover of *W* to the little-league soccer practice taking place by the stadium, it doesn't feel like a big fish is about to arrive in a small pond. It feels like a whale is about to splash down into a bathtub.

Not that the complex is not well appointed. It houses a tennis arena and a velodrome. In the distinctly corporate reception area there hangs a huge photograph of a recent occasion where the pitch was covered in dirt for the staging of a motorcycle event.

'Pretty cool, huh?' says a passing employee.

Can't see it catching on at Real Madrid's stadium, is one's first thought, but so polite and gentrified is the atmosphere that it is impossible not to murmur assent.

If you are used to thinking of football grounds, even when empty, as partially held together with the sweat and tears of generations of supporters, then you might find the Home Depot Center something of a departure. No doubt the 27,000-capacity stadium is a repository of tribal passion on a match day, but the fact that the Galaxy share it as a ground with their bitterest rivals, Chivas USA, ought to indicate just how very mannerly the place seems.

It is an atmosphere that permits the existence of food stands with names such as Goalie's Grill, where fans can purchase a $12 beer, or perhaps a margarita, during games. So how quickly do things spill over into mindless violence? Do they keep a lid on it till after the final whistle? Or can things kick off as soon as half time if the Galaxy are one-nil down and there's been a dodgy sending-off?

'Well, about 200 of us do stand up for the whole game,' laughs Eddie Garcia, who, along with his friend Jeff Skinner, is a founder member of the Riot Squad, the club's most vocal supporters' association. Their motto is *Veni, Imbibi, Vici* (you don't get that in the Shed at Chelsea), they all sit in block 138 of the ground and as a group they consider themselves the club's most hardcore fans. Think of them as the Galaxy Ultras, only polo-shirted, unarmed and totally benign.

'We only kill our own,' explains Eddie, a graphic designer, in reference to several rituals involving beer kegs. Unusually for Galaxy fans, they like to talk about football the game, as opposed to football the family picnicking experience. 'It's so great watching [the former Real Madrid coach] Fabio Capello and [the England manager] Steve McClaren having to eat their words about Beckham's form,' these two local men agree over two black and tans in a pub called the Fox and Hounds, whose traditional English decor would be totally unremarkable were it not located in the middle of Studio City, Los Angeles. Jeff, a film editor, underscores his dedication by revealing that he took a month off work last year to follow the USA team round Germany for the World Cup. He's still taking their loss to the Czech Republic fairly badly. 'I don't have good memories of Gelsenkirchen,' he sighs. But then, which of our great footballing nations does?

Unfortunately, for some, this kind of extremism spoils it for the rest. Margie Banuelos, a teacher from Pasadena, is involved with alternative supporters' association the Galaxians, and offers a flavour of the security protocols in place for local derbies.

'When we play Chivas, the fan clubs now sit on opposite sides of the pitch,' she explains. 'We used to sit next to them, but people ... people got out of hand.' How out of hand? 'Some people chanted against each other,' she reveals darkly. 'Some of them yelled.'

Happily, Galaxy games are preceded by a loudspeaker announcement that foul language will not be tolerated. It's fair to say that Posh has probably heard That Chant for the last time.

More representative still of the game's support base in this country is Greg Delgado, a local father of three who coaches an after-school girls' soccer club and epitomises its wholesome and family-oriented image. So thrilled is Greg at Beckham's arrival – 'the best thing that could happen to soccer in the United States' – that he wishes to immerse himself in anything that might make him feel at home. 'We really admire the Brits for their football chants,' he says. 'We're going to start copying them here, so we can sing them at Galaxy games.'

Really? Looking at the apple-pie pretty 12-year-old girls practising their keep-ups, it feels far from seemly to imagine them passing unflattering judgment on the referee.

'Actually,' admits Greg, 'I'm not familiar with some of the words in them.'

His daughter Kendra, 12, outlines the task facing US soccer's newest ambassador, in a country where it drags so far behind NFL and baseball in the popularity stakes that declaring you want to be a soccer player when you grow up is likely to make your parents question where they went wrong.

'It's mostly a girls' sport,' she stresses, 'because boys get really competitive, so they change to other stuff when they're 15.'

For her father, though, the revolution is already under way. 'You know, because of David,' he beams, 'they're now going to get the players special matching jackets and ties to travel in when they go on the road.' Aha, the club travelling kit. A fine tradition. 'Exactly! We had no idea you guys did that, but now we're going to too. It's just those little pro touches he's bringing.'

There is something genuinely infectious about being in the company of people who are thrilled at the innovation of the away-game suit and it would take a hard heart to warn them that they are setting out on a road that ends in Rio Ferdinand signing for Manchester United apparently dressed as John Travolta, then going on to announce: 'The music, the fashion, the TV – it all goes to make up Rio Ferdinand.'

As far as visions of the Beckhams mingling with the grassroots go, Greg is a realist. 'They are completely different to the rest of the Galaxy couples,' he laughs. 'They're already superstars.' He speculates that Victoria will prefer to hang out behind the glass of the Stadium Club, a members-only restaurant at one end of the ground. 'It's all hardwood floors and brass, and you can look down from your table while you're eating dinner,' he explains. 'It's a really nice place to watch soccer.'

The Riot Squad have alternative plans. 'We thought it would be funny to buy a season ticket in Victoria's name,' explains Jeff, 'so we've done that and we're inviting her to come sit with us.' There is even talk of making it into a throne, 'because we've seen her wedding photos and she likes that kind of thing ... We figure she may not actually sit with us on every game,' they concede. 'So the rule is that whoever gets her seat has to come in a Posh wig and an extraordinarily small Spice Girls T-shirt.'

Whatever Victoria's decision on her seating arrangements, the club may have a job on its hands enforcing the rigid apartheid system that keeps LA's celebrities from having to share facilities with its civilians. To read the reports, you'd think every star in town had bought one of the season tickets, which have gone up from around $660 to $860 for the best seats. As the Galaxy coach, Alexi Lalas, confirms: 'We're expecting a lot of beautiful people in the Home Depot Center.'

Quite apart from newly minted Beckham fans such as Tom Hanks, there is a thriving football scene among British expats in LA. Robbie Williams has his own pitch and team – Hollywood Vale – while Lalas himself turns out for the former Sex Pistol Steve Jones's Hollywood United, a side that also features Vinnie Jones, who is still amusingly convinced that anyone over here has the faintest clue who he is. And then of course there is the Beckhams's new best friend, the enduringly sane Tom Cruise, who was last month spotted clapping regally down from the Bernabeu stands as Real Madrid won La Liga. He was wearing sunglasses at 11 o'clock at night, naturally, and you mightn't want to get trapped in a conversation about the offside rule with him. But it's all bums on seats, isn't it?

Though David and Victoria seem rather keener on establishing a support network in this particular echelon of LA society, Lalas has been keen to stress how close-knit the Galaxy are. 'It's a down-to-earth family,' is the coach's claim. 'Victoria will just be one of the wives.' And so, inevitably, to the Galaxy Wags, as the club's website now offically refers to them.

'They get a kick out of what's happening,' Lalas recently explained, 'but they also have a perspective that, maybe, is lacking in players' wives around the world.'

As if to back this up, one of their number recently added that she was sure Victoria would join them for the 'chips 'n' dips' get-togethers they host when their husbands are on the road. Yes, you get the feeling this woman has better things to do than indulge in a designer-handbag arms race with the likes of Alex Curran. But she may find herself with excess guacamole when Victoria declines in order to spend the afternoon shopping for Bentleys with Jennifer Lopez. Or, come to that, to be Scientologically audited with Katie Holmes. Say what you like about the old girl, she's certainly given herself some options in this town.

However great the lifestyle chasm between Beckham and his new colleagues, it is important to remember that he has always been the most popular of team players wherever he has been. Nevertheless, driving out to the Home Depot training ground along the route Beckham will take from the £11m house he and Victoria have bought in Beverly Hills, one conclusion seems unavoidable. Namely: he's going be taking a helicopter.

Even if he does decide to endure the unbearable traffic for appearances' sake, it is difficult to see how his presence can avoid causing a small amount of resentment in his teammates. Beckham has been allocated the dressing-room locker next to erstwhile cock of the Home Depot, Landon Donovan, whose public statements detailing how excited he is to have been so spectacularly usurped in the fame stakes may or may not have been made through gritted teeth. As for Quavas Kirk, the erstwhile wearer of the number 23 for the Galaxy, he informed Margie Banuelos that he had been strongly encouraged to give up his shirt for the new arrival.

But Beckham's true challenge will be effecting what he was hired to do: widen soccer's appeal from a niche sport or one for kids. Even on the level of physique, it's intriguing to see how one culture's idea of athletic perfection is another's idea of a wimp. As part of a cross-promotion campaign, Galaxy's newest star recently appeared with the NFL star Reggie Bush in an Adidas advert, in which he taught the New Orleans Saints running back how to take free kicks and Reggie showed him how to throw a pass. Were gridiron fans dazzled by the sporting Adonis that is David Beckham ?

'Look at his tiny arms,' sniffed one contributor to the popular sports website Deadpsin. 'He's like a goddamned T-Rex.'

Hop around a few of LA's sports bars and you hear the same deaf-ening indifference. As far as their denizens are concerned, if you wished to hide a map giving Osama bin Laden's precise location, inside a Major League soccer event would be the place to do it.

In the end, there is no shortage of people on either side of the Atlantic who are hoping the Beckhams fail in their latest endeav-our. But what are our LA debutantes if not forces of nature? It would hardly be their style to worry about the odds.

JULY 17 2007

Boris the serial liar and sociopath for mayor

POLLY TOYNBEE

David Cameron has just made his worst mistake. He will bitterly regret the day he encouraged Boris Johnson to stand as London's mayor. What does it say about the desperate state of the Conservatives that they will put up a clown to run a great global city? London is the nation's powerhouse and a city of daunting complexity. Tories running top City firms and Conservative boroughs won't find the Boris Johnson candidacy charmingly funny. Some may or may not agree with his rightwing views, but they will wince at serious London politics treated by the Tory leadership as a celebrity Eton wall game.

This will blow back on Cameron dangerously. No doubt the Boris bandwagon will be good circus entertainment and his japes may be endlessly forgiven with one of his rumpled 'Cripes!' apologies. But everything foppish, buffoonish and essentially unserious about his raffish progress through London will mirror exactly what people already think about Cameron and Osborne's Etonocracy. Everything they are trying to shake off will be writ large as Boris represents the Cameroons. They are struggling for gravitas, but Boris will strip it away from them.

Of course if a monkey can be elected mayor of Hartlepool, Boris Johnson might be elected mayor of London. Jester, toff, self-absorbed sociopath and serial liar, the man could still win. Even Conrad Black called him 'a duplicitous scoundrel', and he should know. But it's truly alarming that he who has never run anything except his own image could be in charge of this mighty financial centre – and some of the poorest, neediest boroughs in the country.

It would be good for London to have a serious contest: a third-term shoo-in for Ken Livingstone would be a miserable election. But it would be a disaster for London if a charming fool, with no interest in ordinary Londoners' lives, were to win it as another feather in his celebrity cap. If London is competing with New York, how does Boris shape up against Bloomberg in the big league?

The danger is that politics is so despised and politicians are so loathed that anyone who manages to seem 'not one of them' starts ahead of serious contenders. It's why female candidates start with a natural advantage, according to pollsters. Hartlepool's H'Angus, after all, wasn't even a person, let alone a politician. Ladbrokes yesterday made Johnson's odds just a shade longer than Livingstone's.

But with humour and wit in short supply in politics, a little goes a long way and Johnson has a lot of both. So does Livingstone. Johnson would have the old 'throw-the-bastards-out' insurgency advantage, but Livingstone has earned respect with the bravery and skill of his congestion charge, his London bus revolution and his imposition of 50 per cent affordable housing on every development.

Johnson's best asset is the devoted support of London's only proper newspaper. The *Evening Standard* – same stable as the *Daily Mail* – detests Livingstone: no surprise they gave Johnson front-page and leader-column coverage, with an article by himself (all about himself, not much policy) and lavish praise from the rightwing columnist Andrew Gilligan: 'Boris has come to save our great city from Ken's ghastly empire of bureaucrats, bendy buses and earnest Cuban festivals.' The *Standard*'s never-ending campaign against Livingstone led to a famous fracas when he likened one of its reporters to a concentration-camp guard: the reporter was Jewish.

But when it comes to gaffes it'll be a no-contest win for Johnson, who can't resist the temptation to be (charmingly) offensive in every column he writes and every lucrative speech he makes. (He earned more than £400,000 last year in journalism and after-dinner speaking, on top of his MP's salary.) Can he stop himself making jokes about poodle-eating South Koreans and Papuan 'cannibals'? No, but that's part of his well-honed USP as 'not really a politician at all'. Don't be fooled. Despite that designer shambolic demeanour, Boris is not called blond ambition for nothing, with a gargantuan appetite for everything: fame, women, money, praise – and power. There's nothing wrong with ambition; the question is: what is it for?

Underneath the whimsy and the Greyfriars pastiche prep-school banter, he is a deeper and more passionately romantic believer in 19th-century Conservativism than most of his front-bench companions. He is not an embarrassed Etonian, but a

Bullingdon Club believer. Perhaps because he was not born to great wealth – unlike Cameron and Osborne – he revels in everything elite – intellectual, social or monied.

Jokes make outrageous views acceptable, but the general tenor of Borisisms reveals his political cast of mind – the endless mock-cockney attacks on "elf 'n' safety', on children's car seats or, notoriously, Liverpudlians wallowing in their victim status. He hints at utter contempt for the NHS, with USSR comparisons. Though liberal on matters of sex (what else could he be?) and drugs ('I'm instinctively inclined to liberalise'), his politics are right off the Cameron scale. Here he is on education: 'I am in favour of selection ... So is every member of the British ruling classes'; and on universities: 'I believe passionately in academic inequality.'

Just before the grammar-school row he complained: 'We have taken away the old ladder of social mobility, the academic selection that used to form a way out for the bright children of poor families.' How will London parents react to the tone of this? 'Masters of the Universe' should 'endow new schools for improving the education of our feral children to reduce the risk of being despoiled of their squillions by a hoodie'. As a rabid Europhobe, how would that play with the Olympics or the Tour de France?

What about Boris the sociopath? Apart from being caught often lying to all and sundry – he was fired from the *Times* for making up a quote – how has he survived the Darius Guppy scandal, when he was recorded agreeing to find a journalist's contact details, so his old Etonian friend Guppy could have the man beaten up? How badly? Guppy suggested just a few cracked ribs. Later when Guppy was jailed for a £1.8m insurance fraud, Boris explained his role with: 'Oh poor old Darry was in a bit of a hole. He was being hounded.' Can Cameron really get through nearly a year's mayoral campaign by just laughing and saying, as he does, 'Boris is Boris'? If he were to win, Cameron would be in a worse hole still.

JULY 19 2007

Insurgents form political front to plan for US pull-out

SEUMAS MILNE

Seven of the most important Sunni-led insurgent organisations fighting the US occupation in Iraq have agreed to form a public political alliance with the aim of preparing for negotiations in advance of an American withdrawal, their leaders have told the *Guardian*. In their first interview with the western media since the US-British invasion of 2003, leaders of three of the insurgent groups – responsible for thousands of attacks against US and Iraqi armed forces and police – said they would continue their armed resistance until all foreign troops were withdrawn from Iraq, and denounced al-Qaida for sectarian killings and suicide bombings against civilians.

Speaking in Damascus, the spokesmen for the three groups – the 1920 Revolution Brigades, Ansar al-Sunna and Iraqi Hamas – said they planned to hold a congress to launch a united front and appealed to Arab governments, other governments and the United Nations to help them establish a permanent political presence outside Iraq.

'Peaceful resistance will not end the occupation,' said Abu Ahmad, spokesman for Iraqi Hamas. 'The US made clear it intended to stay for many decades. Now it is a common view in the resistance that they will start to withdraw within a year.'

The move represents a dramatic change of strategy for the mainstream Iraqi insurgency, whose leadership has remained shadowy and has largely restricted communication with the world to brief statements on the internet and Arabic media.

The past three months have been the bloodiest for US forces, with 331 deaths and 2,029 wounded, as the 28,000-strong 'surge' in troop numbers exposes them to more attacks.

Leaders of the three groups, who did not use their real names in the interview, said the new front, which brings together the main Sunni-based armed organisations except al-Qaida and the Ba'athists, had agreed the main planks of a joint political programme, including a commitment to free Iraq from foreign troops, rejection of cooperation with parties involved in political institutions set up under the occupation and a declaration that decisions and agreements made by the US occupation and Iraqi government are null and void.

The aim of the alliance – which includes a range of Islamist and nationalist-leaning groups and is planned to be called the Political Office for the Iraqi Resistance – is to link up with other anti-occupation groups in Iraq to negotiate with the Americans in anticipation of an early US withdrawal. The programme envisages a temporary technocratic government to run the country during a transition period until free elections can be held.

The insurgent groups deny support from any foreign government, including Syria, but claim they have been offered and rejected funding and arms from Iran. They say they have been under pressure from Saudi Arabia and Turkey to unite.

'We are the only resistance movement in modern history which has received no help or support from any other country,' Abdallah Suleiman Omary, head of the political department of the 1920 Revolution Brigades, told the *Guardian*. 'The reason is we are fighting America.'

All three Sunni-based resistance leaders say they are acutely aware of the threat posed by sectarian division to the future of Iraq and emphasised the importance of working with Shia groups – but rejected any link with the Shia militia and parties because of their participation in the political institutions set up by the Americans and their role in sectarian killings.

Abd al-Rahman al-Zubeidy, political spokesman of Ansar al-Sunna – a salafist (purist Islamic) group with a particularly violent reputation in Iraq – said his organisation had split over relations with al-Qaida, whose members were mostly Iraqi, but its leaders largely foreigners.

'Resistance isn't just about killing Americans without aims or goals. Our people have come to hate al-Qaida, which gives the impression to the outside world that the resistance in Iraq are terrorists,' he said. 'We are against indiscriminate killing – fighting should be concentrated only on the enemy.' He added: 'A great gap has opened up between Sunni and Shia under the occupation, and al-Qaida has contributed to that.'

Wayne White, of Washington's Middle East Institute and a former expert adviser to the Iraq Study Group, said it was unclear, given the diversity within the Sunni Arab insurgency, what influence the new grouping would have on the ground. He added: 'This does reveal that despite the widening cooperation on the part of some Sunni Arab insurgent groups with US forces against al-Qaida in recent months, such cooperation could prove very shortlived if the US does not make clear that it has a credible exit strategy.

'With the very real potential for a more full-blown civil war breaking out in the wake of a substantial reduction of the US military presence in Iraq, Shia and Kurds appreciate that the increased ability of Sunni Arabs to organise politically and assemble in larger armed formations as a result of such cooperation could confront them with a considerably more formidable challenge as time goes on.'

JULY 27 2007

Think before you build

JONATHAN GLANCEY

By definition, flood plains flood, which is why it has never been a particularly good idea to build houses on them. But when push comes to tidal shove, we do know how to build on or above water or on land that at certain times of year is transformed into lakes by heavy rain.

Houses can be raised on stilts, whether traditional and timber or concrete and ultra-modern. It might, in fact, be rather nice to live in a refined modern apartment block, along the lines of those designed by Le Corbusier in France or Oscar Niemeyer in Brazil, with wonderful views across riverbeds and flood plains, while carrying on with life as normal. Such homes could be equipped with dinghies or boats. Here we might lead a form of modern Venetian life, safe from flooding.

Equally, we know that building too many new homes on great tracts of land in an ever-increasing sprawl is a silly thing to do. And yet it seems we simply cannot stop ourselves, despite all the warnings from Yorkshire and Gloucestershire. Build, build, build is the mind-numbing political mantra of today. Three million new homes must be built by 2020, many of them in floodplains along the Thames and elsewhere in low-lying parts of southern England. Call them 'eco-homes' (stick a wind turbine on the roof) designed for 'eco-towns' (all traditional settlements used to be 'eco-towns', without having to crow about the fact), trust that technology will keep floods at bay, and we will all sleep sound and dry.

I would, however, firmly advise anyone unfortunate enough to live in any of these new homes to invest in buckets, boats and thigh-high waders. Why? Because the evidence of our eyes alone tells us that new housing is being raced along contrary to every concern raised about long-term changes in our weather.

The problem is firstly one of sprawl. If we continue our shallow-minded policy of building suburban-style developments across acres of land that no one before has ever wanted to live on – the Thames Gateway is only the most dramatic example – we will soon find ourselves in very deep water indeed. Sprawling estates of 'traditional' homes are pretty much all we know how to build today. These require a mass of concrete to be sunk into the ground as a foundation. This helps to prevent rain from sinking into the ground or washing away naturally. Houses on these glum estates, meanwhile, are too close to the ground for rainy-day comfort.

In any case, sprawling new estates are a part of the very problem of global warming. Most are dormitory suburbs, offering few jobs within walking distance. Few are served with schools, nurseries, clinics or proper shops. Here the car is king. These gormless, supermarket-bound developments are gas guzzlers, contributors to global warming, yet useless when the floods invade their artless cul-de-sacs.

What we need to build are true eco-towns – in other words, modern versions of traditional settlements. Instead of seemingly inevitable sprawl we could build just a very few new towns, preferably on high ground, each a compact and delightful cluster of homes, businesses, places of worship, areas to relax. Each could be walked across in no more than 20 minutes. Each could be a rival to the old, much-loved and floodless hill towns of Tuscany and Provence, or of Buckinghamshire and Derbyshire.

And, if we insist on building on flood plains, because these offer cheap land, then we must use our imagination to design new towns – just a few – that could stand happily with their foundations in water, but with homes well above it. We need to think before we build, build, build. More of the same sprawling junk that we have become accustomed to will lead only to floods. And tears.

JULY 31 2007

Memory failure

MICHELE HANSON

Fabulous news: our little memory lapses – known as 'senior moments' – are not senior any more, they are any age. They are even hip, with a Homer Simpson name – 'D'oh moments' – and are nothing to do with gender or intelligence either, but everything to do with stress and busy lives. They happen up to 30 times a week, to anyone. Thank you so much, Finnish researcher Maria Jonsdottir and your team of psychologists for these revelations. What a relief for us older persons who have, until now, been mocked and assumed to be losing our marbles.

We even believed it ourselves, it happens so often. I listen to my answering-machine messages, I press delete, the messages have gone, but so has the memory, within seconds. Same with call waiting. Who called? Who did I promise to ring back? Haven't a clue. I look up a word in a glossary, I reach the glossary, I've forgotten the word. But it doesn't matter any more, because the darling Ms Jonsdottir says so. The brain is at fault, says she, but there's nothing wrong with the brain. To her, memory loss isn't a sign of decrepitude it's just a normal 'storage failure' or 'action slip'. (I do love Ms Jonsdottir's heavenly new terminology.) And it's on the increase because of our busy lifestyles and high levels of stress.

Perhaps all this will silence those show-offs with perfect recall, who are always banging on about my memory and taking its lapses personally. Rosemary thinks my memory ought to retain details of her week's schedule; my mother used to think it should remember whether she wanted a cup of tea or not; and numerous others think it should remember their names and birthdays. Or that I should have told them such and such a thing, because I'd told everybody else, and I'd even told some people twice, because I tell so many people everything that I can't remember who I've told what to and probably thought I'd told them already and didn't want to repeat myself.

All these people have been insulted by my 'storage failures'. To them, I wasn't having a common memory blank, it was a personal slight – a subconscious truth surfacing and giving the game away. They are sure that I didn't remember them because I didn't really love them, was not interested in their lives and couldn't be bothered to pay attention.

Well, think again, you people. Those were just plain 'action slips' and nothing more. Why would one do such a thing on purpose? My friend Fielding had a terrible 'storage failure' last month. He and his family set off on holiday; they'd left stinking London and got all the way to Salisbury when Fielding realised he'd forgotten his vital blood-pressure pills. The family showered him with abuse and they drove all the way back to town, but poor Fielding couldn't remember where he'd put the pills. It was just an 'action slip', deserving of sympathy rather than reproach. And reproach just makes people panic, which causes more stress, which causes 'discrimination or sub-routine failures', like putting a tea bag into your case instead of your pills.

I think that once upon a time I may have written something about this before. But did I? Can't remember.

31 JULY 2007

Ingmar Bergman: no one made films like him

THOMAS VINTERBERG,
FILM DIRECTOR

I watched *Fanny and Alexander* three hours ago. I think it's the best film ever made. I showed it to a person a lot younger than me and she was in tears and said it was the best film she'd ever seen. She's 19 and I was curious to see if it was too slow for her, if it was outdated, but apparently not.

I talked to him some years ago. He was very, very uplifting, a happy man, actually. He was fooling around, very light-spirited, playful. He gave me a lot of good advice, such as how to handle success, and how to handle failure. I remember every word of it. He asked me if I'd decided what to do after my film and when I said no, he said, 'Well you're fucked,' and I said, 'Why?' and he said, 'One thing that can happen is that you fail, and it won't be good for your self-confidence. It's much worse if you have success – you're absolutely paralysed by it. So you always have to decide your next movie before the opening of the present one.' And he was so right. You don't turn into a career pilot, trying to navigate by success or failure, instead of deciding from your heart.

The thing that interests me as a film-maker, having trouble deciding whether I'm supposed to make Danish movies or English-language movies, is that Bergman stuck to his own project – he made films in Sweden, in Swedish, with his own actors, and instead of trying to become someone by leaving his country, he stayed and made his country something, which is a very proud thing to do. Of course, the world was bigger back then: London and New York were further away. But still, it's inspirational. I think he's definitely the biggest inspiration in Scandinavia, ever, in film-making.

Fanny and Alexander was the film that had the biggest emotional impact on me. I saw his first eight or nine movies at film school and I was a bit bored, because I was restless and too young. I also think he grew better and better. And then, when I saw *Fanny and Alexander* a couple of years after film school, I fell completely in love. My main inspiration for *Festen* was *Fanny and Alexander*. I admitted to him that I stole a scene from it and he laughed. And either he or someone else told me that he stole it from *The Leopard* – the one where they're dancing round the house. It's a common tradition in both Denmark and Sweden, so it's like stealing a tradition, really. But still, it was definitely a robbery.

The thing I liked about *Fanny and Alexander* is that I got to know a whole family as if they really existed. Those are people I'll never forget. I'll always relate to them. I'll always remember the weird uncle farting. It's a piece of life, really, and that's what I adore.

HARI KUNZRU, NOVELIST

One afternoon a teacher decided to use double General Studies to show us *The Seventh Seal*. I saw Max von Sydow playing chess with Death on the beach (the most heavy-metal image ever committed to film) and knew I'd try to see everything this director had made. I haven't yet, but Bergman has popped up at several key moments in my life, always as a revelation. I saw *Scenes from a Marriage* in a stifling flat and asked myself what I was doing with the woman beside me. Von Sydow, playing the tormented artist in *Hour of the Wolf* (more compact, more threatening, the name, in Swedish, is *Vargtimmen*), said: 'A minute can seem like an eternity – it's beginning now,' and I realised something was being taught to me about making art: here was a minute of screen time, an experience shared between the characters and the audience. Bergman was good because he was so literal, able to put things down so precisely.

SHEILA REID, ACTOR

I had been playing Mrs Elvsted in his *Hedda Gabler* at the National Theatre. His PA rang to say he wanted me in his film. When I realised she wasn't joking, I was thrilled: I'd have gone anywhere to work with him again. I think I'm the only Briton to have been in a Bergman film. It was a small part in Ingmar's first English-language film, *The Touch*, with Bibi Andersson, Max von Sydow and Elliott Gould. Oddly, I played Elliott's sister: she was tall, dark and Jewish; I'm small, Scottish and fair.

I had one scene, in which Andersson visits me. I'm an alcoholic and I have a problem with my hands. On set Ingmar asked me: 'What would an English apartment look like when you're about to move house?' I said: 'I might have somewhere to put the bottle, a chair, some curtains I've only half removed.' He said: 'Yes. That's what we've done. What would you say if somebody rang the doorbell?' I said: 'Come in. I can't make you a cup of tea.' We improvised the scene like that.

I have a photo of him just before he said 'Action'. He has his hands on my shoulders and intense concentration in his eyes. You can see he's putting his energy into my body and I'm receiving it. Six months earlier I met him for dinner. I asked if he wanted to talk about my part. He said: 'No. You know her already.' I did – he had written the part for me, because he had observed me when I auditioned. I was rather unhappy then and he noticed that.

On set everybody from the prop boys upwards paid attention when a scene was being shot – unusual for film. There was incredible energy on the set. He was the same on *Hedda Gabler*. We rehearsed from 11am to 4pm with only a 20-minute lunch break, so no concentration drop after lunch. He really stretched us. He gave me very helpful notes that said things like 'She is a candle that never goes out' and 'She has a screen inside her up to her neck'. I was extremely fortunate to have worked with Ingmar in both theatre and cinema.

DAVID THOMSON, FILM CRITIC

Long before the end, Ingmar Bergman elected to live on a small island off the coast of Sweden. It was a way of saying he was alone with his work and his lovers – and probably no one knew the loneliness better than the lovers, and the children, who saw how he put their smiles, their eyes, their meals, their untidy beds on the screen. They had to live with his ruthless and obsessive use of their smiles, their faces and their youth. It was not unkind, but it was not kind either, in the way of reassurance or loyalty. It told everyone that everything changes, yet remains the same. So he would live on an island and then perhaps the foolish film festivals would stop asking him to come and be honoured. Didn't they know that making the films was the only thing that kept him alive or anywhere near calm?

The way Bergman's work and Bergman's pain were in equation struck me early on and almost by chance. In 1957 he made *Wild Strawberries*, in which a great man, a professor, is going to a kind of film festival to be honoured for his career. He is Isak Borg, played by Victor Sjostrom (the pioneering figure in the Swedish film industry and Bergman's mentor). But as he travels toward his honorary degree, so Borg dreams and remembers and feels shocked by his private failures. We can see that he is a cold man attracted to the warmth of others – and I think Bergman saw himself the same way.

Wild Strawberries is a great film, struggling to reconcile inward failure and outward success. I realised that it was the same 'story' as a film I had seen two years earlier – *Citizen Kane*, in which an old man dies and has his last thoughts filled by the same grim debate: was I wretched in all my glory? Maybe all great films say the same thing.

Bergman saw the resemblance between the medieval Dance of Death and the modern waiting for apocalypse. But that tension was only the larger projection of a small, ordinary anxiety: will love last or betray itself? The director who strikes me most as a direct descendant is Andrei Tarkovsky – the latter's *The Sacrifice* is as true a Bergman film as Liv Ullmann's *Faithless*. But every great director, every one committed to the work and prepared to live on an island, as opposed to the Beverly Hills Hotel, has surely found themselves making their own variant of a Bergman film.

Cast an eye back over the great Bergman pictures, from *Sawdust and Tinsel* to *Fanny and Alexander*, from *Cries and Whispers* to *Smiles of a Summer Night*, and this is how you know them – there is hardly a special effect in the canon. Save one: the human face in joy and terror, lost or in flux. For Bergman , the face was always the same: always constant and always fresh.

AUGUST 2 2007

No story too flimsy

OLIVER BURKEMAN

This week the Sun *has been reporting sightings of great white sharks off the English coast. It can mean only one thing: silly season, the traditional*

August news drought, is upon us. Oliver Burkeman offers a sneak preview of some of the other scoops you'll be reading over the coming weeks.

AUGUST 3
Survey: August is best month for surveys

Public relations firms desperate to generate media coverage for their clients should release dubious survey results in August to guarantee maximum exposure, according to a survey conducted on behalf of the travel company Airtours. The survey also reveals that British people would rather have a nice mug of cocoa than spend a night of passion with a Hollywood film star, although what they like best of all is going on package holidays with the travel company Airtours.

August is also the ideal month for beleaguered academics to announce that they have discovered the scientific formula for boiling the perfect egg, making the perfect cup of tea, having the most perfectly attractive face, et cetera. A spokesman for the Higher Education Funding Council for England said such important discoveries were always taken extremely seriously when determining how to apportion cash for research.

AUGUST 6
New blow for Cameron

The Conservative party leader, David Cameron, faces new calls for his resignation today after a radioactive dirty bomb decimated his constituency of Witney while he was hundreds of miles away in Sunderland, nodding understandingly at some poor people in a shop. Defending his decision not to return at once to Oxfordshire, Mr Cameron said he was learning 'important lessons' over the course of this week, which he has spent sharing a one-bedroom house with a low-income family of six. A spokesman pointed out that Mr Cameron was even going so far as to drive himself back to Newcastle's Malmaison hotel each evening, rather than using the services of a chauffeur.

AUGUST 8

Radio 4 recruits listeners for national survey

BBC Radio 4's flagship *Today* programme is urging listeners to 'get involved!' in an exciting new project to identify and classify every pebble in Britain. 'There are thousands, maybe even millions, of pebbles on these islands – but amazingly, there's no single pebble database,' Bill Oddie said in an on-air interview. 'And that's where you come in! We want you to track down pebbles in your area and log them on our PebbleWatch website. This will create a vitally important national resource, and more importantly, it's a great way of keeping busy.' Mr Oddie promised a prize for the most assiduous pebble-watcher, but a BBC insider, speaking off the record, predicted that it would probably be awarded to a junior member of the production staff posing as a member of the public.

AUGUST 13

Speculation mounts over PM's holiday plans

The breathless annual guessing game over where the prime minister will spend the summer has begun – even though Gordon Brown has already announced that he will be holidaying in England and Scotland. 'Will it be Sir Cliff's Barbadian beach paradise? Silvio Berlusconi's house? Or Bee Gees frontman Robin Gibb's Miami mansion?' several papers wonder today. 'No,' a spokesman for Mr Brown responds. 'It will be England and Scotland.' Speculation-watchers speculated that the speculation would soon move on to the question of whether Prince William is secretly back together with Kate Middleton.

Students celebrate A-level success

A strikingly attractive 18-year-old girl has done fairly well in her A-levels, according to a report in every local paper in the United Kingdom. The 18-year-old's photo dominates the front page of the paper and shows her punching the air, perhaps in front of a recognisable local landmark. A picture spread in the *Daily Mail* reveals that there was jubilation, also, for a set of triplets from the home counties, who each got 14 A-grades and will all be heading to Oxbridge, followed by careers in hedge-fund management, the purchase of several four-wheel-drive vehicles and a life ultimately devoid of meaning. But there was disappointment for other students, because they are ugly and thick.

Meanwhile, critics of the government's education policies said the high number of A-grades proved that standards were slipping. 'Every year, the results are either better or worse than the year before, or roughly the same,' said Nick Seaton, chairman of the Campaign for Real Education. 'That's a savage indictment of a world in which pupils can no longer recite the waist sizes of every British monarch from Edward the Confessor onwards, like they could in my day.'

Ed Balls, the schools minister, rejected the criticism, arguing that everybody should just get along and be happy and proud and not worry about anything, ever.

AUGUST 18

New website is latest online sensation

A brightly coloured new website has become enormously popular with teenagers, because it allows them to perform a fairly mundane aspect of their lives – such as discussing music or shouting abuse at others – via the internet. The website has 230 million members in Britain alone, but some critics are worried that it could be used by bad people. It was designed by some Americans and is estimated to be worth approximately £1bn. Celebrity members include David Miliband.

AUGUST 20

Country-dwellers demonstrate in London

A group of rustic folk launched an angry protest about something or other outside the Houses of Parliament today, but Londoners were too busy discussing the latest festival of new writing at the Royal Court theatre to notice what it was. The Countryside Alliance said 10,000 people joined the protest, while police estimates put the figure at nine.

AUGUST 23

Gatwick terror panic

The government has banned airline passengers from wearing green hats after a man in a green hat was arrested at Gatwick airport carrying a bottle of potentially lethal hydrogen peroxide. Holidaymakers who flout the new rule face severe penalties, although hats of other colours will still be permitted, as will rocket-propelled grenade launchers.

The terror alert led to half-mile queues at airport security checkpoints, but tourists caught in the chaos proved phlegmatic. 'It's not really any bother for me, because I come from a Scandinavian country and therefore have an essentially imperturbable temperament,' said Finnish gap-year student Ari-Pekka Sjostrom, who spent the night trying to sleep on a bench outside Burger King in Gatwick's south terminal. 'Also, I'm on a gap year, so hanging around airport terminals talking to journalists is about as constructive as anything else I could be doing.'

A defiant group of Britons interviewed by ITV News also refused to be cowed by the threat of terrorism. They said it was crucial for the survival of liberal democracy that they press ahead with plans to spend the weekend getting life-threateningly drunk in the lap-dancing clubs of Tallinn.

AUGUST 24
Bank holiday travel chaos misery

The United Kingdom was facing a weekend of traffic jams, rail delays and family breakdown as train companies announced a barrage of engineering works that threatened to bring the nation's transport infrastructure to a standstill.

'After several high-level reviews, we've once again decided that the best time of year to shut down our most popular routes is precisely the weekend that most people want to use them,' said a spokesman for First Great Western. 'But passengers should be reassured: a large fleet of coaches will be waiting for customers outside stations across the network, ready to pull away and depart approximately four seconds before you make it across the car park with your suitcase.'

Meanwhile, East Coast line operator GNER sought to turn the situation to its advantage, offering a 'Just Outside Central London' getaway package ticket for £109, promising the unique experience of being stuck in a stationary carriage a few hundred metres from King's Cross Station for most of the weekend. The deal includes stunning views of Alexandra Palace and a free packet of crisps.

AUGUST 26

'Bohemian Rhapsody' triumphs in 'top 100' lists

'Bohemian Rhapsody' by Queen has been named the Greatest Film of All Time following an administrative mix-up among Sunday newspapers preparing this weekend's plethora of 'Top 100' lists. The glam-rock band's celebrated anthem also won the title of Funniest British Comedy of All Time and Most Powerful Person in the British Media. A source at the polling company contracted to produce the lists blamed human error. However, a corrected version of the Best Musicians list still showed Arctic Monkeys several places ahead of the Beatles and Johnny Cash, a result that pollsters attributed to people these days having absolutely no taste whatsoever.

AUGUST 30

Animal spotted in surprising place

A whale, tiger or escaped pig caused hilarity or uproar after it was spotted in the Thames, on Dartmoor, or openly wandering through the streets of Nottingham, according to prominent reports in all newspapers. The surprisingly located animal became an unlikely hero and was given a cute nickname as the whole country watched the drama unfold on Sky News. But eventually specialists concluded that they had no option but to put it down.

'We did our best,' said a veterinary expert from University College London. 'In the end, though, we decided that the only humane thing to do was to put "Benjamin" out of his misery. Although, by the way, it turned out he was a she.'

Media organisations expressed relief that the story had come to an end before the beginning of September, when real things might actually start happening again.

AUGUST 8 2007

Early death in Valley of the Immortals

RORY CARROLL

For centuries Vilcabamba was a South American idyll. The valley boasted a lush and tranquil setting in remotest Ecuador, a year-round balmy climate, pristine mountain water, abundant fruits and grains. The inhabitants lived long and healthy lives.

So long and so healthy that from the 1950s scientists have flocked here to study the hardy mountain farmers as astonishing specimens of longevity. The publicity gave Vilcabamba a nickname – the Valley of the Immortals – and put it on the map. Backpackers visited and so tourism wound its way into the valley, bringing paved roads, vehicles, hotels, restaurants and internet cafes.

And then something else happened. The famed elders – the *longevos* whose vitality defied the ravages of time and inspired scientific papers and dreams of eternal youth – began to drop dead. All of those who were said to be over 110 have succumbed and there are few making it past 100.

'We're dying younger,' said Maria Cabrera, 91. 'It's not like before. We feel we're getting weaker.'

A census is expected to confirm the widespread impression that there are far fewer centenarians. Levin Perez, said to be 105, died five months ago.

'They're disappearing,' said Franklin Carrion, the district coordinator. 'The new generation isn't lasting as long.'

A melancholy entourage at the cemetery – a silent hillside where stone crosses vanish under weeds – bolstered that view. It was the family of Vicente Pilco, who at 107 is probably the oldest inhabitant, laying flowers on the grave of his daughter, Soyla Pilco, who died from a blood clot two months ago, at 72.

'I don't think any of us will live as long as my great-granduncle,' said Jorge Carpio, 22, of Vicente. 'He is still fit, but he is the last of that generation.'

The cause of the longevity was never pinned down. Some scientists credited genes, others the hard labour and vegetable and fruit diet. Sceptics said the elders exaggerated their age.

There is wide agreement, however, on why the phenomenon seems to be ending: modernity and its sins – noise, chemicals, pollution and stress. Nelson Jurado, a gerontologist in the capital, Quito, said a 'tsunami of development' had damaged Vilcabamba's fragile ecosystem. 'Now these people live at a faster pace and that has affected their quality of life and longevity.'

What was a sleepy hamlet has in less than a generation become a tourist centre. Just a 45-minute drive from an airport, the permanent population has almost doubled to 4,200 and is swollen by hundreds of tourists who pack the more than 30 hotels and hostels. Mules wander the streets, but they are outnumbered by 4x4s, taxis and young people drinking beer. There are dozens of restaurants and bars, two nightclubs, and a shopping centre is due to be built. Few places serve *guarapo*, sugar-cane juice, but most serve Coca-Cola.

Nestor Carpio, 89, sits on the porch of his adobe home wincing from the rumble and dust of the lorry delivering cement and bricks to the house opposite, just one of dozens being rebuilt with modern materials.

'Not so quiet any more,' he sighs.

Outsiders have long been drawn by the valley's natural splendour – it was known as the 'playground of the Inca' for hosting royalty of the former empire. The Moon travel guide has a plaintive plea for visitors: 'You have a beautiful place balanced on the edge. It's one of those places travel writers hesitate to describe too lovingly, lest it become loved to death. By all means come, inhale the air, ride a horse, leave a little healthier – just please, tread lightly.'

Signs in English for spas, yoga, treks, massages and colonic irrigation testify to visitors' health quests, but their very presence puts strain on the ecosystem, said Mr Carrion. 'When there is more people there is more contamination.' He stressed that outsiders were appreciated for bringing money, jobs and opportunities. But in making life easier they had also made it shorter.

To meet growing demand farmers are now using pesticides and other chemicals, and some of the mineral-rich streams have become so polluted that the *longevos* hesitate to bathe in them, let alone drink the water. There are no studies to verify it, but locals cite food 'contaminated' by chemicals as causing deaths earlier.

'Everything used to be fresh, but now children are eating and drinking badly,' said Augustin Jaramillo, 98. By keeping to an organic diet he hoped to make it to 150, he added.

Another concern is that foreigners are pricing locals out of the housing market, with even the Cerro Mandando, a sacred Inca mountain, being snapped up for holiday homes. It also has a mobile telephone mast.

'Some people call this development, I call it destruction,' said Carol Rosin, president of the Association for the Defence of Vilcabamba's Elderly. A 63-year-old American aerospace executive, she is a passionate if unlikely protector, as she runs a 30-room hotel, one of the biggest developments. Using mules to build it and serving only organic food, among other measures, puts her on the locals' side, she believes.

Guests seemed unaware that the famed elders were dying off. New-age Americans, Britons and Spaniards attending a workshop on 'physical immortality' hailed Vilcabamba's sense of physical and spiritual nourishment.

'I can feel the energy,' beamed the workshop leader, Sondra Ray.

AUGUST 14 2007

India's golden age

RANDEEP RAMESH

A few years ago, I visited an Indian software millionaire at his headquarters in Bangalore for a story about the country's effervescent computer industry. Software is modern India's spice, a precious commodity craved by the rest of the world. The businessman took great pleasure in showing me around.

I marvelled at rows of programmers working in Japanese. I gawped at the basketball courts and pizza eateries imported to give the company an authentic Silicon Valley feel. After an hour or two, the conversation got personal. In the unselfconscious, nononsense manner of many educated Indians the entrepreneur quizzed me on which university I had gone to (Cambridge) and the subject I had studied (physics), before triumphantly declaring that I had been 'born in the wrong country'. When I protested, he raised his palm.

'The British system has come to this – taking scientists and making them journalists,' he said with a smile. 'What a waste. Just imagine the opportunities you missed by not being born here.'

In my youth I would have laughed that comment away as misplaced optimism in a country that could not even get its trains to run on time. I had grown up shuttling between my birthplace, London, and India, my parents' homeland.

My earliest memories revolved around the open sewers and the endless slumlands of my father's Mumbai – or Bombay as it was then known – and the tropical sloth of my mother's home in Kerala. It is fair to say that nothing worked in the India of yesterday. There were phones, but the lines were mostly dead. Frequent blackouts meant the inside of the fridge was invariably hotter than the air outside it. India appeared to be a place that, like my grandfather's battered Fiat, went faster backwards than forwards.

I spent my childhood apologising for having any connections with India, a country that in my lofty opinion needed major surgery. But a decade ago, while the rest of the world was looking the other way, India reached some kind of tipping point, and change began to happen – fast.

The signs were easy to spot. By the mid-1990s, the Marks & Spencer underwear and ovenproof CorningWare dishes my parents had always brought as gifts for relatives were politely returned or left unopened.

'We can buy this here,' sniffed my auntie in Bangalore.

My Indian cousins, who had diligently studied science subjects, began to leave India for jobs with management consultants and computer companies in places such as Singapore and California. Friends in Britain started to climb the social ladder by having arranged marriages with Indian women who were often smarter, more sophisticated and better-looking than they perhaps deserved.

Since I pitched up in 2003 to live and work in Delhi, I have witnessed firsthand the arrival of a golden age. The making and spending of money has become respected in a country where poverty was once revered. Middle-income westerners now feel poor in the upmarket postcodes of India's big cities.

Yet it would be wrong to think that India has become just like everywhere else. Yes, an economic miracle is under way. Yes, there is now an elite as capable as any in the west. The paradox is that this is a modernising nation, but one still steeped in myth and legend. Indians tend to ascribe the country's rise to its unique, ancient civilisation and in the process tend to be rather dismissive of anywhere else.

This does tend to blind Indians to the real problems faced by the country. Venality abounds and the widespread acceptance of corruption tarnishes the pride that Indians take in their most tangible achievement – democracy – and saps the energy with which they express it.

The abuse of public office for private profit reaches comical proportions in India. Family connections, privileges of caste and a pathological willingness to break the law characterise many social relations. In the dirt-poor state of Bihar I once visited a local politician who was in jail awaiting trial for numerous murders: he was campaigning from behind bars for re-election. Mobile phones and lime juice were brought by the guards as we spoke; they bowed in deference to my thuggish interviewee.

Hanging in the air, too, is desperate poverty. To the naked eye India appears not just an underdeveloped society, but an extremely unjust one. There are 260 million poor people in the country, and more than 1,000 children die of diarrhoea every day. The capital's streets are lined with ragged children and beggars waving handless stumps. Every day 22 farmers in India commit suicide. Official poverty numbers are going down, but not fast enough for anyone to notice. Yet the flow of good news keeps on coming. A top news story here last week was about a Punjabi businessman spending 1.55m rupees (£20,000) on a bespoke mobile-phone number.

Living in India sometimes feels like living in the midst of a cult, with hundreds of millions of souls convinced of the country's inevitable rise to global, nuclear-armed power. The nation's privileged classes and castes have been gripped by a psychology of ascendancy, anticipating the greatness that imperialism and the cold war denied them.

In fact, development for most Indians is a state of mind. Many simply sweep aside doubts by asserting the supremacy of the country's customs and traditions. I have heard my own family here in India discuss people with contempt just because of their background – be it class, caste, race or religion. When I protest, they simply tell me that I am not an Indian, so how could I understand?

During my time here I have come to realise that Indians have little interest in the British now, or in a British Asian like me who has returned to his parents' land. My affinities with the country, too, have their limits. I have come to realise that despite a common heritage there is little I share in experience or beliefs with the millions here.

America, the first British colony to break free, is the model now. Long gone is the view that Britain is a country to be admired or emulated. Like the American people, Indians have become more confident and assertive, citing stories of those who triumph against the odds to balance their nation's shortcomings.

They see glasses half-full, not half-empty, here. India wakes up with a smile on its face each morning, because its people know that the past may have been yours, but the future belongs to them.

Absurd. Enjoyable

PETER BRADSHAW

Bourne again! That super-lean, super-mean CIA tough guy Jason Bourne is back in this enjoyable piece of postmodern action mayhem. It is kept at a wildly frenetic pace by the British director Paul Greengrass, who I can only suppose drank his own body-weight in espresso each day before starting work.

This is the role that turned beardless young Matt Damon from boy into grizzled man. He is the terrifyingly well-trained operative – with high, tight pecs in a dun-coloured T-shirt – who had his memory erased, but who is on the trail of those faceless pointy-headed executives on his own team who betrayed him – and now want to take him out before he gets his memory back and blows the whistle on their illegal death squads. (The movie conforms, incidentally, to the post-9/11 Hollywood rule that only Americans are allowed to be effective bad guys.)

What is especially gratifying is that Bourne teams up with a dashing young investigative reporter from this very newspaper, who is also on the trail of the CIA conspiracy – played by Paddy Considine. What made them cast this actor? It wasn't his initials was it? I personally like to think it is an overdue acknowledgment of the essentially glamorous and exciting nature of our jobs here at the *Guardian*.

There is a nail-bitingly tense scene when the *Guardian* journalist has to report to his superior, who does indeed resemble our own distinguished editor. He and Bourne then go on the run, tracked from our office in London by an agency surveillance spook who has chillingly given the order to 'prepare rendition proto-cols'. Yeah? Bring it on mate. Guantánamo doesn't scare *Guardian* employees. We are unflinching in the face of danger, and this film proves it. Our heroes wind up in London's crowded Waterloo Station where they have to duck bullets from a rogue CIA sniper.

Bourne's adventures take him to Paris, London, Madrid, New York and Tangier, where Greengrass uncorks some gobsmacking stunts and OTT action sequences. All the time Bourne is being observed by a team of geeky laptop-watching agents based in the United States, who shout out details of Bourne's latest escapades to the incredulous CIA chief, played by David Strathairn. ('Sir, he just drove off the roof!' 'Whaaaaat?') However, there is a nice CIA boss, played by Joan Allen, who wants to bring Bourne in alive.

In the traditional way of these things, Bourne can keep going for days and days without sleeping, without eating, without shav-ing, and he has a kitbag with an infinitely expandable Tardis-like interior, in which he keeps an endless supply of guns and kit. Jason Bourne is always waltzing into CIA buildings to nick files, using what appears to be his own ID swipecard to work the turn-stiles. Er ... didn't human resources get the email about cancelling the guy's card?

It's all very absurd, but there's no doubt about it: the Bourne franchise delivers more entertainment-bangs for your buck than anything else comparable. And it's an action movie with an IQ.

Acknowledgments

Thanks first to Alan Rusbridger, the editor of the *Guardian*, who asked me to assemble this year's selection. Also to Lisa Darnell, who runs Guardian Books, and her managing editor, Helen Brooks, who have been invaluable in guiding me through the process. Countless colleagues on the paper helped me with suggestions for pieces for inclusion – apologies to those whose suggestions did not make the cut, there was simply too much good stuff. David Eldridge drew a delightful cover and the template for the text, Jonathan Baker laid out the text, while Barry Ainslie contributed to the design work. Ian Pindar copy edited and Amelia Hodsdon proof read. Roger Tooth, the *Guardian*'s picture editor, selected the pictures. Huge thanks to Ian Prior and the rest of the team on the sports desk, who did the hard work of getting a section out every day while I was otherwise engaged. Finally, in the interests of transparency, I should point out that Paula Cocozza, whose piece 'Maggie Thatcher pinched my shoes' appears in this collection, is also my wife.